Cuba:
A Brief History of the End

Tomáš Klvaňa

Cuba:
A Brief History of the End

Tomáš Klvaňa

Academica Press
Washington~London

Library of Congress Cataloging-in-Publication Data

Names: Klvaňa, Tomáš (author)
Title: Cuba : a brief history of the end | Klvaňa, Tomáš.
Description: Washington : Academica Press, 2024. | Includes references.
Identifiers: LCCN 2024936139 | ISBN 9781680533033 (hardcover) |
9781680533040 (e-book)

Copyright 2024 Tomáš Klvaňa

Dedicated to the memory of Petr Přibík (1937-2014)

Contents

1. **Mind Maps.** *Prague* 1

2. **Everybody Run!** *Havana* 5
Casas particulares 10
Filiberto 17
The Che Myth 28
"Everything Here Is Boring." 38

3. **Unless You're a Foreigner.** *Havana* 43
Waiting in the Boat 48
The Revolution Is Losing its Color 53
The First Raid 59
Cuesta Morúa 67

4. **Tierra Caliente.** *Santiago de Cuba* 77
Jimena 81
Pilgrims of Pico Turquino 90
Cajun Haiku 101
"History Will Absolve Me!" 115

5. **Sword of the Liberator.** *Holguín* 123
Birán 126
Excalibur 132
"I Lived in a Monster." 140
Life in Luxury 149

6. **Leodán.** *Jamaica* 155
Переход 160
In Ocho Ríos 165
Defibrillator 173
34 Dead 179

7. Seminar with Fidel. *Ciego de Ávila* 183

Those Who Left... 184

The Inverted Tree 189

Never, Never, Never! 203

The Raid at Martha's 212

8. Bay of Pigs. *Playa Girón* 219

Maura the Witch 228

Fernandina de Jagua 240

Brigada Asalto 2506 248

9. Hostage at Bella Vista. *Viñales* 261

Tripods and Weavers 263

Cyclone 268

At the Mercy of Greasy Hicks 275

Editorial Note and Acknowledgements 283

1.

Mind Maps.

Prague

The journey to the Caribbean begins in Nekázanka, a cozy corner of Prague's New Town. On a narrow connecting street, surrounded by grand bourgeois palaces, it is less cold in winter and less hot in summer than elsewhere in the neighborhood, and for the last ten years I have associated Nekázanka with Cuba. When I close my eyes, I see palm trees, white sand, and tropical vegetation. I also see a lot of terrible things, but let's not get ahead of ourselves.

A cold shiver runs through my thick coat as the large window of the Čedok travel agency, located in a house not far from the pedestrian zone, appears before me, illuminated by the approaching Advent season. I'm getting a visa to enter the Republic of Cuba, and for many reasons that will become clearer in the following chapters, it's better to get it here than at their consulate.

My travels to Cuba began as a humanitarian endeavor and were no different from those of other travelers, mostly from Europe. Many Czechs have traveled to Cuba with similar goals. Our shared past allows us to better understand the Cuban present. That is why Czechs feel a kinship with Cubans, despite their very different temperaments.

Right now, Cubans are the image of defeat. Above all, people are human in defeat; in defeat they touch their humanity; in humiliation they realize their own imperfection, finitude, and transience. The answer to the question of what I am looking for on the island is somehow related to the ability to find the better in defeat. I go to the people who are the true Cuban elite. They weren't afraid to stand up to the government. They are called dissidents, but I see them as mainstream, as a continuity of the Cuban culture, its civilization that the regime almost destroyed. Meeting them is uplifting.

They have spent years in dirty, infected, and overcrowded prisons. Some have gone on hunger strikes that have permanently damaged their health. Others have been beaten and tortured. Some have given up and gone into exile or even secretly collaborated with the regime. But there are still some who have not lost hope or strength, several thousand of them. They live in all fourteen provinces and work under difficult conditions. Just a couple of years ago, Internet access was incredibly expensive - four hours cost a normal monthly salary. Traveling between cities in a country 1,250 kilometers long is an ordeal; public transportation is expensive and inadequate, trains are overcrowded and run slowly on crooked tracks.

A travelogue is life, and in a book, life is never enough. Life does not suffice. It has no form, no plot, no gradation, it is difficult to manipulate, produce and direct. But it does not lack an inner tension, arising from experience and its reflection. The content of the following chapters are my experiences from my trips to Cuba in the last ten years. I have talked to dozens of people, driven thousands of miles, and crossed the island in all directions. I make no claim to objectivity; on the contrary, my view of Cuban life is proudly subjective. But I think it is of general importance.

In the twentieth century, Cuba became the geopolitical center of the world, the stage for a dramatic and highly photogenic contest between superpowers. The pictorial appeal stemmed from an unusual mix of life-and-death politics, great historical figures practicing it in the alluring backdrops of historic cities, and nature that is some of the most breathtaking to be found on the planet. Even the characters themselves were endowed with photogenic qualities and encountered a historical moment influenced by the emergence of television news. More than before, politics have become theatre and film, with the directors themselves cast in the lead roles: Fidel Castro, Fulgencio Batista, Ernesto Che Guevara, Camilo Cienfuegos, Huber Matos, John F. Kennedy, his brother Robert and other politicians with the look and character of movie stars. Cuba has given rise to myths. Some survive, even though the situation has reversed and today almost no one cares.

My subjective view of Cuba is non-ideological, or better yet, anti-ideological. It is not based on any muster, but on close observation. At the same time, however, this view cannot but be an indictment of totalitarianism and Marxist-Leninist ideology, which have spectacularly failed, destroying the lives of two generations of Cubans in the process. That the Caribbean dictatorship has survived its death and continues to destroy whatever comes to hand is a tragedy. I am not attempting to answer the question of why this is so, I am merely suggesting where we might look for possible answers. I'm not even trying to predict. On my first trips there, I had the feeling that the regime was coming to an end. It looked promising, the situation was reminiscent of the 1980s in Central Europe. Today I no longer think so. Parallels may exist to illuminate certain phenomena, but every historical situation is different. I do not know when what Plato called tyranny will end in Cuba. Nor do I know how it will end and what will come after it. I only know that we are witnessing the last phase of Cuba's momentary form, that we are witnessing its end. I wanted to capture a small, brief history of one end.

Then there is the question of why write about Cuba today, about its men and women facing a reign of evil. Haven't stories of similar people been told many times elsewhere in countries that, one by one, have gone through the same trajectory of decline? I have two interrelated answers to this question. Our world is full of new ideological battles based on various mental maps, some of which I consider dangerous.

But it's good to put down any mind maps from time to time and go to the territories they map to see if they are still any good. A map is not the terrain, and the terrain, in this case life, is constantly changing. We are too entangled in social and other networks. It is therefore useful to break out of them and look at things more closely.

The second answer concerns politics. This is not a political book, it doesn't want to be political, it wants to be a book about life in a part of the world that is both magical and trying. If there is any policy recommendation to be drawn from it, it is a reaffirmation of the age-old postulate that any policy must be measured by the results it produces, not by rhetoric or proclaimed good intentions. The deplorable results of Castroism are encountered in Cuba today and every day.

The basic plane of my travelogue is my last trip to Cuba in December 2022. In this plane I am inserting reminiscences of my past trips since the summer of 2012. As this is a personal book, it includes memories of my childhood and adolescence in the 1970s and 1980s in Czechoslovakia. I include them so that younger readers in particular will have a fuller context for understanding what is happening in Cuba. The essayistic and historical passages serve the same purpose.

At Čedok, the assistant hands me my passport and visa, a simple piece of paper with a stamp and dates that will hopefully entitle me to enter Cuba. I look at the big world map on the wall, which always and in all circumstances arouses in me the desire to pack up and go somewhere far away. It's a reflex built by the people who once built an iron cage around us. People who have passed into history in Czechia but still haunt Cuba. I'm going out to the Nekázanka and on towards the subway. Time to pack up. My head is swirling with the recommendations of colleagues, with whom I have been preparing this last trip, about what to pack. Surprisingly, food is among the recommended items this time. Politics and Covid have brought Cuba to the bottom.

Well, bon voyage, I say to myself, and head into town.

2.

Everybody Run!

Havana

Occasionally before falling asleep, I imagine Cuba as an island at the end of its breath. Like the ending of Breathless, the Godard film. Belmondo stumbles down the street, blends in with the Revolution, runs with a capitalist's bullet in his back, grunts, falls, his cheguevara-beautiful face tightened with pain. *C'est vraiment dégueulasse*, the Revolution breathes its last. It is dead. In the streets of the cities and villages they write of its eternal victory, but like all posters, this is only decoration. Like Che Guevara on a T-shirt. Cool Cat, this Che, builder of concentration camps for gays.

"Cubans have a bare ass," my plain-spoken grandfather František Beneš used to say, God give him eternal glory. I'd like to write that he meant well, but it wouldn't be accurate. My grandfather met the Cuban workers at the Avia in Letňany, where the Communists sent him after February 1948, when they took away his bakery and apartment building in Libeň, Prague, after he was a successful baker and a major league soccer player. My grandfather referred to his Havana comrades as Cubasí, which I thought was an exotic slur until I later realized that he was quoting half of a contemporary slogan: *Cuba sí, yankee no!* Forty years later, I look at the Generation Y blog of the well-known journalist Yoani Sánchez and my jaw drops in amazement. Yoani is in Brazil and the revolutionary youth around her are staging a kind of civilised form of the repudiation act. Whistles, raised fists and chants:

"*¡Cuba sí, yankee no!*"

Acts of repudiation (*actos de repudio*) have accompanied the Cuban revolution from the beginning, and the regime has practiced them against dissidents, although less today than in the past, because almost no one wants to participate. It is a group of comrades who gather around the house of a human rights activist or other imperialist worm, fuss for half a day, sometimes for a day, sometimes overnight, threaten with clenched fists, make noise, throw stones at the windows, pour paint or even more trenchant material on the house, and show how hated that enemy of the revolution is by the people.

"Dissident Librado Linares was recently subjected to an act of repudiation," blogger Yoel Espinosa Medrano told me in Santa Clara. "Horse and pig excrement was thrown at his house."

In the Brazilian conference centre Sánchez smiles amusedly. Her straight, dark hair flows down her back like a wet scarf. She will write that the Brazilian welcome was sent to her remotely by the government in Havana. Maybe. And maybe not. There are still plenty of people in South America, and elsewhere after all, with leather balls for heads who willingly wear Che Guevara T-shirts and believe the propaganda of brothers Fidel and Raúl Castro about education for all, free quality health care, women's employment and other regime lies.

Like my grandfather, I first saw my first living Cuban in a factory. It was in the 1980s, at the so-called summer activity, a part-time job at the PAL Kbely national plant, where I spent part of my high school holidays. I was scared of the burly black guys. They had the sleeves of their overalls rolled up, revealing their long, veined forearms. They were notoriously allergic to any work, hiding all day long, arriving first only in the cafeteria, where they walked with a swinging stride straight to the window without regard for the line behind them. No wonder they were not exactly popular among the honest working men and women in the factory. I sometimes remember this when someone starts speaking Czech to me in Cuba.

"República Checa? I was in Czechoslovakia, amigo..."

No longer do they inspire fear. They're pitiful. Grandpa's description is cruelly precise. They've got nothing, they try to force anything on you, drag you somewhere for a promised commission, sell you a box of stolen cigars, their sister, a cup of hot water in the attic. This is also why a visit to Cuba is a mixture of inspiration and frustration. Walking the uneven, broken, sometimes missing pavement of Havana's old town brings disappointment. One has to want a lot to perceive it romantically, to gush over the shabby post-colonial atmosphere one knows from the photographs taken here. Gone is the charming spirit known from the films of Wenders & Co. The bare reality is without magic. To achieve the right mood, Old Havana needs to be mediated, removed from reality and conveyed through a camera or laptop keyboard. You have to bring it to life at will, preferably to the sound of swinging music.

The buildings in the centre of the capital can be divided into two groups, the decaying and the dilapidated. Some windows on the upper floors of apartment buildings look straight up to the sky through the non-existent roof. Trees and bushes grow out of once plastered walls. Piles of trash and rubble, beggars, prostitutes and tourists; kids playing baseball with crappy sticks and PET lids for balls, and stray dogs and stunted cats that look like aged kittens running among them. I pass a few run-down buildings with balconies jutting out of them that you're afraid to walk under. In a few places there are only remnants of a torn balcony. Three buildings away, suddenly just a remnant of a perimeter wall and a pile of broken bricks inside. We in the Czech Republic were lucky that our dictatorship lasted only forty-one years. The prosperous, bustling metropolis of Prague could mutter to itself if it looked at Havana: There but for the grace of God go I…

When I first arrived in Havana and walked along the pedestrianised Paseo del Prado, I noticed the damaged and torn down balconies on some of the buildings. I walked through an avenue of mature trees, but the closer I got to the sea, the fewer there were. Some were just holes in the ground, destroyed by a cyclone that hit a few years before my visit. I had a local escort, a young man who told me about it. He said that's why the Malecón and the Prado are still so ruined. A cyclone? I'm asking what it was. In America, every tropical storm has a name, the first letter of which determines its order in the season: *Andrew, Baker, Connie, Dog, Easy.* But I'm not waiting for an answer. I know the name of that terrible storm. *Fidel.* The biggest and longest cyclone to devastate Cuba to this day is surely Cyclone *Fidel.*

Life in Cuba is life on the street. People stop, talk, sit on doorsteps, yawn.

"What's up, Pepito? How's the young one? Still sleeping?"

"How are you today, sir? You want cigars?"

"Get out of the way, dumbass, can't you see I'm carrying an old exhaust?"

The man huffs under the weight of a huge, leaky piece of iron. In our country, we'd call it a former exhaust of fond memory, but here it's still an exhaust. Tomorrow it will be mounted under a truck, or some American car from the late 1940s, and it will serve for a few more years. In Cuba, everything serves, in Cuba, nothing gets thrown away.

"*¡Coño!*"

"How are you today, sir? You want cigars?"

A few spruced streets and restored squares in Old Havana trick the senses, and for a moment you don't feel like you're in Beirut at the end of the civil war. Eusebio Leal Spengler, the city's official historian, the man chosen by Fidel Castro in the 1990s for the task of renovating Old Havana (La Habana Vieja), has received UNESCO recognition for his efforts, certainly lobbied out for him by the regime. Through the state-owned company Habaguanex, he gave a face back to a certain set of houses and streets such as Calle O'Reilly and Calle Obispo or Plaza de la Catedral. Leal is one of the elite who live a high life on the backs of the 99 percent of the rest of the country. His son, Javier, once ran a tourist agency and gallery in Barcelona. The hotels around Parque Central, neoclassical edifices between the Prado (Paseo Martí) and the Capitol, a faithful replica of Washington's Capitol, have been renovated. Tourists can get drinks for six euros at the Floridita bar where Hemingway used to go, and the Ambos Mundos hotel, where the master lived and wrote in corner room 511, boasts that former US president Jimmy Carter and actor Jack Nicholson stayed there. You will read in some Western newspapers that more than a third of the old town has been renovated, which is misleading. La Habana Vieja, the original old town founded in the sixteenth century and once surrounded by walls, is a relatively small part of the wider historic centre.

From Calle Obispo, a small street in the old town that is a gathering place for tourists, I turn in the direction where I suspect the train station is. After a while, the neat cobblestones end. The packed dirt and the smell of stray mini-cats welcome me back to the demolition site. More than half a century ago, the revolutionary regime declared war on all things non-revolutionary. The result is a decay even worse than ours in the 1980s. It is taking on Soviet dimensions. The economy is on its knees, sustained here by the Bolivarian boys in Caracas and their cheap oil, there by the scraps from the table of Putin and his oligarchs, and in recent weeks and months perhaps by the awakening Chinese dragon. I'm going through more of the smell, fending off the chasers. A traveler usually comes here for the colors, the smells, the atmosphere. The revolutionary color has faded, decomposing like a dead dog at the end of summer under a pile of cracked bricks.

However, other colors were not touched by politics. Generation after generation of girls have been adorned with the fragrant mariposa, a white jasmine called "butterfly," Cuba's national flower. Legend has it that in the wars of independence, girls adorned themselves with them to show purity and defiance. And if one is immune to the scent of mariposa, one is seduced by the fire of red-orange hibiscus burning along the roadsides. Or the shriveled clumps of the crowns of royal palms, growing up to forty metres, which in ordinary light are green, but by the magic of the sun and tropical fever can turn into grey blue, and against the blue-green sea and the white sand of the beaches can be golden, who knows...

There is a difference between authentic Cuba and a tourist reserve. Most foreigners here go to the Varadero Peninsula in the province of Matanzas, about a hundred and fifty kilometers east of Havana. It's a noodle of more than twenty kilometres (Varadero is about a kilometre wide on average), lined on one side by white beaches of azure blue and pale green ocean. Until recently, ordinary Cubans could not access it without special permission. If you spend two weeks just in Varadero, your impression of Cuba will be different than if you venture just a few kilometres further south. I woke up there early one morning, walked out of the beachfront guesthouse that's attached to the back of a famous steakhouse, and as I crossed First Avenue (Primera Avenue), I noticed how clean it glistened in the rising sun. On either side, fabulous trees lean over the well-maintained road. The glass-walled shops are still closed; they open around nine o'clock. Their range of products is far superior to those outside the peninsula.

Not that one would not recognize that one is in an economy of real socialism. I once had my suitcase wander off on a flight to Varedero. I went to get a toothbrush and toothpaste, which turned into a half-day shopping trip. If I had wanted a mountain bike, rum, cigars, leather bags with Comrade Che's face burned into them, or a sombrero, it would have taken me twenty minutes, but a toothbrush proved scarce. Eventually, after many hours, I took a small child's toothbrush. Still, Varadero, with its large Western-style hotels, is an artificially maintained reserve compared to the rest of the island, where misery doesn't lurk around every bend.

Casas particulares

After the revolution, the government despised tourism. It was a supposed bourgeois vice that brought in drugs, mafia, gambling and prostitution. But a tropical stretch of land in the Caribbean is too picturesque for anyone not to come and see. "Workers from the camp of peace and socialism" started flying in for a "well-deserved vacation." The tourism boom came in the 1970s. Later, the Soviet Union ended subsidies, its bloc collapsed and tourists from the East discovered previously forbidden destinations. The local economy collapsed. That's why Fidel took Western tourism in his stride. In the 1990s, Canadians, Western Europeans and Mexicans began to visit. Before the Covid pandemic, there were over two and a half million a year. It's not a staggering number, with between six and eight million tourists visiting Prague alone in a good year, but it does boost the economy considerably. They went to hotels in Havana and to destinations such as Varadero, Cayo Coco or Guardalavaca, north of the eastern metropolis of Holguín.

A little economic relaxation has allowed Cubans to run private guesthouses, the so-called *casas particulares,* where you can stay overnight and get breakfast much cheaper and often better quality than in the big state-run hotels. *Casas* are marked with a blue canopy-shaped emblem and are found in all towns and cities. On Havana's buildings, which look deserted at first glance, white plaques with blue canopies hang next to the shabby entrances. The rooms, available for rent from twenty to thirty-five euros a day (five extra for breakfast), are clean and usually have hot water. One must not be put off by the damaged exterior of the house. *Casas* are also in the villages, especially the coastal ones.

At the western end of the Valle de Viñales tourist paradise, in a valley with tobacco fields, tobacco curing sheds, houses with palm leaf roofs that look like straw from a distance, horses running around and water buffalo, there is a village by the sea called Puerto Esperanza. You can swim there by a long wooden pier. The small bay in Puerto is postcard-perfect, and a sunset experience with the sea and palm groves should only be by special permission. I don't recommend eating ice cream for a few pesos unless one is inoculated against cholera, but if you resist, you'll miss out on a great experience. Also here, in Puerto, I discovered two guesthouses and had a grilled crawfish dinner in the house I stayed in, which resembled a low, cubical hut on the Sazava River. The elderly lady who runs the bed and breakfast boasted to me that it was listed in *The Lonely Planet*, a popular guidebook. After dinner, she put it on my heart not to say anywhere in the village that she had given me crawfish. I'm told to say that she prepared roast chicken. The lobster was caught on the sly.

It pays to be patient when looking for accommodation. You can find shelter without a reservation even at night. Late one evening I was slowly driving through the Malecón, the waterfront at Havana Bay, looking for a place to stay. It's a shame not to stay in the more beautiful parts of Havana, if only because they are no different in price. I park right in front of a big sign with a blue canopy on the wooden gates of a broken-down apartment building. I enter the unlit arcade, walking carefully along the treacherous sidewalk, careful not to fall into some hole that surely leads to hell. The sharp air from the sea settles at the root of my nose before being replaced by the smell of stale where the sidewalk meets the crushed foot of the house; I pound on the door, then ring the bell. Help comes not from the front, but from the side, where smiling mouth and bulging eyes appear in the darkness.

"Accommodation? Room?"

When I nod, he leads me away. In Cuba, you develop a defensive reflex against yawning shysters, so I almost automatically refuse. I don't want to go around the corner with him, not even "just here, next door, really in the next block of houses," which always results in a walk halfway across town.

"No, I'm not going anywhere, I wanted to see if there was a vacancy here on the Malecón."

The bulging eyes tries to convince me that it is here, only the entrance is from the other side, from San Lázaro Street.

"Bjútifl vjú. Malecón, sí, San Lázaro, evryfink!"

He looks plausible. And he knows Milan Baroš, the Czech soccer hero. We walk around the block and enter an eight-story apartment building on the other side. We enter the elevator, its hard metal surface painted a pale industrial green. In the gloomy lighting of the corridor and the elevator, I feel like I'm in a hastily copied Soviet film. The elevator is missing half its roof. We can see into the ominous shaft above us. Bulging eyes presses the button, the belly of the elevator machine is overwhelmed by a noise like a giant's belch, and the decades-old monster moves up surprisingly fast. A staircase wraps around the elevator shaft, drowning in darkness and greasy, dusty grime. On the seventh floor, in front of apartment nineteen, there is a locked grate. No one answers the bell.

It's around midnight. I think about looking for something else, but bulging eyes is talking me out of it. He goes to find the owner and begs me for five minutes of patience. In the end, I'm glad I waited. Soon Manuel comes in, a good-looking, slightly emaciated man in his early forties with thick, greying hair. My guess is that he has an erotic attraction to the same sex, as I will later see when I catch him watching gay porn with his friends. I cross the threshold into a huge apartment. It spans the entire length of the apartment building. From the living room, painted some suspicious shade of cool pink, I open the door to a tiny balcony, beneath which I can hear the surf of the Florida Straits. On the other side, a similar balcony overlooks a dimly lit city.

Upon waking, Manuel's apartment offers a view of the sea and the city, refreshed by the morning before the heat hits. The blue bay licks the cliffs of the Malecón to Vedado and beyond, where you can't see. On one side of the panorama, the high-rise of the Habana Libre Hotel rises skyward; on the other, at the tip of the peninsula, is the Moro fortress and lighthouse that has guarded the bay for half a millennium. I walk into the green-tiled bathroom, where a small window smiles at the ceiling, just an opening with small wooden blinds, through which the sound of the sea waves and the smell of the salt air drifts in. The surf, breaking against the rocky shoreline and the concrete wall of the street seven floors below, can be heard clearly, more clearly than the aggressive noise of passing cars. I'm high above the houses, and their golden clutter on the roofs evokes the optimism familiar from the beginning of every day: there's still time.

A four-walled dome sits on the roof of a nearby waterfront structure. It's gilded. What time has taken away from the golden color, the clawing sun adds to the top of the sky. The scene has a Moorish feel. The dingy brick color of the rest of the roof is like an unmaintained clay court in the suburbs, ravished ten times over by a cyclone. A pile of rubble and the spikes of old planks sprouting from it, adjacent to one wall of the dome, half-hides an empty, rusting barrel. On some of the roofs stand wooden huts, various other outbuildings and blue water tanks. Through the yellowish veil of the sun I can see mainly the blue of the tanks, the faded red of the roofs and the age-stained whiteness of the plaster in an unintended, random combination of Cuban tricolor. On another trip in Havana, I stayed near Manuel's guesthouse a few blocks from the Malecón, almost on Prado. From my second-floor balcony, I watched the roof of the house across the street and the flapping, drying laundry on it, with the occasional loud snorting pig running underneath. In the wooden coop, the hens were currently competing in a tournament for the loudest cluck.

This is what a metropolis with 2.2 million inhabitants looks like. Havana is a crumbling chaos. Havana is both happy and tired faces. Havana is contrasts. You walk through a vast arcade, and if it's under a cloud, it's almost dark. Two or three steps up a ramshackle flight of stairs, ten metres down a flat plain full of holes, round a pile of planks, then round a pile of stones, and round some more (we'd rather not describe), then down three steps, and so on. The phones that are stuck to the walls of houses in arcades and on corners next to shops don't work much after rain. Although calling them shops might cause confusion in your head, as they are more like dark holes leading from the gloom of the arcades to the inside of the houses. They're full of people and monotonous goods. There are many other people standing around, yawning. Their official occupation, whatever it may be, does not encourage them to be active. Only the daily struggle for dollars, which can buy exponentially more than the peso, can do that. They fight for them in touristy places using a technique called sticking it to the stranger.

"Hello, sir, how are you today? You want cigars? *¡Puros! ¡Cohíbas!*"

"You like salsa, my friend?"

On the Prado, under the canopy of mature trees, two cloudy eyes stare at me. A black youth on drugs has blue irises and behind him stands an attractive girl with a rose in her hair. If I were bolder, I'd take their picture and disappear.

"Today festival of salsa, my friend. You interested? My sister - great dancer!"

The fact is, there is no salsa festival. It is one of many creative lies to lure a tourist with an expensive camera and sell him a dancer.

Havana does not have a coherent face, no one parable fits it. It is neither a symphony nor a jazz improvisation. One can walk around its 730 square kilometres and fifteen districts for days and will pass places that have nothing in common with others just a few hundred metres away. In its eclecticism, Havana is a typical American metropolis. Just take a taxi - agree on the price in advance! -, drive through the centre via Vedado to Miramar along the sea, drive to the Ernest Hemigway marina and you're in a different environment. Majestic villas from the first half of the twentieth century, set in a never-ending park of mature trees and flowering shrubs. Even the elegance here is marred by decay. The villas, which look magnificent from a distance among the palm trees and jasmine, are shabby up close, though they are far from the ruins of Old Havana. Quinta Avenue, Fifth Avenue, intersects the Miramar in the form of a boulevard of grass, shrubs and trees in the middle of two strips of road. While waiting at a red light, I noticed beauties standing on the grass, peering meaningfully at drivers. They're not the only prostitutes in the neighborhood; a number Cuba's top Communists live here, too. They've moved into the villas and palaces of the businessmen, which they have stolen from them and drove them out of the country. A banal variation on the banal history of the workers' and revolutionary movement. Judging by the density of policemen in a neighborhood teeming with the colors of nature, you can guess that you're passing by the house of someone really VIP.

Parks, playgrounds, the bizarre brutalist concrete tower of the Embassy of the Russian Federation. You can see all the way to the White House in Washington from the ambassador's office, the joke goes. There's also the Karl Marx Theatre, before the revolution the Teatro Blanquita, for five and a half thousand people. For that renaming alone, the Castros deserve the electric chair. Its glass façade, with a gigantic replica of the philosopher's signature, reflects the sky and sea in front of which it stands on Primera Avenue, the First Boulevard. In 2001, the Manic Street Preachers performed here. Fidel was also present. When he was warned that there would be noise, he flinched:

"It can't be louder than war."

In front of the refined Miramar is the Vedado, which is crossed by the famous La Rampa (Calle 23) with its restaurants and cafés. Intellectuals, artists, gays and the upper echelon live here. You walk past a cinema showing the latest Tarantino to an ochre-colored villa with a fine Japanese restaurant (dinner is worth one month's salary of a qualified surgeon, just under US$35 per person), and before you ascend to the first floor, where a culinary grove proudly spreads out, you see the Thomson Reuters news agency's office behind a locked grille on the mezzanine floor. From another restaurant in New Vedado, on the fifteenth floor of a modern high-rise building aptly named the Fifteenth Floor, you can see the skyline of Havana Bay, La Rampa Avenue and the Habana Libre and Nacional hotels below, the metropolis' first luxury hotel, built in the art deco style on Taganana Hill in 1930. Below it is a memorial to the 274 victims of the Maine cruiser disaster, a United States warship sunk in the local harbour, apparently by a naval mine, in February 1898 during the War of Independence. The Fifteenth Floor is one of many private restaurants in the capital called *paladares*.

Like guesthouses, *casas particulares, paladares* were created as a response to economic liberalization two decades ago as mostly family-run restaurants in private apartments and houses. They are small establishments of a few tables that serve tasty meals, much better than the often-inedible dishes offered by state-run restaurants. The easiest way to find out where there is a *paladar* in your area is to ask. Taxi drivers and chasers receive commissions from the owners for customers, and these will be reflected in your bill, which can climb into the tens of dollars for a dinner, as mine did at Fifteenth Floor. Fortunately, I didn't have to climb to the 15th floor itself on a muggy evening; there was a clean and reliable elevator. I shortened my wait by reading the bulletin board in the corridor, where, in addition to a revolutionary leaflet demanding the return of five Cuban spies imprisoned in the USA (*¡Volverán!*), there was a list of rent debtors. The Ramírezes owed 500 national pesos.

Other Havana neighborhoods and districts resemble bloated small towns. Arroyo Naranjo, Playa, Santa Fé and Managua have grown into nature and merged with it in a picturesque symbiosis of an island on the edge of the third world. The colors, the smells and the stench, the decadence of the revolutionary tropics, the people with their supple movements, gliding along the sidewalks and streets with the dance step of a film footage that is slowed down compared to reality. Happy, tired, curious faces. Cynical looks. This is what people look like, frustrated but determined not to let reality change their own make-up, which genes and history have drawn from Spanish, African and Chinese reservoirs and endowed them with a casual optimism. Every Cuban gaze is a gaze into the abyss, but one that defies the Nietzschean bon mot. Don't let the abyss stare you down. It may be that this attitude, along with civilizational anti-Americanism, is what allowed the Castro brothers to subjugate the country for so long. If Cubans had been less patient, less cheerful, and less prone to complacency, they might have been free a few years ago. Exactly what is keeping the regime alive, what combination of items, is difficult if not impossible to figure out in real time. Society is not a lab. The variables and unknowns are many. Not even a California supercomputer could handle this equation. After the regime falls, several theories will emerge, each emphasizing a different item. The international situation. Failure of economic vitality. The desire for freedom. The loss of will of the elites.

Filiberto

December 2022. Filiberto slides the frames of his glasses up the bridge of his nose. Beads of sweat break out on his forehead from the determination with which he has tackled the breakfast prepared with his own hands. His wife, Julia, is at the clinic and Filiberto, a civil engineer by training with a diploma from Havana Polytechnic, has for years been acting as master of the house, accommodation manager and breakfast cook for visitors to his residence in an alleyway in Havana's old town.

"Finish it," he says, looking meaningfully at my empty plate, where an unpleasant puddle from scrambled egg and black beans remains.

To set an example, he takes white bread in his hand and carefully wipes the surface of his plate with it. He then places the soaked bread in his mouth like a host, closes his eyes and swallows it devoutly. I couldn't think of anything else except to fib about my heavy stomach and indigestion. It's actually a half-truth, because the digestive problems I often have in Cuba were only delayed by three charcoal pills. These black pills are an instance of last resort if Imodium and Cristal beer in a green can don't work.

"That's what my dad taught us. I come from the East. Bayamo. You know? We had to finish every last bite and then clean the plate like this. We couldn't get up from the table without it."

Filiberto's is the voice of the chastiser. He doesn't care that we're his customers. Daniel, who sits to my left, directly opposite Filiberto, nods his bald head knowingly.

"Child of poverty."

Filiberto protests. Methodically, he puts down his fork, raises the index finger of his right hand and declaims:

"We were not poor! My father was rich. But he had his principles. He worked his way up to be a wealthy merchant."

He pauses, takes a deep breath and looks at me curiously. He's known Daniel for a long time, but this is the first time he's seen me. I arrived at his house a few streets south of Havana Bay late last night. I parked in the dark right in front of the house, walked up a narrow and very steep staircase to a spacious hall with a high ceiling. At the back, where we are now sitting, I saw an atrium dividing the kitchen area from the living room with large windows facing the street. I let Filiberto show me around. On the walls of the hall hung large canvases of famous places in Cuba. Inspired by the style of Le Douanier Rousseau, the painter had composed a tribute to Viñales National Park in the west of the country and several other sites. When I mentioned to Filiberto that I had been there, he began waving his arms and praising the natural beauty of the reserve. His language was sincere, free of the verbal gripes of a tourist promoter.

Now, after breakfast, the December light is streaming in through the skylights into the hall, and the master of the house is watching me closely from behind his glasses. The glass needs cleaning. His forehead is boxy and the long sleeves of his brown-and-red shirt end neatly at his wrists, where any free impulse is cut off by the buttons. Filiberto does not look Caribbean. I remain silent. I know exactly where he's going, but who knows who he's meeting? Who's he talking to?

"Then they took everything from him. Our family had nothing left. Revolution. Communism."

He sighs.

"It was a different time," Daniel remarks, taking a sip of his black coffee.

There's no milk or sugar on the table. If there was a wall clock on the wall, you could hear it ticking. But most Cuban wall clocks in the halls of colonial houses don't. And there are none in Filiberto and Julia's house. I wonder what Daniel's somewhat clichéd conversational intervention means. Daniel is an Englishman in his sixties who visits Cuba often and knows it well. Before the meal, he blurts out that in Havana he always stays at Filiberto and Julia's place, just not here, but at the house down the street. He comes here for breakfast and is satisfied. It doesn't pay me to look for something else, he says. His stay is coming to an end. He has to go back to London for social security, but then he'll come back again depending on how expensive the flights are. He paid only £300 for his current one, which arouses my envious interest, as I paid more than three times that. In the waning days of the Covid pandemic, flights are still expensive.

"But only here," Daniel says. "One-way ticket, not return." He tries to reassure me. I know London well, we used to live there for some time, so

Chapter 2

to save us from his witty remarks, I ask where he lives. He surprises me a second time.

"On the boat. Yes, in London, or rather in Greenwich on a boat."

Later that day, Filiberto reports in Daniel's absence. The Englishman is said to be in love.

"That's the problem. Especially at his age. He falls in love easily and quickly, and with a Cuban! But they're not exactly the ideal *chicas* for a relationship."

I nod for understanding. Daniel has several children in England and at least two in Cuba, each with a different woman. One of whom he says he built a house for in Santiago. He says he's sunk some £300,000 here over the years. This information of Filiberto is without guarantee. Daniel doesn't look like someone who'd splash out £300,000 on pure love. Daniel doesn't look like the type to ever have £300,000. But who knows.

Filiberto picks up the thermos and pours himself the rest of his coffee.

"Mister here is from the Czech Republic. He must know a lot about communism."

I don't respond, and he cuts to the chase:

"Or do you miss it? Did you like communism?"

"Of course, I do not miss it."

Filiberto's face brightens. He raises his clenched fist and touches mine across the table in a salute of non-leftist solidarity. Fist bump. Then he looks at Daniel.

"Daniel used to be a Communist."

The Englishman writhes uncomfortably.

"When I was young. I was an idealist. It was a different time... but social justice, that's what I was after. Even today, it's about social justice, ain't it? In today's system..."

Around the table conciliatory sentences flow from all the participants in the morning conversation. Youth. Naivety. Idealism. Then the talk turns to the present, more specifically to the possibility of obtaining a work visa in Europe. Filiberto and Julia aren't living too badly by Cuban standards. They rent a few rooms to travelers for euros, American or Canadian dollars. Their downtown abode may be in a run-down building, but their apartment inside, behind iron doors and metal bars, is cozy, clean, in good condition. Julia is a respected doctor, head of a department at a well-known clinic, and Daniel advises trying Spain. Attestation, language and all, he says. The couple are fed up with the Cuban situation.

"Do you know how much my wife makes a month?"

I'm guessing $35. Filiberto's taking a moment to recalculate. Today's exchange rate of the peso to the dollar on the black market is about 175 to 1. After thirty years of working in Cuban health care, which the government continues to promote as something of a miracle, Julia's monthly income is a full twenty-eight dollars and fifty cents. She is therefore well below the internationally recognized extreme poverty line of $1.90 a day. Filiberto and Julia have had enough and are trying to leave. This makes them no different from millions of Cubans with the same intentions. In this year alone, 2022, nearly 300,000 people left the country, an estimated quarter of a million to the United States and the rest mostly to Spain.

"Everybody's running," Julio, the hitchhiker, tells me in the car. "Everywhere is better than Cuba."

Later I go with Filiberto to the airport, where I have to do some errands, and the man of the house offers to accompany me and navigate. It's a sunny, windy day, the waves of the Florida Straits crashing against the concrete seawall, and in several places a spray of saltwater hits the road and passing cars. I welcome his navigational aid. In the car, Filiberto is talking. He spent time in Portugal as a civil engineer. He worked for a university where he commuted by bicycle every day more than twenty years ago. Twenty kilometers through Havana there, twenty back.

"There was no petrol, no public transport. But I was in good shape."

Near the third terminal of José Martí Airport, we drive through a park and see prefabricated buildings painted green among the trees. The color of the dilapidated plaster, shining through the branches, is barely visible anymore, and when we get closer Filiberto starts to wail.

"Jesus, look, the building is destroyed! There's nothing left! That was one of the university buildings, I worked here for over ten years. And now there's nothing here."

Filiberto is right, literally. Instead of windows, all we see are empty holes through which we can see inside, where there is also nothing.

The international terminal of Martí Airport resembles a bus station. It is similar in style and design to the one seen at Prague's Ruzyně Airport in the 1980s. Paul Theroux has an observation in one of his travelogues that the culture of a country is best experienced in a railway station, because today every government in the world, even the most miserable and corrupt, can spruce up an airport. Paul wasn't in Havana! Outside the entrance, taxi drivers are jostling for tourists, there are a few bouncers and uniformed police. Although the winter season has begun, there are only a few flights in and out of Havana each day. Still, you can wait a solid hour or more for your suitcase. Tourists besiege the sloping luggage belt, one you don't see much in normal airports anymore, because when suitcases don't fall out, they accumulate in several places, blocking others that the dispenser spits out at irregular intervals. People are jostling. Retirees from Germany, Poland and Canada heading to seaside resorts predominate. And then there are the Russians. They now have limited travel options and one of their favourite destinations is the one whose name their fathers used to pronounce with a tear in their eye. On my arrival there was a blonde Russian girl in her mid-twenties, dressed in a shiny fur coat, waiting at the baggage belt. I waited for her to take it off, it was after all well over twenty degrees centigrade, but no! She stayed in it the whole time. Maybe she bathes in it on Varadero.

I do what I need to do and meet my guide at the car park. He holds a plastic bag without a logo and shows me its contents. Three or four things at the bottom, I recognize the instant coffee.

"Twelve dollars! Twelve..."

He repeats it so that I don't miss the information, but there's no need. Filiberto's English is good, conversational, which is unusual here. Whenever I hear someone I don't know speak such good English, I immediately think of the worst. A cop? A spy? Agent? A few years ago, I arrived in the southern metropolis of Cienfuegos, parked in the picturesque Martí Square in the centre (about half of all Cuban objects bear his name...) and went in search of accommodation. I didn't have to look long, right in the square near the provincial parliament one blue canopy logo adorned the well-kept, white-painted front door: *la casa particular.*

The owner offered an excellent room at a decent price, added breakfast for a small extra charge, and watched me curiously as I trudged out of the car with my luggage. He was an athletic-looking man in his fifties with a bald head and youthful expression, dressed in an expensive designer collared shirt and khaki pants. He spoke English with almost no accent, so I figured he was one of the Florida Cubans who had decided to do business in Cuba after the economic climate had eased slightly, but I didn't dare ask. I just got a weird feeling about him. He looked like a retired Cuban counterintelligence agent. So, on my next trip to Cuba a year or two later, I parked in Cienfuegos on the complete opposite side of the vast plaza and found another *casa* there. A young woman in an apron, probably a cleaner, answered the door and checked me in, saying that the owner was not at home but would be coming soon. What the devil, the owner was again our bald debonair. A little tingle went through me as he looked me over and then asked if we knew each other. I said I didn't remember. I later learned from a friend that he would introduce himself as a former "diplomat and journalist" and that he had even been to Prague at one time during the existence of Czechoslovakia.

Diplomat and journalist. Just the connection! I don't know for sure, but I think that some foreign correspondents of the Communist Czechoslovak Television and Czechoslovak Radio went to the West covered by a diplomatic passport. What is certain is that they worked for the State Security. It is therefore possible that Cuban "journalists" have a similar cover. In any case, I have vowed that the next time I come to Cienfuegos I will stay at a safe distance from Parque Martí, because the home ownership there lacks a certain type of diversity.

Although Filiberto speaks good English and asks questions about everything under the sun, I don't have a similarly uncomfortable feeling about him. On the way from Havana airport to the city centre, he tells me how he quit his job with the state more than a decade ago and has been renting ever since. I ask how much tax he has to pay on the rental income, because a *casa* owner told me some time ago that after deducting all the fees, taxes and bribes he is left with about ten percent of what he earns. Ninety percent is taken by the state. Filiberto brings clarity to the situation.

"When we started, we had to pay about $300 a month. No matter how much we made that month. Then they reduced the amount to $150. Today, taxes and fees are about 50 percent of income."

We drive through the suburban neighbourhoods around Parque Lenin and the impressive set of modernist buildings of the Palacio de Convenciones, the Congress Centre. Filiberto commands me to stop several times at vegetable stands, but almost every time he returns to the car empty-handed and angry. Either they don't have what he needs or he's not willing to pay inflationary prices. I notice that the indicator light shows my tank is half empty, which means I need to look for a gas station.

There is a fuel shortage in Cuba these days and weeks. The generous supply of cheap Venezuelan oil, paid for in part by the government in Havana by sending Cuban doctors to poor neighborhoods and in part by sending thousands of "Interior Ministry experts" who have helped Hugo Chávez and his successor Nicolas Maduro stay in power through dirty tricks, has ended. The Venezuelan Government paid the Cuban Government doctors' salaries in hard currency and at the rate usual in civilised countries. Havana pocketed most of the earnings for itself and paid its doctors a much smaller amount in convertible pesos. But that currency has since been abolished, so today what is left of the "Venezuelan" doctors is paid in the worthless national currency, the Cuban peso. The socialist government in Venezuela, with the help of Cuban spies, has brought its economy, potentially one of the richest in the world because of its oil reserves, to the brink of beggary. The brotherly pipeline has dried up. Today in Cuba, only the interior ministry workers, the military and government officials can rely on a regular and sufficient supply of petrol and diesel, which they fill up their cars at special pumps that are inaccessible to anyone else.

In August 2022, lightning struck the largest fuel depot in Matanzas province at a supertanker port, causing the worst fire in the country's history. It threatened the already meager fuel supply, and worsened the electricity supply, as oil is mainly used to generate it. Power outages, particularly in the east, extended for several hours each day. Electricity problems are also caused by a lack of maintenance of the grid, in which the government - as in almost everything that does not somehow concern the army, the interior and the living standards of prominent people - does not invest. Cubans are thus left to shuffle from pump to pump and say their prayers: Lord God, let them have petrol and electricity at the same time. Because if there is petrol but no electricity, you don't fill up. And if the power is on, but there is no gasoline, you will also leave empty-handed. As I am now from several stations. Filiberto jumps out of the car at each one and goes to look at the terrain. He comes back with some valuable advice, of which the most hopeful is "perhaps in Vedado." We're on our way to Old Havana and El Nuevo Vedado is on its way. It's early afternoon, traffic sparse as a scant number of Cubans own a car. An exact figure is not available but estimates hover below five percent of households. In the Czech Republic, the figure was 76 per cent in 2020.

On Cuban roads you mostly see Ladas, Moskviches and other Soviet cars from the 1970s and 1980s. Most of the orphans of the Soviet automotive industry are in good to excellent condition, their owners taking care of them, cleaning them, covering them with rugs, blankets and fuzzy steering wheel covers. If you collect this category of vintage cars, Cuba is the perfect place to hunt for them. Even today, some lively Moskviches will give Korean and Chinese rental cars a run for their money. On the highway from Santiago to Palma Soriano, a green Moskvich with a big King of the Road sticker passed me easily up the hill, because my little white Hyundai looked like it had just decided to take off the right rear fender, scaring me enough that I'd better slow down to seventy kilometers per hour.

At the end of 2022 you see a bit more Western and Asian cars than a decade ago. These include mainly old Peugeots, Hyundais, Kias and Chinese Geely cars, which don't feature much in Europe despite the carmaker owning Swedish family jewel Volvo since 2010. Another change in the fleet that I've noticed since my last visits is the relative abundance of small electric motorcycles. There are more of them than in the Czech Republic, and you recognize them by not hearing a thing until they hit you from behind and there's a bang.

We arrive at a gas station of the state-owned Cupet company called El Tángana. It also happens to be the name of a well-known Spanish rapper who creatively combines flamenco and trap. I hope that Tángana will also cut a few litres of special for me, in a relatively quick cadence. The gas station is located almost on the Malecón between O and N streets. It is surrounded on one side by pale yellow and pale blue prefab apartment blocks with blue balconies. The petrol station itself has the green and red Cupet-Cimex logo displayed on the white plaster of the semi-circular single-storey building. Next to it is the Spanish and English words "Your Friend for 24 Hours." Especially in its current state, it sounds tragicomic.

The pump is besieged by cars, which form more of a huddle than a queue. But it does mean they have at least some fuel. Unlike almost everyone else waiting, I'll be filling up with special, higher quality and more expensive fuel. Normal is forbidden for rental cars, probably because the state rental bosses know all too well what is mixed into normal and how it ruins the engine. As a result, there's a much shorter queue for special. We park and Filiberto stands in solidarity with me in the all-male line. You must first negotiate how many litres they will allow you to load, pay and then head to the designated number stand. In the queue Filiberto again asks all sorts of questions. The main thing that sticks in my mind is his question about how to fill up with petrol in the Czech Republic. I don't immediately understand what he means.

"What does it look like when I run out of gas?"

He nods.

"I'll come to the gas station, fill up and pay."

"Don't you have to pay first?"

"I don't remember having to pay first anywhere in the Czech Republic. It is possible. It happens sometimes in worse neighborhoods in the States and in Britain, if I remember correctly."

"And you can fill up all you want?"

"I just pull up to a free rack and fill up the tank. There are a huge number of petrol stations in the Czech Republic, I would say we have one of the densest networks per capita. Sometimes I pay with a credit card right at the pump."

Filiberto gasps, slumping his shoulders, and I get the uncomfortable feeling that I'm showing off. The men in line pay no attention to our conversation in English. They wait impatiently for their turn. Most of them pay with business or company credit cards.

"Our petrol is very expensive now," I say to Filiberto, because I feel the need to add something to spoil the picture of the Czech paradise. Filiberto doesn't react, just looks behind me towards the sea, which is still at its highest today. A free wind is blowing over it, seagulls are flying, and I can see cargo ships in the bay. The combination of the vast expanse of asphalt the color of lead and the blue of the Caribbean in front of me would deserve a good camera and a wide lens. Unconsciously, I reach into my pocket, stroke my sweating phone, and let its battery rest.

My comment about expensive gasoline is a merciful lie, because fuel is only cheap for us in Cuba. If you earn five thousand pesos a month, which is a very decent salary for an educated professional, and you pay fifteen hundred for a full tank of gas, on the black market it's only nine to ten dollars, a ridiculous amount for us, but for a Cuban it's a third to a quarter of their monthly income. Let's keep in mind that these are calculations based on the black-market exchange rate, reflecting the real state of the economy and purchasing power. The official exchange rate is different, but it is worthless and almost no one sane buys pesos at it.

Filiberto doesn't have a car. He says he doesn't need one now, maybe later. But he has a brother who has a small restaurant nearby.

"My brother's restaurant isn't much. It's mostly students who go there for sandwiches."

He states it clearly, emphatically, in a way that doesn't sound like an invitation. Finally, it's our turn. The salesman gives me 25 litres, not a drop more. That's enough. As we pull out onto the street, Filiberto mentions only in passing that Julia's shift is about to end, and she's not far from us. I nod. Why not? We can stop for her. Compañero pulls a smartphone from his belt pouch.

"I have a car. Hm. I see. Yes."

Turns out Julia's shift isn't over yet. Julia is in a meeting and can't talk much. We're not picking Julia up. We're heading towards the Revolution Square district. We pass Martí's neglected park and athletic stadium on the waterfront. It used to be a colorful sports ground with green grass, the pride of central Havana overlooking the sea. I imagine what it must have been like to play baseball here or practice 400 meters. I'll skip the hammer throw. I look toward the dingy bleachers, slowly crumbling.

Chapter 2

The grassy area has become a yellowish, deserted patch. Every time I drive by this field, I think of the phenomenal track runner Alberto Juantorena. According to Filiberto, Cuban sport is in decline. There's no money. Sometimes there aren't even athletes.

"Everybody's running."

We're finally getting to baseball. Unlike me, Filiberto also follows amateur competitions and reports that the Czech Republic is doing well.

"You have one of the best teams in Europe."

Later I look at the rankings and find that our national team is seventh in Europe and in the top 30 in the world, and that cannot be said about soccer. Cuba and baseball is quite a different story. The Cuban league is excellent, but even here there is a drain of talent. Many Cubans play professionally in the United States. Filiberto mentions Yuli Gurriel of the Houston Astros.

"He played for Sancti Spíritus. Then in Japan before he went to the States."

"Did he leave legally?"

"Nope. Illegally. Most of them leave illegally. But now one young player went to Japan and the Japanese paid a mountain of money to the Cuban Federation for him."

In 2006, the ESPN sports channel reported that the young Yuli Gurriel had left Cuba for Colombia, which turned out to be a false alarm. American television was a decade ahead of its time. It wasn't until February 2016 in the Dominican Republic that Gurriel ran out of patience with Cuba. He and his teammate and brother Lourdes first finished the Caribbean series, then relocated to neighboring Haiti. There, Yuli met another Cuban, Yordan Álvarez, a future teammate in Houston. By the end of 2016, all three were headed to Major League Baseball, the legendary competition that is the dream of every kid who has ever faced the pitcher with a focused eye. This year, exactly six years later, Yuli became America's champion for the second time, winning the World Series. His base salary earned him eight million dollars a year.

The Che Myth

I stop at a red light in the wide expanse of the Plaza de la Revolución. There are several armed police and soldiers patrolling. An obelisk rises in the centre, in front of which is a white marble statue of the kneeling Martí, a knock-off of Rodin's Thinker. Filiberto points to the white building of the Ministry of the Interior with a linear stylized portrait of Che Guevara and the inscription *Hasta la victoria siempre* (Until the final victory), and the building of the Ministry of Information and Communications with a similar depiction of Camilo Cienfuegos and his quote, *Vas bien, Fidel* (You are doing well, Fidel). These quotations unintentionally capture the different natures of the two revolutionaries. While Che was a doctrinaire ideologue and radical, Camilo had a playful disposition and a sense of humour.

There is an anecdote related to his quote from the time of Castro's coup. At a rally in January 1959 after the overthrow of Batista, Castro spoke to the crowd. Judging by the reaction of the audience, he noted Camilo's popularity, which some witnesses said exceeded his. It was Cienfuegos who, along with Guevara, brought the rebels to the capital. The Castro brothers and Huber Matos and their troops set out from the Sierra Maestra in the opposite direction, taking first the eastern capital, the second largest city, Santiago de Cuba.

At the time, Castro added to the chaos by saying that Santiago would again become the capital of the country after a few hundred years. He had an emotional attachment to it, having gone to high school there, and in 1953 he and a band of adventurers tried to take over the barracks there. He's buried in Santiago. In January 1959, after taking Santiago, Castro and his band of rebels made a triumphal march west, only to enter a jubilant Havana eight days later. Comrades Guevara and Camilo were waiting for him there, and Fidel changed his mind about the capital. Someone had the presence of mind to say that the capital is wherever Fidel is! It remained Havana. Castro was speaking at that meeting with Camilo behind him, and at one point he turned to him and said: 'How am I doing, Camilo?' He grinned and said, "*Vas bien, Fidel.*" You always do well. The inscription now adorns a building whose officials are in charge of controlling communications in the state.

Chapter 2   29

After Castro's guerrilla takeover, a power that dictator Fulgencio Batista had unceremoniously left lying in the street and disappeared with a bundle of money, the non-Communist rebels, Matos and Cienfuegos, grew less and less fond of the growing influence of the Marxists in the leadership, especially Raúl Castro and Guevara. Matos was relegated by the clique to the central province of Camagüey. There he became a big fish in a smaller pond. Nevertheless, from the summer of 1959, he criticised the Communist tendencies of the ministers in question. He came into conflict with Prime Minister Fidel, who, although he claimed not to be a Communist, did nothing against the Marxists in the cabinet. Above all, he could not bear criticism. According to the testimony of his long-time bodyguard, Juan Sánchez, Castro was under no circumstances willing to give way to another opinion. He called people with different views idiots.

In Havana, 1959 is a dance of shadows, a play on the reflection in the mirror. In front of the world, Castro claims he has nothing to do with communism. He, Raúl and Che meet Soviet intelligence agent Nikolai Leonov in Mexican exile a few years earlier. The impressionable US television network CBS comes to Havana and Castro allows himself to be filmed with his nine-year-old son Fidelito in his pyjamas, a family man. On *Face the Nation,* he lies that civil rights will be preserved in Cuba, that he will declare free elections. Meanwhile, behind the scenes, executions are taking place without due process, purges are underway of those the new regime labels as pawns of the former government.

The dispute between Castro and Matos lasted several months. According to Matos's memoirs, the two men met on the anniversary of the attack on the Moncada barracks on 26th July at the Havana Hilton (now Habana Libre), where Matos handed in his resignation. Fidel did not accept, noting that there was still much work to be done. Fidel admitted that Raúl and Che were flirting with Marxism, but countered that Matos was not powerless either, after all he was in control of the situation in his province. For Fidel's part, it was a cover-up, an evasive manoeuvre, a play for time. Matos's criticism and Camilo's popularity were more than Fidel's ego could bear, and this proved fatal to both former comrades-in-arms. He had Matos arrested, tortured, and then imprisoned for 20 years for alleged counterrevolution. Matos didn't get out until 1979. He retreated to Miami, where he became an activist in the exiled democratic movement. He died in 2014 at the age of 95. The man who arrested him in 1959 on Castro's instructions was Cienfuegos himself. He carried out the order, but before that he listened carefully to Matos. Matos warned him about the Communists, and also bluntly told him that Castro would never put up with an arrangement in which he was overshadowed in public. This happened on October 21, 1959. A week later, Camilo boarded a Cessna in Camagüey with a destination of Havana. The small plane was lost somewhere over the sea. Camilo Cienfuegos's body was never found.

Green. I put the car in gear and drive between the statue of Martí and Guevara's likeness out of the vast square.

"Plaza de la Revolución," Filiberto says dryly. "This is where Fidel spoke and the Cubans listened to him religiously. Oh Fidel, what a beauty! They listened to his nonsense. He spoke for eight hours, and people hung on his lips and swooned with happiness. Cubans are fools. Most people are stupid," he says, more melancholy than angry.

"You've never been a Communist?"

Filiberto comes out almost offended:

"Me and a Communist? Never."

"Not even as a student?"

"My father explained everything to me in time. Before he was arrested. They let him run his shop for a while, which they took away from him, and then they charged him with embezzlement and put him in jail. He did time here in Cabaña too," pointing up the waterfront to Fort Moro. In its stone cells, Castro imprisoned prominent political prisoners, among them Matos and the poet Reinaldo Arenas.

I have some suspicion that Fidel's "eight-hour speeches" are an urban legend. Not that he's known for his ability to get right to the point. Speaking for four hours was a piece of cake for him. Shocked and subsequently mortified eyewitnesses to the UN General Assembly could tell the story. He spoke there for the first time for four and a half hours. Possibly his longest is a speech at the Communist Party Congress in 1986, which is said to have lasted 7 hours and 10 minutes, but this figure is without guarantee. He also managed to be relatively short. His funeral oration for Guevara here in Revolution Square on 18 October 1967 may have lasted just over an hour.

The Castro brothers and their group met Ernesto Guevara, a trained doctor and motorcyclist, in Mexican exile. They got used to him slowly. Socialist internationalism is nice in theory, but the Cubans didn't understand why an Argentine would be interested in the conditions on their island. Castro's group had had a baptism by fire after the failed attack on Moncada, which had brought them together, and suddenly here was an outsider with a different experience, a different accent in Spanish, and looking so impossibly beautiful to boot! Competitor. Speaking of looks, I'm convinced that their appearance as elegantly unkempt Hollywood stars, that incredible photogenic quality, was one of the reasons for the popularity of the Cuban coup in the leftist world. Picture the young *barbudos* Guevara, Cienfuegos, Matos and Fidel Castro side by side. One as the other could play alongside Paul Newman his accomplice in a bank robbery in a Metro Goldwyn Mayer production. Initially, then, Guevara was something of a rival. Intra-Latin American dynamics also play a role here. Argentinians have a reputation on the subcontinent for being uppity. My Brazilian friend Luiz told me that there is a joke about Argentines back home: What is the difference between an Argentine and God? God does not think he is Argentine.

Guevara was arrogant. He was also a committed Marxist. He was interested in Cuba as one of the third world countries where a Communist revolution could win. He sailed from Mexico with eighty revolutionaries on the desperately overloaded yacht Granma. It's a wonder they didn't drown. The seas were rough, the weather was bad, the wood of the old barge was cracking, the rebels were seasick. After several days of horror, they landed in southwest Cuba in what is now the province of Granma. They were immediately attacked by soldiers and not twenty of the rebels survived this first battle. Guevara then fought in the Sierra Maestra. Because of his education, he also served as a field surgeon. In almost two years, through hard work, intelligence and charisma, he developed into one of the guerrillas' leading figures. In Santa Clara, Che commanded a unit that captured an ammunition train, and on January 1, 1959, a group of rebels under his and Camilo's command entered Havana.

In the new government he became Minister of Economy and for a time also head of the Central Bank. He would explain to the US intelligence investigators who would later interrogate him after his capture in Bolivia how he, a physician and revolutionary, had become the first banker of the revolution. Fidel was chairing a cabinet meeting and was in the process of finding a bank chief. He asked his comrades if there was an economist among them. Guevara immediately raised his hand. But he misheard. Instead of the Spanish word *economista*, he heard *comunista*.

The banker Guevara did not deny the Communist in him. In 1960 he co-ordinated the persecution of people who did not conform to his doctrinaire definition of the new socialist man, including homosexuals, whom he branded as sexual perverts. He sent them, along with other class enemies, to be re-educated in the first concentration camp at Guanahacabibes. The government organized the camps under the slogan "Work Will Make a Man out of You." Its similarity to the Nazi "Arbeit macht frei" was not accidental. World Stalinism had many similarities with German Nazism, but in one respect it surpassed it, namely in the number of innocents murdered, not to mention the decimation of the economy and the destruction of the lives of entire generations.

Like the prisoners of the Gulag, the Cuban inmates were cheap labour, who could - as was the case - be tortured at will and raped. However, the Cool Cat Che, the hero of the Left, was not only homophobic. In his diaries you will find cruelly ironic descriptions of black Africans who, he said, "maintained their racial purity through their lack of passion for washing." As a proper Argentine, Guevara considered whites of European descent a superior race not only to Africans but also to Mexicans, who granted him temporary political asylum. He labelled them "a bunch of uneducated Indians."

In power, Guevara set a comradely example. He had himself filmed harvesting sugar cane with a machete. Half-naked, he ran at a great pace from one machine to another in the factory. Ideologically it was certainly correct, aesthetically less so because of his growing apparatchik belly. His visit to Moscow, where, as minister in charge of the economy, he was officially negotiating economic aid but behind closed doors arranging the route of a certain cruiser to Havana, became crucial. It had 36 nuclear warheads in its hold, each one with the destructive power of fifty Hiroshima bombs.

Guevara was a true adventurer. He didn't enjoy governing. After Nikita Khrushchev gave in to Kennedy and withdrew nuclear missiles from Cuba without consulting Havana, he began to turn against the Soviet Union. It seemed to him that Moscow was not doing enough for the world revolution. Castro, who was also offended at first, was bribed by the Russians with economic aid, the Hero of the Soviet Union medal, and the 'triumphal' trip across the Soyuz, but Guevara could not be swayed. At a time when Cuba's economy was becoming woefully dependent on the Soviet money supply, he began to openly criticize the Soviet Union, not only in Cuba but also during foreign travels in third world countries. He even compared Moscow's policies to those of the archdevil north of the Florida Straits. The Russians, of course, did not like this. Well, admit it, tovarishch Castro, where is his gratitude? What would he be without us? And by the way, what would you be without us? The 1990s gave the answer to the last question: nothing. Nothing in the form of a devastated economy, in the form of a country where people have nothing to eat.

But let's not get ahead of ourselves, we are only in April 1965. Fidel invites Che Guevara on the carpet, but he suspects the Argentine is no puppet. Their conversation behind closed doors lasts for hours. Long hours. I'm imagining a real Latino exchange. Both of their foreheads are furrowed, they are scratching at their hairy cheeks, at times shouting at each other, saliva bouncing from their mouths into the revolutionary space between them, then they're begging for sanity again. At the end of this episode, Guevara comes out of the office of the *comandante en jefe,* the commander-in-chief of the revolution, and he is no longer a minister, no longer a member of the Cuban government, he is just Comrade Guevara. Fidel will later announce that Che can return when he is ready. That will never happen. The life of apparatchik was not for him. He moved from Cuba to the Central African Congo, but there his efforts to turn a guerrilla war into a socialist revolution failed miserably. In late 1965, plagued by asthma attacks and dysentery, he withdrew from the battlefield. What now? What's Plan B? Plan C? He didn't want to go back to Cuba. Was he afraid to look Fidel in the face after the African fiasco, or was he simply fed up with the leader's hectoring? For six months he took refuge in the Cuban Embassy in Dar es Salaam, Tanzania, and then went to Prague.

It was his third visit to Czechoslovakia, but this time he did not come at the head of a government delegation as in 1960. The second time he was there almost secretly in the spring of 1965, apparently staying at the spartan Solidarity Hotel in Prague's Strašnice District. The third time he came to see his mistress, Tamara Bunke, a Jewish German from Argentina known by the nom de guerre Tanja. The Czechoslovak secret service took care of her, including training, false travel documents and visas, which they produced and provided. According to the investigative journalist Stanislav Motl, Guevara's small entourage stayed in the village of Ládví near Benešov in a safe house of the Ministry of the Interior. The rebel has changed his appearance completely. He shaved, cut his hair, put on dioptric glasses to avoid the attention of Western agents, and did not trust much even the StB, the Czechoslovak State Security, the secret political police which officially covered him. He posed as the Uruguayan businessman Ramón Benítez. He rested in Czechoslovakia from March to July 1966. He frequented pubs outside the capital and, according to the investigations of the former Argentine ambassador to the Czech Republic, Abel Posse, quoted by the Czech news server iDnes.cz, he did not like Czechoslovakia.

"Everything here is dull, grey and lifeless ... This is not socialism, but its failure. The whole of Prague is like a room from the Titanic. There is nothing left of the glorious days of the revolution," Guevara is said to have vented according to Posse.

From Prague he headed to South America and took refuge in the mountains of Bolivia, where he again tried to foment trouble. When the Bolivian president learned who was operating in the jungle, he asked the United States for help. President Lyndon Johnson dispatched CIA advisers to Bolivia who helped capture Guevara. One of them was Félix Rodríguez, an officer of the US intelligence agency who had participated in the 1961 anti-Castro military operation by exiles in the Bay of Pigs. He interrogated Guevara shortly before his death and, according to his later statements, tried to persuade the Bolivians to let him live. In vain. On the orders of President René Barrientos, Guevara was shot by a detachment of the army under the command of General Alfredo Ovanda.

Fidel took his time in publicizing information about the death of his rebel comrade. It took a week for the regime's media to announce it. Perhaps he wasn't sure if it was not an intelligence ruse. Maybe he was meditating on Guevara's legacy, planning how to handle it. In any case, the last competitor from his days fighting in the Sierra Maestra, still capable of eclipsing the radiance of his own star, had fallen away. Camilo was missing, Matos was squatting in the dark, and his younger brother Raúl was no competition. All his life he had moved in Fidel's shadow, faithfully fulfilling all his wishes. As the only one of the first set of revolutionaries, Raúl lacked the will to lead and the charisma. He knew this about himself, and it is possible that he dissipated his feelings of inadequacy with powerful doses of alcohol.

On 18 October 1967, Fidel held a memorial service for Guevara in the Plaza de la Revolución, launching the production of one of the most monstrous myths of the twentieth century, an age not exactly thin on myths. In his heartfelt speech at Martí's statue, whom Guevara remotely resembled with his martyr's death wish, he recalled his former banker as one of them, as a lad from the Granma, on whose deck in rough seas Che suffered unbelievably from asthma. He also recalled his alleged heroic deeds in battle and assured the assembled audience of his undying hatred of imperialism.

"Che represented the highest expression of revolutionary sacrifice, militancy and international spirit," he thundered from the podium.

For the avoidance of doubt, Fidel stressed that Che had not abandoned Cuba, but had merely embarked on a new stage in the spread of the world socialist revolution. He tactfully left out their final quarrel behind the doors of the Palace of the Revolution. The man who sent gays to concentration camps was now to become an example for all Cuban children.

"Be like Che," Fidel will repeat in the future with his typical obstinacy, and the regime's propaganda will display this statement alongside the portrait of the handsome guerrilla in a beret on hundreds of walls, posters and billboards alongside roads and dirt tracks from east to west along the length of the long island.

The revolution needs martyrs. After the war, the Czechoslovak Communists manufactured the myth of Julius Fučík, a Communist journalist and propagandist who was murdered by the Nazis. They published *Reportage Written on a Noose*, Fučík's properly ideologically adjusted notes from Pankrác prison, had it translated into dozens of languages and promoted around the world. Like Che, Fučík was good looking, and in the 1950s he was to become a symbol of youth, prematurely ended, but symbolically leading a new generation into a future without wars, into a world of socialist revolution. Compared to Guevara's similarly fabricated myth, Fučík 's was unlucky in that it operated in the territory of a small language circle. Despite more than three hundred foreign editions of the *Reportage*, in my travels and extended stays around the world I have not spoken to anyone who has read it or knows anything about Fučík, even if only his name. Everyone knows Guevara. Progressives wear him on their chests and write glowing pieces about him in their revolutionary publications. Any amount of those texts and images, including Hollywood's treatment of the Guevara legend, cannot hide the artificiality of the charade.

There is no myth like myth. Unlike the organically generated cultural myths, ideological myths are not vessels of knowledge, they are war cruisers of control. They are not encoded with authentic human agency that could be fruitfully interpreted and studied on levels that would tell us something new and interesting about ourselves. The ideological myths such as Guevara's and Fučík's are tautologies, referring only to themselves. Unlike authentic cultural myths, which are open to knowledge, dialogue and interpretation, ideological myths are closed systems. If you immerse yourself in them, you will soon recognize their shallowness, consisting of a limited number of platitudes. It's as if you want to go on an interesting journey of discovery, but you soon hit a wall. The distinction between the authentic myths of a given culture and the ideological myths of propaganda works here like the contrast between artistic statement and kitsch. Like aesthetic kitsch, the ideological myth, designed for superficial political polemics, relies on the appeal available to the greatest number of recipients. Handsome Che. Handsome Fučík. *Tomorrow there will be / dancing everywhere / when our victorious red flags / fly to the flagpoles of the world.* Made in the same sweatshop.

Alberto Korda's famous photographic portrait of Guevara, *Guerrillero heroico* (*Heroic Guerrilla*), was taken on March 5, 1960, at the Christopher Columbus Cemetery in Vedado. The occasion was a memorial service for those who died in a munitions explosion in Havana harbour the day before. In violation of safety regulations, the Cubans began unloading Belgian-supplied shells and ammunition from the French ship La Coubre right at the dock, and it was not long before the first explosions were heard. The vessel, loaded with 76 tons of explosives, turned into a huge bomb. Around a hundred people were killed in a series of explosions and rescue efforts. Castro was immediately clear: sabotage by the American imperialists! Although the US defence secretary denied that his country was involved and the Cubans presented no evidence, the version of the alleged sabotage is still circulating today.

In Korda's picture, Guevara wears a black beret with a Communist star, a jacket zipped up to his neck, and a look of the finest melancholy. Perhaps his mind is racing with memories of the previous day, during which he spent several hours treating the wounded at the port. The left cheek is a little less clear in the photograph; it is in shadow, the hair flowing unruly under the beret. One can hardly imagine a more iconic portrait of a revolutionary than this. Hundreds of later reproductions, cuts and filters have shifted the atmosphere of the original photograph, and with it its meaning. Almost imperceptibly, but still. There is less gloom and soft sadness, but more determination and hardness.

On Revolution Square, I take one last look at the metallic outline of Guevara's head at the Ministry of the Interior, and it occurs to me that this is the right way to do it in their iconography. The content of the face has disappeared completely, as has the original sadness for the lives lost. After all, the Interior Ministry isn't here to mourn the dead! The Interior Minsitry is the iron fist of the working class. Gone is the face of the doctor, mourning the dead whom he saw up close only the day before, whom he treated with his own hands, and in its place is the abstraction of the soldier of a better tomorrow.

"Everything Here Is Boring."

I'm shifting gears and disappearing towards the Malecón. Traffic is light, yet the waterfront is one of the busiest boulevards here. A strong wind blows in from the sea, moderating the air temperature, which has risen to thirty degrees. Filiberto persuades me to take advantage of the afternoon for a swim. He recommends the beach of Santa María del Mar, one of several east of Havana known by the collective geographical name of Playas del Este. I respond evasively. Filiberto insists, extolling the beauty of the beaches.

"You'll be there in twenty minutes by car."

"I'll think about it," I blurt out faster than I want to. I manage to end the awkward conversation. I have a different agenda for the afternoon, one I don't share with my conversation partner. On my right, we pass the tall building of the Ameijeiras Brothers Municipal Hospital near the university in the San Lázaro neighborhood. This is where dissident and political prisoner Orlando Zapata died in 2010 after an 80-day hunger strike. We cross the point where Belascoáin Avenue meets the waterfront, and on our right, we have once elegant colonial buildings that are slowly crumbling, falling apart, and some are already literally gone. Filiberto watches them in silence, as if he were seeing them for the first time, as if he had not lived here and was therefore not used to the dismal sight. His house is only a few minutes' walk away. I praise the beauty of the Malecón, and I don't mean that ironically. If the Cuban government were just a little bit normal, the Malecón would be one of the most captivating places in the world.

"The Malecón is beautiful, but look, my God, it's ruins. Ruins!" Filiberto's unfeigned lament for the city's departed beauty hits me with emotional intensity, especially since he verbalizes it in English, but with a Spanish "r" that still rattles with a sad echo under the car's roof. Rrruins!

"They are building new hotels near the Riviera Hotel, but nothing for the people. Communism, the most terrible thing in the world."

I cross San Lázaro Avenue, pass a few apartment blocks north of Paseo del Prado and drive slowly, because the streets are full of slow-moving dark-skinned people. In the afternoon sun on the dusty, dirty pavement surface, filled with potholes and garbage across its width, they evoke the graceful movements of tired predators, friendly, smiling predators, beasts that have long forgotten to hunt. They couldn't even roar properly anymore. Children in tattered shirts with logos of European football clubs and white shirts with red young pioneer scarves play in the smell of garbage. Cats and dogs weave between them. I stop in a guarded parking lot in a gap on Avenue Italia, a few hundred meters from the sea on the way to the main square, Parque Central. I bargain the amount for parking, without result, with the fleshy black man guarding the car park. I'll walk the rest of the way. I hand him the key and he honestly writes out the bill. Filiberto says goodbye. He goes to his residence. It's a short walk, just around the corner, and I make my way toward Havana's main square, with palm trees, fancy hotels, the Capitol building in sight, taxi drivers, cigar and prostitute matchmakers, drivers of restored American cars, rickshaw drivers, and a few tourists playing the role of victims of strategic hustle and bustle.

In the square I reach the light blue building of the Telégrafo Hotel. In its bar, I watched the Euro soccer final between Italy and Spain in 2012 with a few tourists, paying outrageous prices in convertible pesos for cocktails and internet access. I sit down in the garden of the hotel restaurant overlooking the square and am approached by a teenage boy from a barrier on the pavement. Moving his hand to his mouth, he indicates he wants money for food. I'm wary of this type of beggar. An acquaintance of mine offered food to one, he took offense, swore obscenities and walked away. As in many southern metropolises, there are organized groups of begging agents, children and women designed to arouse sympathy in foreigners, aka walking purses. Before I can react, the waiter chases the boy away.

The square is a palette of colors. Green palm trees, red and pink paint on old cars, blue sky with an honor guard of Cuban technicolor trains. I think of Guevara in Prague in 1966, which coincidentally was just a few months before I was born in September of that year.

"Everything here is dull, grey and lifeless."

Yes, my childhood. Growing up in the Prague of the seventies meant socializing to grey. Guevara was badly mistaken in his judgment of the character of our society, which was not a failure of socialism but its quintessential form. According to Posse's account, Guevara remarked at the time that nothing remained of the glorious revolution in our country. Nonsense. The "glorious" revolution of 1948 steered the ship of Czechoslovakia into just such a mushy bay. It was a necessary destination for her. Ships from every socialist country, from Vietnam to Poland to Venezuela, were headed for the glajchshalt-laden wasteland. New and new waves of leftist intellectuals, grasping at proverbial straws in their ideological drownings, claim that our communisms were in fact not really communisms at all, but deviations from the right path. Something went wrong somewhere and our regimes became perversions of a worthy idea. They do not say where and what supposedly failed.

And then there were the half-empty stores. The government had to respond to them. Even it felt the need to explain to the people why it had failed to produce this and that, to stock the shops on time, to have enough toilet paper, bananas and tangerines. Some items, common today, I didn't even know existed. I first ate broccoli in 1990 in Norway, when I was twenty-three. But their explanations were not really explanations, they were just excuses. First they talked about sabotage by imperialists. Later it was fashionable to ride on the ignorance of individual workers, always safely low on the power ladder. The Party had manufactured a conceptual apparatus for criticizing alleged deviations from the right path. At the end of communism, my university classmates and I used to joke about it. When, then, did we have unadulterated real socialism without mistakes, we asked mockingly? After the February 1948 "Victory" came the cult of Stalin's personality, a time of "mistakes" and "blunders." The 1960s suffered from "right-wing revisionism." In the 1970s and 1980s there was "stagnation" and "bureaucratic centralism." By process of elimination, the post-war period 1945-1947 came out: it must have been true socialism, the National Front government under Comrade Klement Gottwald! It was, of course, gallows humour.

Every socialist experiment, not only the Czech and Cuban ones, ended in the same failure. That there is something wrong with the original idea of forced uniformity does not occur to today's radicals. They cherry-pick the supposed successes of those regimes and so de facto parrot the old propaganda. *The New York Times* carried an article about the Soviet cosmonaut Tereshkova's trip into space as supposed proof of the emancipation of women in the Soviet Union. Feminists in gender studies departments dust off statistics on women's employment in the Soviet bloc as if it were some kind of proof of progress. Like men, women were not free in the slightest and faced the same sexism in the workplace as their sisters in the free world, except that they could not defend themselves against it. No woman had any real power then. There were only a few pawns.

There was no escape from the grey, figuratively and literally. In the seventies, people had black and white television sets. Most newspapers and magazines printed black and white photographs. No need to mention the boring content. The plaster of the houses was dingy, the streets choked with smog. Whole blocks were surrounded by scaffolding that stayed on the sidewalks for years. That workers would come, erect scaffolding, repair the house in a few weeks and take the scaffolding down again, as is common, was unknown to us. The scaffolding was forever, just like our friendship with the Soviet Union, as the banner that was hung on the scaffolding proclaimed. The behaviour of most people was also grey. We tried not to stand out. It was not a fault in the system, as Guevara believed, it was its fundamental feature. There was one right way, it was determined by the party and the government, and people were expected to conform. Communist ideologues were wary of diversion, deviation, distraction and dislocation. It was a laboratory of control, the opposite of a free society.

I don't like the word capitalism. It doesn't mean what most people mean by it, either admiringly or critically. It is a fixed concept in the vocabulary of Marx and Engels that is no longer able to explain any of the dynamics of today. Only the accident of a long ideological wedge has prolonged its use. If you say capitalism, most people think of it as the opposite of socialism/communism. The dichotomy is false. It suggests that there is a kind of symmetry whereby we have either communism/real socialism or capitalism. But the state of Cuban society proves that communism/real socialism is only a particularly harmful distortion, and its opposite is not capitalism, but a free society, which itself can take many forms according to its natural political, cultural and historical development. The opposite of a Communist economy is one based on free initiative. It can be regulated and taxed in various ways. "Capital" in it can have different functions and forms, according to the democratic decision of the citizens who live in such an economy.

Mirror perception is inherent in the Communists. For them, the world beyond the border is a world in reverse. Their way of thinking judges others by themselves, ascribing to others similar motives for action to which they are guided. They cannot imagine anything different. Surprisingly, this way of perception took hold during the long years of totalitarian isolation and survives to this day.

3.

Unless You're a Foreigner.

Havana

I'm staying at Yosvany's on Ánimas Street. It's a clean apartment on the first floor of a dirty building two minutes walk from the Prado. A large part of the living room with the kitchenette is taken up by a dance floor. In addition to Airbnb, Yosvany also runs a private dance studio. He's a taller, bearded gay man in his 30s, slightly uptight. The night I arrived he nervously watched my suitcase maneuvers around the dance floor. He's afraid I'll step on it. On the walls of the apartment hang posters with dance motifs and photos of ballet creations.

In the morning we sit in the kitchen on bar stools together with a few tourists. The polished wood of the parquet floor reflects the sunlight streaming in from the large French windows. I yawn. The room has a beautiful morning light. The chairs stand in a single row in front of the counter, on which a well-kept lady in her years with a suspicious look places our food. She has everything down to the last egg. No refills of coffee. No encore. Yosvany is not here. The lady is helped at the stove by a young man whom I mistake for his friend. Yosvany's real boyfriend, I learn, is currently in Madrid.

What is so disturbing about the whole breakfast ritual is not so much that they don't have enough food, but that the lady and the young man stand opposite us the whole time and watch us while we eat. Their faces are screwed into smiles that are un-Cubanly artificial. There is no milk in the coffee, the bread has its best days in the past, and the next day there are cracker biscuits instead. The sausage tastes chemical. The omelette is essentially one egg, and when I unwittingly want to top up my diluted juice, a debate arises as to whether it's allowed. Everything here has rules. For example, I can't make my own coffee, which was brought by Jimena

Cervantes, a law student from Central America who travels with me in tandem. Looking at her subtle figure and the size of her huge suitcase, I immediately realise, firstly, that I will be lugging it everywhere and, secondly, that she has six months' worth of provisions with her. She's also carrying used children's clothes to give away to the needy. After all, Christmas is coming.

"You can't go to the stove. Those are the rules set by the owner. But I'll make you your coffee, I haven't had a good imported one in so long..." says the young man slyly. His behaviour is different from that of most Cubans, who are naturally friendly and hospitable.

After breakfast, Jimena and I run down the staircase from the first floor. Something strange is running down it, I hope it's just dirty water. Downstairs we open the iron grill and through the chaos of Ánimas Street we head for the Prado, a boulevard with an avenue and pedestrian zone in the middle. It's flanked on both sides by the dilapidated palaces of Spanish rule. The modernist Cine-Teatro Fausto, which once shone and was crawled over by giant metal ants during a biennial, is abandoned. Compared to my visits a few years ago, I see fewer chasers. People sit on the steps and watch the surrounding clamour. Covid dealt them a hard blow.

At the end of the Prado by the sea, where the boulevard meets the Malecón, is the new luxury hotel Paseo del Prado. When I pass by tomorrow evening, I will see two prosperous men sitting by the window, discreetly discussing something over a drink. There's a deal coming. How does it feel to be rich in the middle of all this misery? I see a shiny black Mercedes parked in front of the Kempinski Hotel, which must have cost a good 300 hundred thousand dollars. Who'd have thought to buy this toy for the local roads? I'm guessing a baseball star who came here for two weeks to have a relationship with the government.

Through Parque Central we go to the alleys of Old Havana to buy a Cuban SIM card. Phoning and texting to Europe is expensive. On the edge of Calle Obispo is the famous La Moderna Poesía bookstore, but I don't look inside this time. It's under renovation. Veils of heavy, cloudy plastic hang over it. There are posters celebrating Eusebio Leal's eightieth birthday in various places around the centre. The signs play with double meaning - *leal* means loyal and Eusebio will remain loyal to Havana for eternity, judging by the propaganda. We go to the ETECSA store a few minutes down the Obispo, beyond Floridita. It's not easy to buy a SIM card in Cuba. There are two uniformed guards at the locked entrance. When they open the door, they ask why we want in.

"SIM card? Then sit down here. You have your passport with you, yes?"

We sit down on a bench in the corner of the vestibule in front of the spacious inner hall. There are only a few people in it, but we're not allowed in yet. Clearly ETECSA is into overstaffing. Several uniformed men walk up and down the hall, their only job is to keep an eye on the situation. I feel as safe as I would at Fort Knox, where they keep some of America's gold reserves. The only treasure I see here is a couple of low-end smartphones in a locked display case. Outside on Obispo, people stroll around and I can either watch the bustle of the street or the commercials for Cuba that run in a video loop on the flatscreen TV here. Images of white sand beaches, Floridita dancers and old churches in Trinidad are interspersed with advertisements for medical tourism. Doctors in white coats smile at the screen and helpful nurses help elderly Europeans to modern machines. Their style is reminiscent of the commercials that were filmed in our country in the 1980s.

We are instructed to move to another bench in the hall closer to the counter where we will be checked in at some point in the near future. But not yet. The overemployment at ETECSA is not about the saleswomen. There's only one. Hence the line. To my right, I get a view of a large video screen made up of several monitors. It runs the same loop as the one in the lobby, but because the video is poorly formatted for the size of the projection screen, the people, buildings, and landscapes on it look distorted like in a fairgrounds mirror maze. Everything is a little flattened and a little too wide. The wide faces of the doctors and nurses. Wide churches. Wide ETECSA assembly worker climbing a stunted but wide mast. Wide are the arms of revolutionary Cuba.

After an hour of waiting, we proceed from our bench to the counter, but we can't complain. It's cool inside, the air conditioning is working, while outside the late tropical morning is beginning to rage. At the counter, it takes another fifteen minutes to fill out all the forms and check the documents, after which the saleswoman, less helpful than the nurses with their promotional smiles, informs us that we have become the owners of an official phone number in Cuba. Armed with a SIM card with the prefix +53, we set off for the Old Town.

In the Plaza de la Catedral, the sun is frying the shadows, reflecting off the peeling plaster, and the last thing one wants to do is work. It's hot that even the grey and white stone of the cathedral is swarming and green as it quietly exhales the dreams of a trying city. I pass book stalls set up on the street. The sun's brightness reflects off the paper covers. This is where I once bought a well-worn collection of poems, *Versos sencillos* by José Martí, which someone in Prague had ordered from me. It was from it that the lyrics to *Guantanamera*, about a village girl in Guantánamo province (guajira Guantanamera), Cuba's most famous song, were written. The lyrics come from four poems published in this collection.

We enter a nearby bookstore. English-language literature here is limited to left-wing radicals and Hemingway. I browse the shelves of poetry. The shop is almost empty, clean, smells of new books. In the corner, a tall teenage girl in a young pioneer uniform stands calmly discussing the book with her parents. I assume it's a family. The father is wearing pressed khaki pants and an expensive Ralph Lauren golf shirt. Since he doesn't have a dude collar turned up, as is customary in the country, I'm guessing he's an intellectual. An official one who knows when and where to use the situationally appropriate lexicon of revolution. The regime rewards him for it. The girl is holding a book and her parents are consulting with her. The father nods and the girl happily walks away with the book to the cash register. Literature for a good grade. It's a momentary and touching glimpse into a normal life that doesn't involve trying to pump you for a few dollars, a serious and, in its own way, comforting episode.

Another poster of Leal hangs in the Plaza de Armas. There are a few tables in the arcade of a stone building. The Air France steward I remember most clearly from my Paris-Havana flight is having lunch here. A short, agile Asian type. Two dogs copulate by the low fence of the park. On the fence, where the canines are enjoying themselves, hangs a banner

'Chevron-Tóxico,' caricaturing the famous oil companies that have displeased the Venezuelan *compañeros*. Now, as I did years ago, I'm looking at the Hemingway plaque on the facade of the Ambos Mundo Hotel. Back then, the sound of a piano came from its bowels. A torrential rain started, a fierce summer storm, and I went inside. A blonde pianist was playing a romantic piece that no one was listening to. I stood a good three feet from the open window and felt the drops bouncing off the sill on my bare calves. The chasers had come here to hide, and the waiters let them their shirts to dry.

A friend of mine aptly said that just as Franz Kafka turned into a kind of Mickey Mouse of Prague, Ernest Hemingway became a Havana Mickey Mouse. The greats impress the more educated tourists. They lend an assumed depth to flat business life: suddenly a hotel is not just a place to stay. This kind of commerce is pushed by genre books that say, where did the famous actor X stay, see, over there, in that corner apartment on the third floor, how those two windows are lit up? And this is where such and such a movie was filmed. By the way, do you know that when Mastroianni walked past the fountain at night, his wristwatch fell into it? But it's gonna be harder and harder to keep up this faux-intellectual tourism. Fewer and fewer people have any idea what we're talking about. Previously, some visitors had an idea in which part of the cultural map to locate Kafka, Hemingway, and the goold soldier Josef Švejk.

"Ah, Kafka! Yeah, Hemingway..."

A knowing nod and a quick search through the folds of the cortex for titles drilled in high school. *A Farewell to Arms...*

Today, there are few such tourists on the streets of cities; reference points have shifted from literature and art to movie blockbusters and computer games. Hemingway is just another name that says nothing, like Jimmy Carter and St. Francis of Assisi. Nine out of ten visitors to Prague know zilch about Švejk. Neither literature nor philosophy has the social status it had the year Hemingway won the Nobel Prize.

In the 1950s, the traditionally educated elite set the tone and theme. Since then, discourse has democratized, with infinitely more people participating who have other interests and less time to read novels and philosophical treatises. Fiction gets diluted in the solution of the larger volume. With diminishing prestige, it has become the domain of *connoisseurs*. The younger generation reads it minimally, sales are down, and familiarity with genres is disappearing. My students at an elite US university confuse the novel with nonfiction. In a term paper, they will calmly write that Aristotle says this and that in his novel.

Waiting in the Boat

One colorful morning the master woke up in room 511. His head ached after a night of drinking. He took a shower, checked if his leather shoes had dried out since the evening, had toast, eggs and black coffee in the café downstairs. He read the paper and ran his eyes over the results of the baseball *gran ligas*. When his metabolism returned to balance, he briskly made his way to the cove where a rigged fishing boat was waiting, including several bottles of Hatuey lager on ice. It was time to hunt. Like wild beast in the savannah the master chases after a triumph. When he publishes *Across the River and into the Trees*, a novel about aging against the backdrop of postwar paralysis in Venice, critics write him off, and he needs to prove to time itself that he is not finished.

He will find his next story here, in Cuba. Not much of a story, really. It tells about an old fisherman from a coastal suburb of Havana named Santiago, whose determination to break through a door barricaded by bad luck leads him to a near-final battle with fish and fate. If *The Old Man and the Sea* isn't required reading here, it should be. In Cuba, in a culture that gravitates toward expansion rather than introspection, the trophy collector describes defeat and vulnerability brilliantly.

The Old Man won the Pulitzer Prize and became a major item of credit to the Nobel Committee when it awarded Hemigway the 1954 Literature Prize. Immediately upon its publication, the novella attracted clever symbolic interpretations. Santiago is said to be like Jesus. No, no, he's like Joe DiMaggio. To this hermeneutic, the author was merciless: 'There is no symbolism,' he wrote to the critic Berenson. "The sea is the sea. An old man is an old man ... Sharks are ... sharks ... All the symbols they talk about now are just bullshit."

José Antonio Fornaris waits in front of the Inglaterra Hotel in the cover of a tourist bus. He suggests going to Sloppy Joe's, a famous institution. From the 1930s to the 1950s, celebrities frequented it as well people fleeing Prohibition and sometimes the law. It burned down in the mid-'60s. The neo-classical building decayed for decades. But as we know from the poster, Leal is loyal. As part of an urban renewal, the bar reopened.

I met José Antonio in the summer of 2012. While looking for his house in the suburb of Managua, I realized how vast and diverse the capital is. I searched about an hour for his cozy abode with an atrium in a neighborhood resembling a forest park. In the days before GPS navigation, such a task was akin to the plots of spy movies. When I finally found it, we settled into a small backyard full of flowers and greenery. Waiting for us was his wife, freelance journalist Amarilis Cortina Rey (some sources give her name as Reyes), who at the time was writing a blog for the Bratislava daily *Sme*. She playfully addressed José Antonio by his surname, pronouncing it in Cuban, without the last letter:

"Fornari!" Amarilis calls into the kitchen, where José Antonio is preparing coffee. When he brings us three cups on a tray, she addresses him with playful assertiveness:

"What do you say, Fornari?"

José Antonio's shorter grey hair, combed up, crowns his shy introvert look. When he regards you, the word loyalty comes to mind. I know him as a considered glossator, and I think to myself that in the Czech Republic he would work in public radio, where he would patiently, without gestures, comment on the elections. The shriller voice of Amarilis, seven years younger than José Antonio, echoes through the courtyard. For a few seconds, we are like a painting called Visiting the Dissidents. A married couple welcomed the guest and isolated him from the war zone behind the fence. The world suddenly seems normal. Amarilis, a woman with an oval face and a prominent nose, tells how she was going to watch the trial of another dissident Julia Delgado in the Arroyo Naranjo neighborhood. Five State Security agents blocked the courtroom door and prevented her from entering. In doing so, they violated their own laws. At the end of the trial, Delgado was given a year in prison.

Amarilis also tasted the act of repudation, at least a version of it. It happened during the regular procession of the Ladies in White after Sunday Mass. In May 2010, she wrote about it in the Slovak newspaper. "We found ourselves in the middle of a crowd that attacked us verbally and physically. We held hands... Along the way we faced racism, bullying and lies from state television. The traffic stopped and passers-by looked at us curiously. Again the poor, hackneyed slogans and repeated insults, racial attacks against the black Ladies in White."

José Antonio and Amarilis worked on the Primavera de Cuba news project but left the team due to disputes with colleagues. Undeterred, they worked with eight other journalists to produce a newsletter, Cuba Prensa Libre, with a circulation of 200. The title is a tribute to the Cuban newspaper, which was published from 1941 to 1960, before Castro banned it. They organised a photography exhibition to mark the anniversary of the first Cuban newspaper. The newspaper was called *Papel Periódico*, founded in 1790 and published as a daily newspaper from 1793. The exhibition was held in the Bridge Gallery at the home of one of the collaborators. They were ordinary pictures of Havana life, as José Antonio says, nothing overtly political. Yet the regime wanted to ban it.

"What didn't they like?"

"Maybe the crumbling buildings in the photos. Or an abandoned dog in the middle of the street. Probably wasn't revolutionary enough."

He was detained for the day because of the exhibition.

"That's the risk of doing business. We have prepared another exhibition, this time not of photographs but of paintings. We are also building a journalism library. It's named after the first newspaper, *Papel Periódico*."

At the corner of Ánimas and Agramonte, José Antonio and I walk into Sloppy Joe's, a stylish bar lined with mahogany wood. In 1958, Hollywood filmed the movie *Our Man in Havana* here, based on a novel by Graham Greene. The menu jumps out at me for an espresso with honey. The creeping gentrification.

"How is Amarilis?" I ask.

"She went to Florida," he says.

After the 1959 coup, the government restricted travel, so Cubans were locked in the same cage as Czechs and Slovaks before 1989. Recently, however, travel has been freed up. If you have money to spend, you can go wherever you want. Due to the limited financial resources available, the ability to fly and afford accommodation around the world is a luxury that is accessible to only a select few. Generally, those who have relatives residing in the United States have the financial backing necessary to undertake such travels. Additionally, dissidents may be able to secure the necessary funds through foreign sponsors or non-governmental organizations supporting their cause. The decision proved masterful on the part of the regime, as it added another bone of contention to an already fractious dissent. Activists keep track of who has been invited where and envy each other's travels. "How is it possible that you've been to Stockholm and Brazil, and I've only been to Bratislava?"

I'm asking if Amarilis is visiting or has emigrated. I can tell from his tone that this is a sensitive subject. Maybe he doesn't know, maybe she doesn't know herself. She says she doesn't like Florida. She's a cleaner and can't get a proper job, he says. He looks out into the street through the milk glass of the bar counter.

Journalist and human rights activist José Antonio Fornaris Ramos is the president of the Association for Press Freedom, which he founded in 2006. He was born in 1952. He studied journalism at the University of Havana and then worked as a radio editor and scriptwriter. He became a dissident in 1998. He wrote for the Cuba-Verdad website and devoted his time to organizing the independent scene. He also writes for the foreign press.

He's drinking a Coke on the rocks.

"Sometimes the cops are nice to me. They play a game with me. They sit across from me and you can see they've done their research. They say to me:

'You wrote in the 1970s about the changes needed. You are a leader who can be critical, but you are decent.'

I don't know what that means. Maybe they're toying with the idea of cultivating an organization that isn't pro-exile. They know my views. They want to survive and provide for their own families. The people upstairs are such historical artifacts already. They're trying to stabilize the situation. They'll do what's convenient for them. Today they smile at me, and tomorrow they might cut my head off."

When Obama normalised diplomatic relations, José Antonio pointed to the zero results of his policy. The left abroad deflects such criticism with labels: what else can you expect from die-hard Castro haters? In his case, however, they are off target. José Antonio's tired, affable eyes are those of a kindly poet. Frustration creeps into his voice at the end of his sentences, manifesting itself in a higher tone and a kind of almost imperceptible question mark that is there even after the announcement lines. It's like asking yourself why you're never quite understood.

"After the 2022 demonstrations, the regime cracked down hard. Some young activists were sentenced to 23 and 28 years in prison for coming out to protest," José Antonio pointed out on a recent visit to Spain. "This is terrible. People have the right to freedom of expression and assembly, Article 54 of their own constitution recognises this. But this is just a theory...The problem is also that there are still people in the world who give Cuba as an example worth following. They do this, of course, because they don't live there and they don't know the situation there. That is clear, from the outside it looks different. People are fleeing, they are selling their houses, even those who live in lucrative Havana neighbourhoods such as Miramar. They're trying to get out because they have no hope. They are fleeing through Jamaica and other neighbouring countries."

He reminds me of Santiago. He's about his age today. He has a sense of journalistic tradition, remains true to it even in rough seas. His fishing boat is under attack by sharks, and with his dwindling strength he clutches the rope that cuts into his palms.

"I've gone too far," Santiago says to himself.

When do we know we have reached the line separating premature resignation from overestimating our strength? Yes, without the Sisyphian toil we will not know the true meaning of things, as Camus and Havel knew. "Only those who risk going too far can discover how far it is possible to go," wrote T. S. Elliot.

Still, sometimes it must be better to pack it all up and run away to Florida. But when? The answer eventually came. Even José Antonio and

Amarilis have hit their limits. Amarilis returned to Cuba from her former residence in Florida and continued her independent journalism with her husband. Recently, however, they both went to Central America, where they knocked on the door of an international nonprofit. It seems their long Cuban chapter is over.

The Revolution Is Losing its Color

Tania Díaz Castro is fighting an unequal battle with her new Dell Inspiron laptop, which she says she got from a friend in Miami. She can't get the program to install and set up properly. For people her age, such tasks are not trivial. She was born in 1939 in the municipality of Camajuaní in the then province of Las Villas. If José Antonio is the voice of a seasoned generation of journalists, Tania is a living legend of independent journalism and the human rights movement. I visited her in her little house in the Santa Fe district of Havana, where she lived alone with her dog and a few cats. You feel like you're in the country. The small buildings are surrounded by green gardens and you have to walk across a piece of land to get to Tania's dwelling, because it is located not in the front but in the middle of the plot. I reflexively look for the State Security surveillance cameras. I'm wearing a baseball cap and sunglasses over my eyes, but it's a truly pofidery camouflage.

"There used to be about seven or eight of us freelance journalists and we all knew each other. José Antonio Fornaris was one of us. With the internet it's easier to organise, there are hundreds of bloggers of different quality. We also have quite a few serious independent journalists, I estimate there may be around a hundred on the whole island. When we wanted to start an independent newspaper, *La Franquesa,* in 1990, we had to steal paper from somewhere and we were only able to make maybe a hundred copies. Sometimes we really only made carbon copies. That was when our dear Yoani Sánchez was still playing with dolls, wasn't it?" says Tania, winking mischievously.

We chat in her small living room overlooking the garden. I look at the shelf where her books are lined up. There are collections of her own poetry, once published by the official writers' union when she was not yet a dissident. *The New York Times* has described her as an accomplished poet. Tania attended a convent school and worked as a reporter for several magazines. Like José Antonio, she wrote radio scripts and also contributed to a newspaper for the Chinese minority in Havana. In 1988 she helped found the Human Rights Party, the first opposition party since the coup. In November of that year, she visited a friend in prison, the poet Ernesto Díaz Rodríguez, jailed for twenty years. Because of this, she herself was sentenced to a year for disturbing public order. She then tried to register the party with the authorities, but in vain. She organised petitions for a referendum on the legitimacy of Castro's dictatorship, and for that she went to jail again.

She tells me about Dr. Alfredo Samuel Martínez Lara, the Secretary General of the party. He was arrested in March 1990 and charged with sedition. He stood trial in February 1991, was found guilty, but received a light sentence of three years "restricted freedom," and then was released from custody.

"Several others of us party members were given between three months and one year of restricted freedom for illegal association."

Dr Martínez was charged with inciting the violent overthrow of the government in collaboration with the CIA, but the evidence presented to the court was ridiculous even by local standards, so he got off with a relatively light sentence. Under the provisions of the Cuban Penal Code, anyone sentenced to "restricted freedom" is subject to various limitations and supervision by the authorities. Tania says they didn't leave him alone even after that and locked him up several more times.

"In 1989 we were in the house of dissident Sebastian Arcos Bergnes when one of the worst and longest acts of repudiation took place there."

Dr Martínez Lara eventually went into exile. He continued his political work there.

"He took care of us as his own, he was interested in us. From there he helped us a lot. He was a great person," Tania says.

"Was?"

"He died in Miami. Sudden cardiac arrest. He was young, only 53 years old."

Tania sees me as an ambassador from a country that has managed to do what Cuba has not yet. In her memories, she keeps returning to the late

80s and early 90s. She asks about the end of the dictatorship in Czechoslovakia. Her generation of dissent was influenced by the ideas of Václav Havel and the strategy of Charter 77.

"At that time I was just in prison, but I felt happy. I had seen the Soviet bloc collapse! In 1976, the activist Ricardo Bofill founded the Human Rights Committee here in Cuba. He was the one who punched the first hole in the wall. In 1988, he was forced to emigrate to the United States. There, President Reagan received him at the White House. We then built on his work and enlarged the hole."

We talk about life in this quiet neighborhood. Tania corrects me, she says it is calm now. But there was a time when there was a car outside the fence with State Security officers. Twenty-four/seven.

"You wouldn't have gotten to me then. They would have picked you up right at the gate."

I look out the window in a slightly foolish attempt to see the surveillance camera. Or at least a curious neighbor. To get my bearings. But Tania says no one here trusts the government anymore.

"Fidel's revolution is losing its color in the minds of Cubans. It's beginning to fade. I'm the only one here in Santa Fe, I think, who watches the TV news every day. I don't know if you can call it news. They present this unreal world. It would be nice to live in Cuban TV news."

Behind the black frames of her glasses I see laughing eyes. Her body moves with difficulty, but her head goes full speed without hindrance.

"I'll tell you a joke about it. You know our anecdotes about Pepito?"

I nod. Pepito jokes are a famous Cuban genre. Tania's gonna do an acting etude:

"Pepito is sitting in his desk, with his hand raised and shouting with excitement, 'Comrade teacher, comrade teacher, our cat has kittens! They were born yesterday! Seven kittens!'

'That's nice, Pepito,' replies the teacher, 'but don't interrupt. Seven kittens, you say?'

'Seven. And six Communists!'

'Wait, Pepito, how come there's only six? What about the seventh?'

'The seventh has already opened its eyes.'"

I remember hearing that joke a long time ago, but it still makes me laugh. Surveillance cameras are far away now. It would be interesting to chart anti-regime jokes across the Communist world. How did they come about? I imagine they used to go from Europe to Cuba with union tours, but they could have gone the other way. Tania's getting back to the serious stuff.

"The history of the struggle for human rights in Cuba is interesting. I am proud to have been there at the beginning and to have been there until the end. The human rights movement alone cannot overthrow a dictatorship, it does not have and will not have the strength to do so. But it can steadily undermine it, and in so doing weaken it. Today, there are thousands of houses in Cuba where the opposition meets. This was not the case in 1980."

When we say goodbye, I ask if she wants to bring something from the Czech Republic. She says she would appreciate photocopies of her articles that are published in Czech newspapers. In 2007, she started a blog on iDnes.cz in which she drew scenes from Cuban life and politics (she closed it in 2016). When I go out into the garden, already in black glasses and baseball cap again, she is still calling to me from the door:

"I know Václav Havel's books by heart. He was the most important teacher for us!"

The former pro-regime journalist and now dissident Reinaldo Escobar is proud of his wife. He once almost attacked a commie apparatchik who publicly insulted her. Escobar challenged him to a duel to defend her honor like a true Latino. His friends had to hold him down on the boulevard near Plaza de la Revolución to prevent the worst from happening. Curses flew through the air and the threat of jail loomed over the scene. Reinaldo's wife is Yoani Sánchez, almost 30 years his junior.

With the internet the age of bloggers came also to Cuba, the most famous of which was Yoani. I tried to contact her on my previous trips, but she was abroad. I was greeted at their apartment in New Vedado by Reinaldo, a black-curly-haired rebel. We talked recent history, but also discussed Central Europe, about which he knew quite a lot. Their apartment, on one of the top floors of a tower block high above nearby

Revolution Square, surprised me with its generous size. It accommodated part of the nascent editorial office of an independent media organization, and there was also a stage made of parquet floors at the end of the spacious living room against the wall for lectures and conferences. Reinaldo mentioned that when the tenement was being built in the 1970s according to Yugoslav technology, he himself was involved in the construction as a temporary worker. He said the technology would allow the high-rise to withstand even earthquake. In Cuba, however, all recent earthquakes have been exclusively political.

In 2007, Yoani founded the blog Generación Y and became an international star. Living in the Spanish language circle has its advantages. Cubans are similar in number to Czechs, above ten million. However, the potential audience for Spanish-language journalists is around half a billion people. Around the world, Yoani is seen as a representative of the movement, invited to conferences and given prizes. Her blog has been translated into seventeen languages by volunteers and read by millions. Later, their web project grew. Today, she and Reinaldo run 14Ymedio.com, founded in 2014 as Cuba's first independent news website.

Generation Y refers to millennials born in the last quarter of the century. The name derives from the fact that many people from that time have names beginning with a y: Yaniel, Yenifer, Yunior, Yulieski, Yoel, Yandra, Yanet... They are variations on common local names, often inspired by American names. The original inspiration was Russian, the first name the most famous, Yuri as in Gagarin, who visited Cuba just months after his famous space flight.

My landlord, Yosvany, belongs to this generation. He advised me to keep my gold chains at home. I wear two, one thicker empty and the other thinner with a cross.

"Why?" I ask. "Is Havana dangerous?"

"Not dangerous. But Cuba is poor. You never know."

Horrifying stories are told about violent crime in Latin America. In countries like Venezuela, Colombia, Ecuador, and even in developed Argentina, there are neighbourhoods to watch out for. It's good to keep an eye on what's going on around you. That's not true of Havana yet. Not once did I feel unsafe. I walked through a supposedly not-quite-safe area at two in the morning, past industrial warehouses illuminated by the tired light of streetlamps, and felt as safe as in the center of Prague at noon. The government has a monopoly on organized crime in Cuba, and it doesn't care about my gold chain. In totalitarian dictatorships, street crime tends to be minimal. I have no doubt that when the government falls and the country opens up to the world and integrates, it will get really dangerous in some neighborhoods. The drug trade will arrive big time. The Cubans who are living in squalor today will say it was better before.

The government still controls almost everything. It has built up tourism, which is organised by the military through the GAESA consortium, but measured in global financial flows and cultural exchange, Cuba is on the sidelines. The internet is getting faster, more and more people have access to it, but the regime has good reason not to let the situation get completely out of hand. As a generation of revolutionaries dies out, their children are enriching themselves while ensuring impunity in the event of a transition from a rigid form of dictatorship to a looser society.

It was only in 2011 that the government allowed people to own, buy and sell cars without special permits. Until then, only vehicles that were already in the country before 1959 could be traded without a permit. The bizarre measure has turned Havana into a de facto museum of old American cars. Many of them, however, have almost nothing original left in them except the ancient chassis and seats. I recently sat in an old Plymouth. The steering wheel and gearbox were from a Volkswagen, the wheels from a Peugeot and the engine, judging by the puffs of black smoke billowing from the exhaust, from a Russian tank. When I once got into my friend's red Lada in the summer heat at the bottom of the hill on which the Hotel Nacional stands, his rusty car was some thirty-five years old.

"And if I want to sell it, I'll get six thousand dollars for it tomorrow."

I wondered how much one of those horrible smelling American cars would cost.

"Ten thousand dollars," he says without blinking, turning onto the Malecón across the double yellow line into oncoming traffic. The value of the Americas is enhanced by their spaciousness. People use them as bulk taxis that can be hitched anywhere and can easily load eight people. They are paid for in the national currency. Unless you're a foreigner.

The First Raid

Two secret police cameras are watching Antonio's villa. That's why I'm not going directly there. Early in the morning, Antonio will pick me up near the Hotel Nacional and take me to his garage. Like in a time capsule, I travel in his car to his house, where I will conduct a day-long seminar on the transition to democracy.

Among dissidents Antonio Rodiles is unusual. He comes from a once prominent Bolshevik family. He studied physics in Mexico and the United States, so he speaks perfect English. His first wife and two daughters still live in the States. When he was a student, he turned against Castro and did something unexpected: He returned home. His anti-regime group, Estado de SATS, operates out of the sprawling seaside villa where he lives with his current wife, Ailer González Mena, and his mother, who is in advanced retirement.

In the hall I meet Antonio's activist friends. There's a black man, Manuel Cuesta Morúa, an independent socialist. He speaks fluent English and has a philosophical bent. He is always willing to exchange views in a friendly, gentle and civil manner, and this is the exception among impulsive Cubans. I also meet José Díaz Silva of the Movement for a New Republic. Two lawyers come in, Vcizant Boloy and Yaremis Flores. Later, the filmmaker and photographer, the elegant and reserved Claudio Fuentes Madan joins. I know Claudio from a brief encounter in the lobby of the Iberostar Parque Central hotel. Estado has launched a campaign called Por otra Cuba, For a Different Cuba, and Claudio shows me on his laptop a promotional video he has produced. At that time, a number of independent journalists and bloggers began making videos, the quality of which was marred by beginner's inexperience. Not his, Claudio is a professional. He edited the video like a hip-hop clip. The artists used it to promote the Voto Unido petition. In the video I see Gorki Águila, whom I know from Prague. His band Porno para Ricardo was a hit at Prague's United Islands festival and Gorki nearly fainted with happiness when he met the famous British guitarist Jeff Beck at the Mill Cafe in Kampa.

We are discussing the restitution of property in our country after the fall of communism. There is no consensus around the table as to whether such a thing is feasible in Cuba.

"Half the buildings in Havana are coming down. People have no place to live. Something has to be done quickly," says Antonio. "Our situation is not very similar to yours. I'm not sure large-scale restitution would work here."

He speaks decisively, energetically, from a position of leadership. His analysis is meticulously precise. He does not deny the technically trained intellectual in him. He sees society as a play of forces and vectors. His views are conservative. He stands by them emotionally but with respect for others at the big round table. During a break, Antonio recalls a public event held here at the villa. It consisted of a panel discussion and a concert and attracted dozens of people.

"Aren't you afraid of secret police agents coming here?"

"Of course there will always be a few of them at these events," he says with icy calm. In his glasses and tousled hair, he looks like a professor from some university in the States, younger than he really is.

"We don't care. After all, this house is almost certainly bugged."

The police tried to disrupt their concert by blasting extremely loud music from the balconies of the hotel next door. Antonio's friends responded the same way. They pulled the speakers out onto the terrace facing the sea and turned up the volume. It was hell for a while. Then the police gave up and left them alone.

Ailer, Antonio and I are thinking out loud about organizing an international conference in his house, combined with an art festival. Ailer would like to invite musicians and artists from Prague. Then in the next few months they will really set up the conference, so I'm planning to attend on my next visit to Cuba. I'm invited as one of the panelists.

I'll be up very early that morning. At the *casa particular* on the Malecón, I throw in an egg and coffee, then catch a taxi. It rained almost all day yesterday, but today looks promising. To my right is the bright blue of the ocean, calm as a lake among the forests. The climate is fresh, the air over the bay full of anticipation. We pass the brutalist Russian Embassy building. The population density is thinning. As we leave the wider center, the landscape puts on the character of an urban periphery. We head towards the sturdy triangle of the Panorama Hotel. Flags of many countries on flagpoles in a semicircle flutter in the wind that blows in from the sea, a few dozen metres away. The more provincial the society, the more international flags around the hotels.

I step into the reception lobby and look for a place to sit. I observe a man with an unhealthy complexion of expired white. Longer greasy hair tied in a ponytail caresses the shoulders of his yellowish shirt. He's lighting a cigarette. A young guy, a biologist I guess, a Russian, which the lobby is full of. His back is straight as if reinforced by the strap of a leather bag that doesn't hang nonchalantly from one shoulder but crosses his chest in a tight, nerdy way. He's straight out of the seventies. Two elderly Russian diplomats with beer bellies stuffed into tight shirts, their nondescript ties barely reaching their navels, entertain a young Cuban woman in accented Spanish.

Antonio's nowhere. He was supposed to be here at eight, but twenty minutes have passed since then. There are two entrances to the lobby. I study the faces hidden behind dark glasses and baseball caps. Forty minutes, and nothing. I fiddle with a white Samsung Galaxy, reserved for emergencies. I walk out the glass door and walk toward the ocean and back. Then I sit back down in the café and order another espresso. The glass and marble interior is full of flowers. Almost an hour and a half after Antonio was supposed to show up, I send a text to Prague to the number provided. I'm instructed to wait. Another glass of orange juice, another sighting of Russian tourists. There's a new batch of them now. I could draw them from memory. Then I get a text from Ailer forwarded to me by Prague telling me that Antonio has been detained by the police and that I should definitely avoid their house. She says it is surrounded by security forces. I pay, stiffened from sitting on the leather armchair, stretch and leave the hotel, which at that moment seems even uglier than in the morning.

I walk deliberately along a side road, the ocean now roaring to my left, and I slowly approach the site of Antonio's villa. It stands near an aquarium where one can see dolphins and sharks, a favorite spot of Fidel Castro, still alive at the time. The aquarium attracts tourists, so I am in relative safety. But I'm interested in other sharks. I don't want to get locked up, but I want to see the situation as close as possible. I pass a shopping mall on my right with a large empty parking lot in the back. The parking lot attendant is wearing a thin leather vest with a faded Habana Club sign on the back, and his head is adorned with two hats at once. The other, more visible, is a baseball cap perched atop a soft khaki hat.

When I get to the aquarium, I'll slow down. On the approach from the exit, I see a police car and two uniformed officers blocking the entrance. I circle around for a while, but eventually I encounter the same scene in all the driveways. I get a chance to see what I missed later on YouTube. The government prevented the conference from taking place and did it their way, as only they can. The police surrounded the house and sent young pioneers into the street with scarves around their necks. Ten-year-old children obediently walked around an imaginary oval in front of Antonio's house, shouting slogans they themselves could not understand, slogans about enemies of the people, worms and subversive elements, and obscenities, which was certainly more fun than being stuck in their desks and listening to a comrade teacher. Some children were given spray paint and then painted the dictated messages on the brick fence in front of the villa.

Antonio lost his temper and walked out of the house. The police picked him up, immobilized him and took him to the van. In the video, I can also see Antonio's mother, an ill woman in a green house dress, walking among the children, who are shouting obscenities at her, her face full of exhaustion and stress. She tries to talk to them. A few people come out of the house and try to drag her back. It's very hot, everyone is sweating twice as much, the air is thickening, the playful morning has given way to the reality of a merciless day.

And then there's Ailer. She sits cross-legged on the pavement in the middle of the street like the daughter of Buddha, her eyes closed. She's absolutely still, a zen surrounded by chaos. Screaming children walk past her.

Almost no one got to Antonio's conference except a few participants who arrived a day early and stayed overnight at the house. Among those detained were two Argentine students who were questioned by the police. An officer searched their smartphones. He found a picture of one of them with the then Argentine President Cristina Fernández de Kirchner. He said it was from a reception, perhaps at the university, but the officer was duly impressed. When he asked the student how it was possible that he had a picture of the President on his phone, the student replied, in a sudden burst of inspiration, that Cristina was his friend. This reportedly stunned the police even more, so they released the two young Argentinians and quietly sent them back to Buenos Aires. Antonio was released a few days later.

I can't get the scene out of my head for a while. Ailer Mena is sitting on the dirty asphalt surrounded by screaming children. Her eyes are closed. She doesn't need the silence of the living room for inner peace, she can pull up a drawbridge in front of her enemies and no one can follow her anymore. The Red Happening is an example of the aggressiveness of a dictatorship that we have not known, because our Communist regime was calmer in central European manner. But it may be an illusion of hindsight. The philosopher and spokesman for Charter 77, Jan Patočka, died in hospital after a long interrogation, and the Minister of the Interior ordered that his funeral be disturbed with the roar of the speedway motorcycles from a nearby racetrack. Meanwhile, Patočka sits up there on the pavement of a street that not everyone will find their way into, smiling, with motorbikes speeding past and exhaust pipes screaming, "*¡Gusano!* Worm!"

At over seven kilometres, the Malecón must be the longest urban waterfront in the world. In the evening, the crowds tend to gather here. People sit on the edge of a concrete barrier that defies the forces of the ocean. In high winds, the waves crash against it, drenching cars and pedestrians with a salty spray. Today, however, the wind is reasonable, just right, not disturbing, cooling sweaty foreheads. Havanese sit in clusters, listening to boombox music and secretly sipping cheap alcohol.

Branded rum is a luxury only available in specialty stores. I walk slowly along the sea. Gusts of wind raise the volume of seagulls shouting their signals to the stone fortress of Moro and the nearby La Cabaña building. In 1961, on the premises of the local prison, a firing squad shot dead the American adventurer William Morgan, a revolutionary who had organised the anti-Castro resistance.

On the way to Malecón I stopped in Vedado in a small apartment building near the coast. I met José Alberto Álvarez Bravo and his wife, Lilia Castañer Hernández. Their apartment is not far from the American Embassy. The street is protected by branches of deciduous trees, arching from one side to the other. Even in the daytime, it's dark.

I knock on the door, Lilia in white opens it. José Alberto is not at home. The energetic woman in her sixties is a member of the anti-regime movement Damas de blanco, founded by her late friend Laura Pollán. She invites me in. I sit on a hard kitchen chair by the window overlooking the courtyard. Lilia is wearing a T-shirt with Laura's likeness on it. We're talking about the raid on Antonio's. We gloss over the deployment of the kids, and Lilia tells me it happened to her too. During the regular procession of the Ladies in White after mass, the police herded children in pioneer uniforms towards them. They yelled at them and made obscene gestures. Lilia got angry, which is risky with her heart problems.

"They behave like our owners. They use Cubans as human material, beggars, homeless people, criminals."

She was detained, beaten and interrogated. Her thumbs got bloody. I'm trying to imagine this lady of years being physically attacked. I wouldn't have believed it a while ago, but another dissident, Martha Roque, of the same generation as Lilia, showed me the stairs of her apartment building where she was dragged by her hair. Lilia was also pulled by her hair, by a young policewoman and a black female soldier on Third Boulevard near the Aquarium and the Rodiles House. She was going to a birthday party for Maria Cristina, a friend from the Ladies in White.

I look around the modestly furnished apartment while Lilia reminisces about her son who emigrated to Spain and then disappeared. Later, she will go looking for him in the United States. She remembers Laura. She was there when the police violently detained her on the street. She describes to me how Laura fought back, how there was a scuffle. How Laura was bitten by a police officer and then, she says, scratched with a poisoned tip. When I ask if she has any evidence for this, she admits she doesn't. Conjecture. Laura was a diabetic, and being arrested was very stressful for her. The police took her to Calixto García Hospital. Lilia visited her there and found her in bad shape. Normally her friend didn't complain, but now she was visibly ill. She said she was on the verge of a breakdown herself. Laura showed her the bite marks and the scar she had sustained during the arrest. The doctors assured them she was fine. She recognized a white-coated security colonel, Fernando Tamayo Gómez. Seven days after her arrest, Laura Pollán died of cardiac arrest in hospital. The official cause of death, she tells me, was dengue fever.

Dr. Oscar Elias Biscet, a well-known human rights activist whom I also met in Havana, discussed the possible causes of Laura's death on his blog. His analysis suggests that her death could be interpreted as either clear misconduct by the treating team or deliberate negligence with the aim of killing Laura. Neither possibility is unique in Cuba. Laura was in fair health prior to her arrest. The combination of tyranny and "advanced socialist health care" resulted in her untimely demise. As in the case of Oswaldo Payá Sardiñas, the government is directly responsible for Laura Pollán's death.

Here comes José Alberto. He's the same age as Lilia, very slim and calm. He'll jump right into the conversation.

"We are a typical example of a tropical dictatorship in its last phase. Towards the end they are the most aggressive. When they feel safe, they can afford a certain generosity and tolerance. But now the spiral of hatred is spinning faster."

And he complains about the elitist tendencies of some of the opposition.

"No one means this badly, but many project leaders use the language of educated people for educated people. They ignore the ordinary problems of ordinary people, the terrible social situation. We want people to express themselves on short videos about the current situation. To say what they think. Everyone, not just intellectuals. We film them and then distribute the videos."

"How?"

"We certainly don't send them to the government. We do not recognize its legitimacy. We started this a few months ago and we have almost a thousand people. So far only activists and artists. Now we have to reach out to normal people as well. A video is better than a petition, it confirms identity better than a signature, it is authentic. A signature can be forged, a face can't. And if someone agrees to be filmed and distributed, they lose their fear of the regime. This encourages others."

His project is called Cuba Exige. The police confiscated several cameras. And they want to evict them. His apartment near the US Embassy is in a special so-called frozen zone. Anyone who wants to live here must have permission from the authorities.

"There is a lot of tension between us and our neighbours. They don't want us here. They have staged a hysterical, completely spontaneous demonstration against us in the street, a repudiation act in which slogans are shouted and stones are thrown at windows. These actions are normally organised by the police, but in our case the neighbours got together on their own."

José Alberto looks alternately at me and out the window into the courtyard, dark eyes sunk deep into eye sockets. Under a high forehead, a prominent nose dominates a small, gaunt face. The rest of the black hair on the sides is beginning to turn to grey. In some of the photos, he's wearing glasses, but now he's sitting there without them. Whatever he does, he does it with seriousness, not letting himself be intimidated. He's a very lean endurance runner whose legs are constantly being tripped by the judges, but José Alberto gets up every time and keeps running.

"I've tried setting up a few projects here. I wanted to turn this apartment into a centre for independent journalism. It didn't work out. I wanted to start the New Hope Academy, but that didn't work either. They chased our lecturers. Then they surrounded the house for days and wouldn't let anyone in. The Academy was finished. I went on hunger strike for two weeks. Then I started a new initiative, the People's Council, I wanted to defend public spaces, squares and parks, for the activities of all citizens. I argued that they belonged to everyone, not just to the 'revolution'. We started to organize public meetings in parks in the suburbs and in other cities. In Camagüey, Santiago. That scared them. Thirteen times they kidnapped me and threatened to kill me. They physically attacked me and Lilia."

Lilia shows me a picture. It's of her arm in a cast. José Alberto continues.

"I went to get bread, for example, and ended up in the clutches. Then I founded the Association of Families Who Disappeared Without a Trace. Thousands and thousands of people disappeared here. Some died at sea trying to cross into the United States. There were times when a police helicopter circled over their vessels and sandbags were thrown at them. Some were simply shot. I estimate that 60-70,000 people disappeared and lost their lives."

The government claims that no one has ever gone missing for political reasons.

"This is nonsense, of course," says José Alberto, producing a large black-and-white photograph of a young man. "Roberto Amelio Franco Alfonso disappeared on May 20, 2009. A well-known dissident. He left home one day and never came back. Leaving behind his wife and eight-year-old child."

Cuesta Morúa

In the square of Francis of Assisi I am looking at a gilded sculpture by the French sculptor Etienne called *Conversation*. It's two seated metal figures engaged in talk. Etiénne works with filled and empty space in a similar way to Olbram Zoubek in his sculpture at Újezd in Prague dedicated to the victims of totalitarianism. Parts of the figures are missing, the sculpture gives an uncontained impression, and the strength of the fragment is in the suggestion that invites conjecture. After Havana installed Etienne's work in 2012, Leal declared that it represented "the dilemma of contemporary society, the need for dialogue." Given the state of the civic conversation, it's not surprising that the statue serves mainly tourists taking selfies. The need to exchange views has given way to the need to flash in front of relatives, Socrates has been displaced by Narcissus. I wonder if the loyal Leal was trying to take a subtle dig at the Castros politburo by mentioning the "need for dialogue"?

I see something similar poking around a little while later. In a small gallery across from the basilica, Nelson Domínguez Cedeño is exhibiting several paintings and sculptures. The miniexhibition is called *Pandemías* (*Pandemics*) and reflects on the Covid tragedy that has taken the lives of millions, often quite needlessly, as they died as a result of politicians' incompetence and human stupidity. Domínguez's large-scale canvases are powerful. The artist paints with muted earth colors, creating a jumble of figures with crosses, praying and kneeling people referring to abstracted illnesses of the past. In a corner of the gallery hangs a text with his artistic confession:

> "Throughout history, people have been victims of countless sufferings due to failing health. Moreover, let us not forget the even greater evils committed by man in his unbridled desire for mammon without regard for the suffering of others; evils that have made it impossible for his fellow man to make a living and led to exodus, to seek a better life in spite of the high walls built to end their dreams, leaving them without hope except to pray to the gods who accompany them in pain, misery and sickness."
>
> Nelson Domínguez Cedeño, Havana, December 17, 2021

Domínguez is not a rebel. He has held positions in the artistic hierarchy and received awards from the regime. But the exhibition and his words speak clearly in the current political context.

Outside, the sixteenth-century stone Basilica Minor of Saint Francis of Assisi casts a merciful shadow over part of the square. It used to be a Franciscan monastery and boasted a praying statue of the patron saint atop the tower, but in the nineteenth century a cyclone took Francis. At the base of the church stands a sculpture depicting Saint Junípero Serra with a naked Native American boy, Juaneño. In one hand Serra holds a cross and is depicted as a youthful athletic cleric. In the eighteenth century, this Franciscan was involved in the continental spread of the faith. His legacy today is contradictory. He was instrumental in Madrid granting legal status to indigenous peoples and protecting them from abuse by soldiers. At the same time, he participated in the cruel punishment of these Indians "for their good and the salvation of their souls." He also became known as a

Chapter 3   69

flagellant. There is a surviving record of him beating his bare shoulders with an iron chain during a mass he conducted. He was a follower of the Holy Inquisition. He suspected Catholics, Mexicans and Indians of witchcraft. Let us quote from one of his letters:

"In ... the last few days a certain Cayetana, a very clever Mexican ... married to the mulatto Perez, has confessed [to witchcraft]-she has been observed and accused of similar crimes ... [She is joined by other] persons ... flying through the air at night, who are in the habit of meeting in a cave on a hill near the rancho El Saucillo, in the centre of the said missions, where they worship demons and offer sacrifices to them. The demons appear to them in the guise of young goats... If we do not confront such evil, a terrible depravity will spread among the poor Indian novices in our charge," Serra wrote to his superiors.

His recent canonization was accompanied by disputes between traditionalists and the woke, and after his canonization someone vandalized his statue in Mexico. Attacks on his other statues have occurred in the United States. The one in San Francisco's Golden Gate Park had to be removed after several incidents. Here in Communist Havana, however, Father Serra, or rather the bronze version of him, can feel safe for the time being.

I'll order a piña colada in the street and while waiting for it, I observe from the counter the interior of the room, which resembles a dingy warehouse with a high ceiling. In the corner is a bright red tall refrigerator that's been chatting with Hemingway, and next to it is a massive ancient metal cash register, the kind that if you dropped on the sidewalk would fall through the surface to the other side of the world. On the wall, the obligatory Che Guevara in a beret grins from a faded photo. The waiter has gone to the back, apparently on a break. After a long wait he comes back and I finally get my iced drink, take it in my right hand, and head further into town.

I have one more visit to do before I leave Havana. I check the exact address where I have to be in less than an hour. Cuesta Morúa, whom I met at Antonio's seminar, lives nearby in the La Victoria district of Habana Centro on Santo Tomás Street. The directions indicate I should be there in about half an hour. We were going to meet the day before yesterday, but he was detained by the police.

I head towards the Capitol, and then around Chinatown towards the Centro area, but I don't go straight. Instead, I dawdle and take a few detours. The streets are busy near Central Square, but after about twenty minutes of free walking, you won't find a single stranger on the sidewalks, and it's still early afternoon. The locals are hiding from the sun. I take pictures, look at the map, pretend I'm a tourist who's lost his way. Everything should be fine, I've communicated with Cuesta via WhatsApp, but you never know.

Warehouses and small factories are appearing, Centro has a suburban industrial character in some places despite its name. I arrive fifteen minutes early. Not a foot on the streets, just opposite my address a few men sit in a tyre workshop chatting. When they see me, they take a cursory look at me without interest. Then they go back to their topics. I cross the house and the next intersection, turn the corner, turn around, look at my cell phone, all the while observing my surroundings. I don't see any surveillance cameras around Cuesta's house. No one's patrolling. Maybe they're watching him from the surrounding apartments, which wouldn't be obvious from the sidewalk. Any time you visit a prominent dissident, you risk getting picked up.

I'm sending him a message. His silhouette in a snow-white shirt appears on a balcony high above the street, looking down at the door. In a few seconds he unlocks the barred entrance for me. Everything works out so that I don't have to wait. We walk up the narrow, steep staircase of a clean building to a small apartment with a shiny floor. We reminisce about the seminar at the Rodiles villa. Cuesta Morúa is in his early sixties - in fact, he is two weeks away from turning sixty that day - he is spry and, as usual, has a polite smile on his face. You wouldn't guess his age. In the kitchen, activist María Mercedes Benítez Rodríguez greets me. A friendly pit bull, which in Prague we call a little nanny, runs happily around our feet.

We sit in the small living room on big green chairs with a bedspread. I sit with my back to the door to the balcony, screened by blinds. Cuesta Morúa places his cup of coffee on a tray with the Heineken brewery logo on the armrest to his right. He is wearing the white shirt I spotted from the street, contrasting with his dark complexion, canvas trousers, socks and brown patent leather shoes. He looks like he's been cut out of a magazine. The large, black-rimmed glasses make it seem that his face behind them is smaller than it really is, that I'm not talking to Cuesta himself but a caricature of him in the newspaper, an exaggeration, perhaps like his friends nicknaming him Kalule. Once upon a time, he briefly took up boxing, and his style was said to be similar to the technique of Ugandan star Ayub Kalule, who became welterweight champion of the world in Havana in 1974. In politics, Cuesta is the opposite of a puncher, but to tire up the metaphor somewhat, let's say that as welterweight champion, he regularly goes up against a heavyweight regime that has horseshoes hidden in its gloves. Occasionally he has help, albeit not a very effective one, from even heavier weights. In March 2016, he met Barack Obama at the American embassy. Other dissidents such as Coco Fariñas, Nelson Álvarez Matute and Miriam Celaya González attended the meeting.

I'm interested in his last arrest, and Cuesta describes how he came out of the house but didn't even make it across the next street, Árbol Seco, and they had him.

"They took me to the station right away. They held me for about six hours. They didn't really want anything, they just wanted to control us."

We talk on Monday and Cuesta says the house was surrounded all day Friday and all day Saturday. I am reminded of the absurd Radio Rebelde official radio show I listened to in the car on Human Rights Day while waiting for gas. An expert from the University of Havana explained that, despite being vilified by the opposition, Cuba is one of the most advanced countries in the world in the protection of human rights, having ratified some 40 of the more than 60 international conventions.

All over Cuba, there are now propaganda billboards with the slogan *voluntad de elegir,* willingness to choose, a slogan that was intended to express the determination of the people to participate in the local elections organised a few weeks ago.

"Of course there was no real election," Cuesta notes. He puts on that trademark smile again, for no one can change the atmosphere so naturally in the stuffiest room. Looking at him, I have the feeling that nothing bad can happen and that Cuba will soon be really libre. I take a sip from my cup of coffee and then place it on the floor next to the chair. The dog has disappeared somewhere. He has correctly deduced that nothing good comes out of me.

"We have tried to participate in elections in the past, but no candidate proposed by us has ever passed the pre-selection process organized by their commissions. This year, one candidate in Palma Soriano did - he passed the selection, but they didn't allow him to be elected. The 'election' did, however, yield an interesting insight. In Havana, only about fifty percent of the people participated. That's not the figure they published, of course, but we managed to get hold of the real participation statistics. It gives a good picture of how people really feel."

It reminds me of the "elections" in Czechoslovakia, organized for the so-called National Front candidates. The Centre monitored who took part in the farce, and those who didn't bother were subject to sanctions.

We speculate where the political situation will go. He tells me that the government will step up its efforts to attract foreign investors from Spain and Canada. The Blue Diamond Resorts group, owned by the Canadian company Sunwing, is said to be in talks with the government about further acquisitions and building new hotels.

"They feel they are losing influence. But if they start talks with the opposition, they will be in a weak position. In my opinion, and I must preface this by saying that this is just my feeling and I have no support for it, they want to improve the economy a little bit within three years. Then there could be a greater opening and the start of reforms."

I look skeptical and he senses it because he adds:

"People really are losing fear. If you just read the Cuban internet, including social networks, you would get the feeling that Cuba has freedom of speech. People quite openly swear at the regime. My friends used to be afraid of me. When they saw me on the street, they preferred to cross the sidewalk to avoid being seen with me. Today, everyone greets me from afar, and people even ask how they can help."

So I ask how we abroad can help.

"Visibility is extremely important. The more visible we are internationally, the more protected we are. The Chinese have a saying:

Those who mention you, protect you. And then there's the second thing. Friends of Cuban democracy abroad should realise that democratic change is a process, not a single visible event. We are trying to build that process gradually, day by day, step by step, but it will take time."

María jokes that one day she will run Cuesta's presidential campaign. In jest I'm volunteering for duty. Cuesta is the only socialist in the world I'm willing to work for. This trained historian is one of the opposition's most charismatic figures. He walks me down the stairs.

"See you in Prague?"

"I'm not allowed to travel."

"They took your passport?"

"No, but they won't let me cross the border."

"How did this happen?"

"Day to day. I was going to a conference in Brussels and then to Brazil. I arrived at the airport. The policeman looked at my passport, looked at the computer monitor, then gave me my passport back and told me I wasn't going anywhere."

I walk out of the darkness of the house onto Santo Tomás Street. An aggressive light hits my eyes. I walk quickly towards where I suspect Padre Varela Avenue, which on some maps is also called Belascoáin. After twenty minutes I reach it. The mood here is different from the quiet of the Victoria district, from which I have just come. Through the holes in the walls, which substitute for entrances and windows of sorts, I can see inside the dark spaces of the half-empty state markets and shops. Time has stopped here. It looks exactly as it did ten years ago when I first walked down Father Varela Avenue. You have to be careful where you step, the sidewalks are full of tricky unevenness of craggy concrete.

The avenue slopes down to the waterfront. The tall apartment buildings surrounding it are built at different levels, creating a mysterious corridor, an unsightly urban canyon. It gives the impression of a chaotic archaeological dig. Scientists are about to excavate the area, and lo and behold! There are still people living here. It's not extinct yet. We'll wait with the excavation. Moscow had a similar atmosphere in the late 1980s - dark, smelly, empty shops. In Moscow, as I recall almost plastically now, and it's been more than thirty years - the brain plays a strange game with you sometimes - people smelled of a mixture of alcohol and sweat; the badly washed filth of empty shops. Havana smells of cars with engines without catalytic converters. Being on streets like this for a few hours is a guaranteed way to a headache.

When I approach Barrio Chino, near one of the original buildings of the Partagás tobacco factory, founded in the mid-nineteenth century, I sometimes see people with Asian features, although Filiberto told me that there is at most one Chinese in the whole neighborhood, since all the sane people have returned to China. On Zanja Boulevard, where the tenements are lower than on Padre Varela, a street hustler talks to me. I make a rookie mistake: I tell him where I'm from. It's the heat.

"Pável Nedved!" he calls to me excitedly from a distance of one meter.

He probably thinks I didn't hear him right, so he raises his voice:

"Pável Nedved!"

I'm giving a thumbs up as a sign that I know who he means. We all love Pável. What follows is a series of questions that are no longer related to the Czech Fury, as the footballer was called in Italy. Does *amigo* need anything? I'm expecting an invitation to a salsa festival, but this trick seems to have worn out its welcome. There's no salsa. I assure him I'm not missing anything. Zanja is an ugly, busy street by Havana standards, which means you really have to look for traffic when you cross it. I enter the roadway with the amigo on my right, walking quickly to give him a bit of an exercise. In the middle of the roadway, I change my mind, turn around, and return to the right sidewalk from which I exited. The Juventus Turin fan rolls his eyes at me from across the street, uncomprehending.

Sometimes I feel uncomfortable with the tricks I use to get rid of street hustlers whose ingenuity is worthy of admiration. Life in Cuba is hard. The ideal is to have access to US dollars or euros, and every foreigner is a potential source of income. But that empathy wears off after a while, especially after one or two of these smart-asses trick and rip you off. You start protecting yourself.

"Hey friend, how are you?"

"*Amigo,* cigars?"

"Hey friend, what is the time?"

Chapter 3

You go on, pretending not to hear. No eye-contact. Even fellow human beings in need have a knack for turning into annoying insects in a certain configuration. I walk slowly, thinking of Cuesta, of his charging optimism. I get back to the Hotel Telégrafo, sit down in the arcade, make sure I can pay by credit card (that the electricity is on) and have a Cristal light lager. Across from me, a French-speaking metrosexual pokes a fork into a huge plate of five-star salad. He's chatting across the aisle with a model-dressed lady in her dotage who sits two tables to my left. To my right, at the end of the arcade, a multi-member band in white shirts and black pants launches Chan Chan, the Buena Vista Social Club ensemble's biggest hit.

From Alto Cedro, I'm heading towards Marcane,
I'll come to Cueto and go to Mayarí.

My hands get heavy when I remember the names of those magical places that Compay Segundo and Ibrahim Ferrer sang about. I set the ice-cold can down on the glass table.

4.

Tierra Caliente.

Santiago de Cuba

The east of Cuba is called *El Oriente*. That was the name of the easternmost province before the coup. The identity of the east is a historical one, but today it is not visible at first sight. It has always been underdeveloped, but today all of Cuba is underdeveloped; poor, but all of Cuba is poor. The poverty of the East, however, is of the category of harsh poetry. And I mean *harsh*. One meditates here on Arenas's childhood, captured in his memoir *Before Night Falls*. As a child, he used to put dirt in his mouth, which resulted in worms in his guts, which then woke him up from his sleep. Years later, he was having intercourse with domestic animals. It was not unusual in his milieu. Sex with animals had become the collective ritual of adolescent boys in the furthest reaches of the Oriente.

I was once wandering the country roads of Holguín province looking for San Germán, where I had a meeting with independent journalist Yosvani Anzardo Hernández. I drove slowly along a dirt road, a cornfield on my left, a grove of low trees on my right, and beyond them the shimmering surface of a river. Between the branches I saw a man on horseback. He rode Indian style without a saddle, half undressed and wearing a straw hat. After a few minutes, a view opened up of the ford toward which the fellow was heading. There were several brown horses jostling in a small space, surrounded by a group of men. The cowboy rode his horse right into the water, dismounted, and set about washing the animal. He was smiling beatifically, a unique type of light in his face. It occurred to me that this was the look of a future saint. The journey isn't over yet, but I'm going right, he says to himself. The brown horse glistens in the afternoon sunlight penetrating through the thick branches towards the ford. On his neck there is a simple halter of ordinary rope. The movement of the horses' hooves muddies the clarity of the river. The *arroyo* is caked with mud. I got out of the car. No one noticed me, the men were absorbed in their own affairs, their own thoughts and sentences, their own task. I managed to take a few quick photographs. As the years passed, almost all of them were lost somewhere, only one remained. *The joy of bathing a horse.*

It was Sunday. I drove through the fields with premeditation, approaching San Germán, a true eastern backwater. I passed a broken-down truck. The open hood partially covered the driver, who was desperately rummaging through the machine, which had been repaired many times. Around the hood of the truck hitchhikers phlegmatically regarded the driver's efforts to squeeze a few extra miles out of the dying machine. This is a scene that the traveller often sees on the side of Cuban roads. A broken-down car, the bonnet open and smoking, the driver groggy and holding a rusted tool, with hitchhikers stranded. It was dry, tractors and trucks in the opposite direction were surrounded by puffs of grey dust and greasy exhaust smoke. A little further along, on the left side of the road, was a cluster of run-down apartment blocks, where many of the people seemed to be heading.

Yosvani lives with his wife Lourdes María Yen Rodríguez and their two children in a neighborhood that includes a huge, abandoned-looking sugar mill, the perfect backdrop for a sci-fi horror movie. You cross a few pairs of tracks next to the train station and pass a nondescript clinic to reach a section of wooden houses with porches and small gardens. The first time I was here was in the summer of 2012. Yosvani and Lourdes told how they don't put their kids in school to keep them from being brainwashed. Surprisingly, the school respected their decision, they told me then. As I said goodbye, I asked what they wished to bring.

"I want to go to Europe so I can have Frankfurt sausages," Yosvani told me. He laughed. The kids showed me T-shirts with Disney characters, neatly ironed and little-used rarities.

I park a few streets away, as the safety policy dictates, and walk down the empty streets to the Anzardo family's house. No one responds to a knock at the front door. I go around the building on my right and try the back entrance. It's quiet, no one's around. Yosvani opens the wooden door and squints into the light. It takes him a moment to recognize me. Black hair disheveled, wearing a faded tank top. He's barefoot. Sleeping? It's afternoon, maybe he's had a siesta. Oh, no, he says, he's in his bedroom watching a film about Nelson Mandela. The room is darkened against the assault of the afternoon sun. He hides from the world in his bunker. He is alone, wife and children not at home, angry that Cuban television portrays Mandela as a Communist.

"He was no Bolshevik! "

Gradually, his anger falls away, and he returns to his spunky, bearish self. He describes the state of affairs in the East.

"There have been more cops on the streets the last few months. Even undercover. They say it's because of criminals, drug dealers and robbers. But that's bullshit. In reality, it's an intensified crackdown."

Yosvani has seen his share of repression as a local activist.

"In 2007 I was kidnapped and beaten. I was supposed to go to Havana to present a petition against dual currency, which I also signed. Against the fact that there is a national currency and a convertible peso alongside it. *(At that time, Cuba had a dual currency, the national peso and the so-called convertible peso, the CUC, which could be used to pay in special, better-stocked shops. However, the CUC has since been abolished by the government, and the special shops now accept foreign currencies only - note: TK)* I was going to attend a press conference there, and then I was going to go to the National Assembly to present the petition. The night before I left, a man on a motorbike approached me. They threw me into a car, interrogated me, beat me up and drove me home. Lourdes thought they'd found me drunk, so she thanked them for their help! I couldn't walk properly. They hurt my knee, something snapped."

Yosvani is a bit of a wrestler. I wouldn't want to get into a fight with him. It's a job for a few well-trained men just to pacify him on the street. In 2009, he spent two weeks in a cell, and undercover officers took his recording equipment.

"They call me in whenever I publish something they don't like. For example, about the closure of the nickel factory in Moa on the north coast or about how outdated the machinery and equipment in the sugar mills is. The cops threaten me and say they can prosecute me for such articles. My team and I run an independent newsletter called *Candonga*. We cover our region and I organise the work from here. I don't do anything that is technically against their laws, so realistically they have nothing against me."

I'm interested in how his team distributes articles and video reports.

"There are movie rental stores all over San Germán. That's where we leave our memory cards and flash drives. That's how we spread the news. That's a model that works nationwide. The government didn't know for a long time, but now they've found out and have closed some of the rentals. And it has also started to organize its own film rental companies, which it has better control over."

Yosvani defies the stereotypical image of human rights activists. He would work well as a character in a Bohumil Hrabal story from the Kersko cabin resort. He's a quirky original from the Oriente, and he's attracted to people of a similar ilk.

"I've always enjoyed writing about people who are a little crazy. They're not afraid to talk to you. I write about homeless people sleeping in the bus station. About social issues. About a family that lives in the mountains above Santiago and is completely independent of the government. They grow everything themselves. I write about vagrants and street jugglers."

Yosvani's life story is also not the usual story of a dissident.

"I used to work as a manufacturer of orthodontic prostheses. Then, in 2006, I met activist and journalist Alexander Santos. He was arrested and I brought him food in prison. They staged an act of repudiation against him. Gradually, I worked more and more with him and did the same things he did. The authorities put me on a list of undesirables. The police then took away my denture-making equipment. But I didn't mind. I found that I liked to write, and I also liked to do video stories. My team consists of six people. They're all people with different jobs. We have a high-tech expert, and we have a farm worker who verifies information for us. For example, we find a woman who refuses to go to the hospital. She's afraid to die there. We send our peasant to check it out. Then there is my sister

Irina, who is a psychologist, my wife, and other family members help us. Everyone on the team knows what they need to know, nothing more. I'd like to do more video reporting and interviews with people in the villages, or maybe even with a policeman if he's willing to talk. Or even a Communist. I won't censor them. Let the commie have his say."

Talking to a cop may seem like a crazy idea. But independent blogger Yoel Espinosa Medrano of Santa Clara once reached out to police sources. He managed to uncover a dark case.

"A cop killed a guy," Yoel told me. "It happened at the Villa La Granjita tourist complex. A conflict broke out between the man and the cops when the guy found out the cops were getting prostitutes for the tourists. The cop beat him to death. The dead man's name was Ernesto Baeza and he was 40 years old. It happened around mid-November 2013. I wrote about it for CubaNet."

Jimena

I'm on my way from Holguín to Santiago. It's hot, but you don't find a working gas station in this region on every corner, so I'm saving fuel and not turning on the air conditioning. Instead, I open the back windows, as they used to do in the Tertiary period. My companion is Jimena Cervantes, a law student from Central America. On the missions I undertake in Cuba, we travel in pairs. It's safer, plus my basic Spanish doesn't allow for more sophisticated conversation, so I can't do without a translator. Most of the dissidents we meet with don't speak English. When I learned that a university student, who was also finishing up her driver's license, would be traveling with me, I became nervous. My Cuban expeditions are nothing like a vacation. Esteban, with whom I had prepared the trip, assured me that Jimena was "very nice" and everything would be smooth sailing. Fortunately, he was right, Jimena has become a reliable and helpful partner. I just didn't let her near the steering wheel after a careful risk assessment, which, at least as I could observe, she didn't regret.

Jimena is, as they say, from a good family. Her father is a physician and her boyfriend a sociologist. Her favourite TV show is *Breaking Bad,* so we immediately find common ground. She's 26. Unlike many of her peers, Jimena has no romantic feelings about the Cuban Revolution, Che

Guevara or other figures of the radical left. But otherwise, like my daughters, who are only a little younger, and like my American students at New York University, she is a typical representative of a wedge generation, a cohort between millennials and Generation Z. It is the first globalized generation, characterized by similar habits regardless of nationality. They're growing up later than us and taking everything more seriously. When I mention a book or a movie, Jimena immediately writes it down.

"Why are you writing this down?"

"So I don't forget the name of the book," she replies quite logically, but I already feel like I'm in a lecture and I'm careful what I say. Even here in a car in the Cuban countryside, I can't just chatter irresponsibly. Getting used to being taken seriously by strangers is one of the hallmarks of adulthood, which to me clearly came late. Sometimes Jimena surprises me with a question that has no easy answer.

"Have you ever touched a chicken?" she asks, for example, as we drive through the farmland.

"Chicken?"

I'll make sure I heard right.

"Yes, hen."

"You mean, did I physically touch it? A live chicken? I think so, on holiday at my grandmother's. Why do you care if I touched a chicken?"

"I've never touched a chicken," she concludes in a rather eccentric conversational intermezzo.

Other times, she complains about sexism in Latin America. I ask what bothers her most.

"Double talk. When I walk down the street, the remarks, the whistling. They have no respect."

I don't doubt for a moment the machismo and sexism on the part of Latinos, but remarks and whistling, I fear, will not be the preserve of men in South and Central America alone. I accept her words with a mixture of hope and frustration. On the one hand, I wish this generation were a little more resilient, with more perspective and a sense of human frailty. They are uncompromising. But I believe that they can change for the better some of the things that my generation takes as fait accompli.

There are a number of advantages to traveling around Cuba with a female co-worker (as opposed to traveling with a male co-worker). For example, when you walk around town, people assume you're a couple. Gone are the inventive and aggressive efforts of many, many prostitutes, *jineteras,* to get you somewhere private and show you... well, the butterfly collection, of course. An acquaintance told me a remarkable story. This was back in the days when normal Cubans couldn't get to the resort town of Varadero. Access was restricted to locals and people who worked there. Others needed a permit to enter. On the way from Havana to Varadero, where my friend had gone for a few days with a colleague, he decided to do a good deed and take three hitchhikers: a grandmother, her adult daughter and a young granddaughter, who all took the back seat. My friend was driving and his partner was in the passenger seat. After a while, he felt like something was tickling his side. And sure enough. He looked down and saw someone's hand reaching into his crotch from behind. The lady sitting in the back must have figured she didn't want to waste any time. Why wait until Varadero? In front of her mother and daughter, she slid her right hand out from behind the driver's seat and aimed her palm straight, how shall we say, straight to the point.

"I figured out why they were traveling in this lineup and why they wanted to hitch a ride with a foreigner. They were hoping that the car with the tourist licence plate would not be stopped by the police at the entrance to Varadero, and they could get there without a permit or without having to bribe. I guess the woman didn't have a babysitter for her daughter. She took her with her and brought her mother. While she does her shift, the grandmother will keep an eye on her granddaughter on the beach."

On a previous mission, I toured Cuba with Jan Gebert, a documentary filmmaker who looks like a movie star. We had some hot moments with the jineteras. Well, for the record, we didn't really enjoy anything, but we had to try hard to avoid them. It's easier with the woman in the tandem. The jineteras stay out of the way, although they still subtly wink at you behind your partner's back. How a young woman enlightened by the #me_too movement feels in such situations is another matter.

"I'm being looked at like a whore again," Jimena complains.

"Not me," I tease gently. "They're looking at me like I'm a real man. Look at Daddy, what a rabbit he hit!"

Jimena doesn't seem to appreciate this humor, but tactfully keeps quiet. It usually happens in the apartments we stay in. While I find the people I meet there friendly and likeable, Jimena has a different experience.

"She looks at me strangely," he says of the lady of the house. "She doesn't answer my greeting at all."

On past trips I've also taken with a female co-worker, we sometimes had trouble finding a room with two separate beds.

"We are not a couple," we tell the owner. "We want two beds."

"Of course you're not, of course..." the owner says slyly, winking meaningfully. "But we don't have a separate bed. Hopefully it'll work out this time, you can stand it, right?"

"It won't. So goodbye, we will find something else."

"But wait! Wait. I just remembered we have one more lounger."

With Jimena we didn't have to deal with that. We were traveling in a time of tourist shortage and our wish was always an order. But we didn't avoid the strange looks. We were a very unusual pair. We each had different passports, I could have been her father and Jimena certainly didn't look like a gold digger. She looks like a typical young Central American intellectual.

"Leave them alone," I comfort her. "Let them think what they want. After all, it's a pretty good cover story."

That calmed her down.

Shortly after noon we stop in a nameless village near a bus stop. It is silent and almost empty. On the opposite bus stop, two teenage girls in denim are sitting, taking selfies. I open all the windows. Behind the bus stop, a guy sits impassively by a tethered horse. Nobody notices us, nobody wants anything. The contrast with downtown Havana is absolute. A fly flies into the car and its buzzing fills the silence, slightly disturbed by the sound of the breeze over the hot roof. I unwrap a plate of a delicacy called *cremita de leche*. I bought it ten minutes ago in another village under a canopy of branching trees that sheltered the road from the attack of the midday sun. A man of indeterminate age and indeterminate dress was selling *cremitas* by the roadside. To call the *cremita* a sweet is almost an insult. Imagine the sweetest thing you can and multiply it by ten. This speciality from the province of Camagüey is nothing more than slow-cooked, mountains of sugar-flavoured milk with a pinch of salt and possibly a dash of vanilla essence. It can also be flavoured in other ways, if there's anything to flavour it with. I unwrap the table, which softens in the heat and sticks to your fingers. When you don't know when your next meal is coming, this is a solid way to patch up your stomach and get a quick burst of energy. Afterwards, you need to have plenty of drinking water in stock, which is not a given, especially in the eastern provinces. Drinking Cuban tap water is a health hazard and bottled water is not available on every corner.

In absolute silence, we finish the *cremita,* drink it powerfully, and then carefully start to move. The eastern roads are divided into those in bad condition and those that are worse. We're off the central thoroughfare, the legendary two-lane *Carretera Central,* stretching over twelve hundred kilometres along the length of the island from Pinar de Río in the west to Baracoa in the east. *The Carretera* was begun almost a century ago by the government of President Gerardo Machado. It became a powerful stimulus to the economic boom between the two wars. In recent years, here in the east, it looks as if it hasn't been repaired since 1927. I have always felt that *the Carretera Central* is a heroic epic, because all those who venture on it are heroes of our time. Oh Carretera Central! I always wanted to exclaim after hours of drudging between cow and horse carts, Soviet trucks smellier than a coyote, cyclists, dogs and goats, moskviches, ladas and chevrolets with fins.

That was before I knew the roads in Oriente. One such, from Holguín to Santiago, now on the map promises a relatively short trip, but as we shall soon see, these are promises worthy of the Castro regime. After a moment of smooth driving that would almost make one sing out loud, I hit a roadblock - a detour to the left. The driver of the old Soviet off-road Lada Niva in front of me decides to ignore the roadblock, simply pulls around the shoulder and disappears into the distance. But what the SUV can afford, my tiny Hyundai can't. So I take a hard left into the hinterland towards La Mensura National Park, and butterflies fly around my stomach. I've wandered a few times in these parts at the end of the world, I know what passes here for a roadway, and most importantly I can't be sure of proper detour signage. In our neck of the woods, a detour is a simple concept. You get off the main route and, thanks to solidly marked orange signs, get back on the main route with a slight delay. I suspect it won't be so easy here. A suspicion backed up by experience. And it is. After more than ten kilometres, the signs just stop. I'm relying on the satnav, but suddenly it's also starting to do its own thing. I do have a navigation app for offline use, which has so far proved reliable, but right here, in the hills on the border of Holguín and Santiago de Cuba provinces, it seems to have decided to take a rest. I'm driving at around 40km/h so that I can get around potholes that could fit the entire front of my car, but I'm braking in places as the road takes on the character of a tank track soon after the live ammunition exercise.

The villages here are unmarked with few exceptions. They are situated far apart, consisting of a cluster of small wooden huts, only a few metres by a few metres, with roofs of palm leaves. The huts crouch on small plots of land bordered by cactus fences. I remember the small green and yellow cactus fences from my previous trips. You'll find them in other parts of Cuba, but for me they're a symbol of the wild east. We stop and ask for directions. Santiago? But you're completely wrong, you have to go that way, what, oh, a detour, yeah. Wait a minute.

Asking for directions in Cuba won't necessarily make your trip easier. There are several reasons for this. First, many natives are not understood because of the local dialect. Second, they often don't answer what you ask; they simply have something more important to say. Third, they don't say anything simply and concisely. They tell stories. They point, they turn in all directions, they play little acting etudes. Some of them run back and forth. And fourth, because almost no one drives a car but rides a bicycle or a horse-drawn carriage, they have a varied estimate of distance.

"You have to go straight, very straight, it's very far, how far? Lots of kilometers, but at the Pinares sign you turn right. Man, you are seriously off!" Thank you very much.

Dusk is falling. It goes fast up here in the mountains. We stop at a few stalls and ask if they have coffee. They don't. Then, in one mountain village, we see a concrete cube in the town square with a sign that says Cafetería. Here, too, we ask for directions and for coffee. Directions they have, but no coffee, and the fact that we ask for it seems hilarious to them. They think I'm crazy. "Who ever saw it, coffee at Cafetería!" They offer chewing gum and rum, whereupon the latter seems to be probably homemade sugar cane moonshine. The perfect drink for drivers on the move.

So move I do. I see signs for Mayarí, Banes, Cueto. And then Marcane. I have to go round in circles, the distance to Santiago is still around two hours, but that's a good two hours! Damn navigation! I feel like I'm in the movie *Buena Vista Social Club*, the sound of shy Chan Chan looking at Juanika playing with the beach sand in my head. *De Alto Cedro voy para Marcane / Llego a Cueto y voy para Mayarí*. The countryside is picturesque, the first stars are appearing in the sky and the air temperature is dropping. I see people by the roadside in their tracksuits and beanies, although it can't be less than 18 degrees. The bad road continues, huge potholes in the broken surface that are impossible to see in the dark. I pray the car will hold. When an engineer designed it in hypermodern South Korea a long time ago, he must have had a different quality of road in mind for it. Fortunately, I have plenty of petrol. The only food we've gotten in many hours has been *cremita* but focusing on the road drives away hunger.

The worst thing is the irregularity. For a while it looks like the road has improved, you pick up speed, and then from somewhere below, surely from hell, you hear a few thumps. I've been going up and down the dirt road for a good fifteen kilometres now, and I have the vague feeling that I've driven this way once before on my previous expeditions, and that I am therefore destined to wander the dirt roads of the Oriente, perhaps to fully experience their artistic imprint in Ferrer's songs. I'll look to my right. Jimena has been silent for some time. I begin to think about the possibility that we might not make it to Santiago today and find a place to stay. But then the dirt road ends and the asphalt, or at least its cousin, rumbles under the wheels again, and the navigation suddenly kicks in again. Only about 40 minutes to Santiago! We arrive in the municipality of Palma Soriano and it's really close to the eastern metropolis, the second largest city in Cuba. Plus, we're getting on the freeway. There are very few of those in Cuba. They started building them in the 1970s, but after less than 20 years and about 600 km, they stopped. They ran out of money. The western section of the highway, called the Autopista Nacional, connects Palma Soriano to Santiago de Cuba and is of poor quality, but compared to what I just drove on, it feels like a test track in Maranello.

I'm descending down the plateau towards the port city. It's pitch black, nothing is lit, not even the horse-drawn carriage that appears from time to time just in front of me. The Cuban freeway has its rules, and the first is that there are no rules. You will meet a cyclist, an ox cart, a lady on Vespa, and even a horse rider. Even in the left lane, which is the least broken, so everybody drives in it, there is no shortage of surprises. For example, you might find that a car in front of you in the left lane suddenly decides to stop *in the left lane*, the driver gets out and starts phlegmatically rummaging through the boot of the car. Apparently he's got a craving for cookies. The other downside to this stretch of motorway is that in places only one lane is working, but you only find out when a car is suddenly coming towards you. No, it's not going the other way, it's fine, you just have to share the tarmac as best you can.

Arriving from Palma Soriano to Santiago is a bit like arriving on the D1 to Prague or arriving on the I-95 to New York, from the direction of White Plains and Yonkers to the Bronx: you descend from the hills and plateaus to the metropolis. It's early Sunday evening, but unlike Prague and New York, traffic here is scarce and the highway is dark and undulating, as if to accommodate the waves of the Caribbean just a few miles ahead.

Santiago is a beautiful city. It's built on the slopes above the bay, so that in some places it resembles the steep streets of San Francisco. It's not as degraded as Havana, although there are places that could be considered ruins. Its main drawback is the great distance from Havana, some eight hundred kilometres. The state of the Cuban roads basically precludes the possibility of covering this distance in one go, unless you want to risk your life.

Chapter 4

I enter the lights of the centre and head towards the main square, Parque Céspedes. We're staying a few blocks away on San Basilio Street above the port. The man of the house, a sympathetic septuagenarian with receding hair, gallantly makes room for me in his garage. He has a gorgeous dark blue 1957 Ford, which he drives with bravado down the steeply sloping garage surface, then watches curiously to see if I can make it up the hill. Parking is not my discipline, so driving the dusty and tired Hyundai inside becomes a collective activity in which the whole street joins in. It's pretty slippery up on the smooth surface of the garage. In the end, a few volunteers push my car to its designated spot. We've succeeded. After unloading our luggage into a room located between the garage and the atrium of the house, we get a restaurant recommendation. The choice is not great. Only one is open at the moment, but fortunately it has a good reputation and is located on our street about two hundred meters above us. We reach it past a loud street party. Speakers are blasting dance music into the street and someone is projecting video clips onto the house next door. Neighbors are having fun, nudging each other, no one is dancing, and I wonder how they can even hear each other on this decibel-laden evening. And also if maybe tomorrow morning, Monday, no one is going to work.

Fortunately, the recommended restaurant is a little further away, and although it is on a rooftop with a beautiful view of the surrounding rooftops, the noise of the street party is only distant. The staircase stinks of urine, but it turns out to be the only drawback to an otherwise amazing establishment. We're the only customers. We sit on the edge of the terrace overlooking the street. I order a beer, which tastes delicious after the long journey. The restaurant is a typical family-run *paladar,* of which there were many in Cuba a few years ago, but with inflation, lack of tourists and pandemics, their numbers have dwindled. I order the shrimp and yellow rice, cucumber salad, avocado slices, fresh Chinese cabbage, pickled green beans and fried *plátanos.* Plus two cans of German beer, all for about eleven dollars. First good meal in the restaurant in days. I was so discouraged by my experience at a private restaurant in Havana that I survived for a couple of days on canned tuna and legume chips brought by Jimena, in ample quantities. This is the first time I've brought my own food to Cuba. I took the good advice of seasoned travelers who described the shortages that now exist.

"You may find a *paladar* with no food after a day's journey. Just drinks," a colleague told me while preparing for the trip. This ultimately did not match our experience. Food was relatively plentiful, but its quality generally declined, as did the number of private restaurants. Their affordability has deteriorated, even for more affluent Cubans, and with few tourists, much of the potential clientele has disappeared. There has been a surprising increase in the variety of imported drinks, from real Coca-Cola and Pepsi-Cola to various foreign light lagers in cans - German, Dutch, even Australian beers, some significantly inferior to the tasty Cuban brands such as Cristal, Bucanero and Hatuey that dominated the market in the past.

We enjoy a quiet dinner in an almost family-like setting. A young waitress with short-cropped dark hair sits at the bar, with two young men at her side. They're only a little older, maybe in their twenties. There's no musician serenading the dollar like there was ten years ago in a packed Santiago *paladar* not far from here. A singer with a guitar walks up to the table where my colleague and I are sitting and launches into the revolutionary "Comandante Che Guevara." We are not amused, and it confuses him. I mean, Che is a global icon? Now a tiny black-and-white cat sits at my feet, hypnotizing the shrimp impaled on the tip of my fork.

Pilgrims of Pico Turquino

Arenas's memoir stands out for its frankness. He wrote them in the United States, where he was dying of AIDS in the late 1980s. His childhood and adolescence, full of disturbing images of zoophilia and paedophilia, are later interspersed with passages of political awakening. He depicts the fateful years of 1959 and 1960, when he was sixteen and seventeen, studied agricultural accounting in Holguín, and participated in regime-organized rallies in Havana. He reflects on the social climate of the time, mixing a positive attitude towards the revolution with a fear of the unpredictable violence organised by the new power establishment.

In every Bolshevik revolution, especially in the first years of its ideological heat, there are innocent victims. Murdered, tortured, beaten.

There is a certain paradox when it comes to Cuba and the nature of the Cuban people in general. As an Afro-Latin culture, Cubans do not give an aggressive impression, they do not have an aura of violence and easily provoked attack around them. After all, the fact that they have endured a regime that has impoverished and oppressed them for over six decades also shows a certain patience and willingness to endure hardship stoically. They resemble their wandering, hungry, lousy and sick dogs. There are plenty of them running around in villages and towns, friendly, willing to run up and get scratched with a good-natured or sad expression. To some extent, stray dogs reflect the culture of their environment, as they have experiences that shape them, and in Cuba it is clearly a relationship of trust between dog and human. Cuban dogs do not expect anything bad from humans. By the way, the most aggressive stray dogs I have met were in Serbia.

This amateur lesson in cultural anthropology has limits to its usefulness. Cuba's wars of independence in the 19th century were very bloody. Batista's policemen were noted for their cruelty to political prisoners, unless their names happened to be Fidel and Raúl Castro. The organised violence of the Castro regime is also well documented. The post-revolutionary killings have been characterized by Castro's propagandists and foreign writers echoing them as logical retribution against Batista's minions. However, as we know from Prague, Brno and other Czech cities in 1945, the retribution against so-called traitors was morally more complicated. Arenas writes that the public trials were more a morbid popular entertainment than an expression of justice. They were "trials" without counsel, without proper consideration of evidence and circumstances. It was enough to accuse someone. More important than the evidence was who the accuser was and whether the victim had sufficiently disgusted the mob.

"People were enjoying the sight of a poor bastard sentenced to death by shooting, whose worst crime might have been that he had once slapped someone who now was trying to exact revenge. The innocent were dying with the guilty. Many more people died than in a war that didn't actually take place."

Arenas is referring here to the fact that after the rebels set off from the mountains in two directions towards Havana and Santiago, there were no major clashes as they advanced through Cuba. Batista's army refused to defend itself effectively. The regime was so demoralized that it surrendered. There were no more than three hundred rebels, and if the armed forces had really organized, they would have had to destroy the band of the bearded. Passivity was fatal to Batista's men. None of them saw what was coming their way. Castro did not have a reputation as a Bolshevik, he was a nationalist, a rebel and a putschist, and he was also a trained lawyer and the son of a wealthy landowner. His first wife, Mirta Díaz-Balart, came from an elite family that was a mainstay of the military government. Brother Rafael was a member of the Cuban House of Representatives and for a time served as Deputy Minister of the Interior. When the Castro brothers were arrested for the attack on the local Santiago military quarters, it was assumed that they did not receive the death penalty because Fidel had married well and was generally considered "one of us" in Havana, a member of the elite. Although Mirta divorced him after his arrest, Castro was given a handsome jail term on Isla de Pinos (now Isla de la Juventud). He served barely two years, and was then subject to Batista's amnesty, declared in 1955. Although Rafael publicly criticised his brother-in-law's pardon, it was of no use to him; Fidel and Raúl were free. After Castro's revolution, the Díaz-Balart family wisely decided that Cuban soil had become too hot for them and retreated into exile.

Mirta, who is in her nineties, now lives in Madrid and, apparently, partly in Cuba. For a long time, she could not see her son Fidelito, and it was only about 20 years ago that she was allowed to visit her homeland on the intercession of Raúl Castro. In exile, Rafael became a prominent anti-Castro figure. When I lived in the United States in the 1990s, some of the most visible Republican politicians there were the Florida congressmen Lincoln and Mario Díaz-Balart, Rafael's sons and committed anti-Castro politicians, whose uncle was the *Líder Máximo* himself.

Fidelito, the boy in pyjamas in the CBS documentary, Castro's second eldest son, suffered a tragic fate. He studied nuclear physics in the Soviet Union and lived in his father's shadow. He married a Russian woman, but the marriage fell apart. As a member of the scientific establishment, he became embroiled in a corruption scandal that eventually cost him a prestigious academic post. Fidel did not stand up for him, and during the scandal he is said to have even remarked that Fidelito deserved to be punished because Cuba was no monarchy. In February 2018 in Havana, at the age of sixty-eight, he committed suicide. His full name - Fidel Ángel Castro Díaz-Balart - sounds somewhat bizarre in the context of modern Cuban history.

Except for providential people like the Díaz-Balarts, the Cuban elite welcomed Castro's revolution in 1959 and 1960. They were fed up with Batista, who had been on the political scene for more than twenty years and was in the pocket of the American mafia, especially Meyer Lansky. They attributed some of the excesses of the revolution to Castro's hotheadedness and expected things to go back to the way they were when Fidel got his way. One telling example relates to the famous Bacardí family, who in January 1959 put up a banner on their Havana building welcoming Fidel's arrival in the capital.

At this point, Arenas' memories of Holguín at the time are invaluable. They leave us in no doubt that his education was designed from the beginning in the spirit of Marxist-Leninist ideology. In addition to professional accounting, economics, and agricultural subjects, he already had to learn the history of the international labour movement and political economy from the Soviet author Nikitin.

"In 1960, while Castro was assuring the world that he was not a Communist and that the revolution was 'as green as our palm trees,' Cuban youth were already receiving Communist indoctrination in addition to military training."

A somewhat amusing part of the "education" at that time was the obligation of students to climb Pico Turquino in the Sierra Maestra, the highest mountain in the country, rising to 1,974 metres above sea level. To graduate as an accountant, young Reinaldo had to make six expeditions to the top of the mountain with his classmates. There was a hierarchy of importance in the education of cadres, as those studying international relations and going into the diplomatic service had to climb Turquino as many as twenty-five times! I am reminded of my landlord in Cienfuegos, a "journalist" and "diplomat." How many times did he have to climb the mountain? During the ascent, the students sang songs in chorus. At first, they were free to choose as they pleased. However, during the last few expeditions, the ideological climate changed, and they could only sing the Internationale and other revolutionary songs. The Marxist processions were meant to bring the youth closer to their role models, the *barbudos* of the mountain jungle. They are good evidence of the faux-religious nature of this leftist ideology.

"Santiago is beautiful. But it's hot. It's a hot country, that's why we call it tierra caliente," says a hitchhiker we stop on the Autopista Nacional. And indeed, it is. I wake up on a hot December day. I walk out of my room into a small atrium with greenery and flowers. There was no one here, just the faint sounds of breakfast being prepared in the kitchen. I see three open Bibles on the coffee table. I investigate one of them. First Book of Samuel, verses twelve and thirteen:

"David's young men set out on their journey home. They came back and told him everything. Then David said to his men, 'Gird each of you with a sword. So every man girded himself with a sword. And David also girded himself with a sword. Four hundred men followed David, and two hundred men stayed behind with their equipment."

The story of the rise of King David and the conquest of Jerusalem. A few meters away, a poster of Guevara hangs on an orange wall. The Bible and Che, the morning remix of Hot Earth. In other words, Monday. Taking advantage of the solitude, I turn on my computer and hastily write down yesterday's experiences. I try to finish it before breakfast. I sit down at a green plastic table, the kind that seems to be sold all over the world. You can find them on the terraces of Czech cottages and in refugee camps in Dunkirk. Breakfast consists of a two-egg omelet and good coffee, with milk and sugar. Who would have thought in 1959 that sugar would be a scarce commodity in Cuba! The lady of the house puts white bread on the table and homemade Cuban cheese, known here simply as queso.

"No, it's not goat cheese," the landlord clarifies, "we don't make much goat cheese in Cuba."

I ask because I've seen more livestock on the road than in the past, including goats. In Holguín, a man was walking down the street with a

Chapter 4

goat on a leash. The cheese is delicious. Then there's the homemade guava jam. Excellent breakfast. And yet the landlord apologizes for its simplicity. He says food is a problem in Cuba these days. What does he think I have on my table every morning in Prague? I ask him why the roads in the east are in bad shape. He gives me a long, somewhat embarrassed look and doesn't answer for a few seconds, so I almost think he misunderstood. But he did not. He stands next to me, puts his hand on my shoulder and sighs.

"You haven't seen the really bad ones. Nobody keeps them."

He winks conspiratorially. He doesn't engage in more specific conversation. In a Communist dictatorship, even trivial topics like the state of the roads are potentially dangerous. He's not a Communist, though he's probably not the one studying the Bible, but his grown son, who wears frayed jeans, speaks decent English, and listens to the blues, a nice change of pace in the local reggaeton lagoons. But what about the Guevara on the wall? A reminder of his youth? A neutral decoration for tourists? Big, faded framed photo, black beret, red star, uniform. We stay on the subject of roads, not the Lord's paths, but the physical state of the roads, and he gives us advice on how to get back to Holguín and avoid the worst. He shows us where to turn and what to watch out for.

"It's a longer route, but you save 80 kilometers on bad roads, or more than two hours of terrible driving."

The time has come for the "Birán" conversation tactic, which I have already discussed with Jimena and for which I have her support. I am proud of this idea. The plan is as follows. In order not to embarrass strangers with direct questions about political conditions, I will try to get their opinions indirectly. Birán is the birthplace of the Castro clan, not far from here in the province of Holguín, a small village in an arid landscape near the mountains. The regime has built a museum there, and although I have been to Cuba several times, I have avoided Birán. The idea is that I'm going to try to ask around and see if anybody will latch on to a conversation about politics. Birán - do you know it? How do I get there? Have you been there? Is it worth seeing? I imagine the conversation going like this:

"Birán? Don't waste your time. Propaganda..."

Or:

"Terrible. Avoid it, commies..."

Maybe even like this:

"Yeah, sure, I know. They're great at museums, but they can't even fix roads..."

Or vice versa:

"Birán! The birthplace of the Commander of the Revolution! You must see it! Beautiful!"

At least I would know where I stand. But the landlord is neutral. Yes, the birthplace of the former president. There's a memorial there, but I've never been there. I can't tell you what condition it's in. Go see it. It's only eight kilometers from the main road.

Hm.

In two hours, the playoff between Brazil and South Korea will kick off in Qatar. Teammates from my favorite London team Tottenham Hotspur, the Brazilian Richarlison and the Korean Son, whose almost rhyming names make me want to write a limerick or a haiku, will face each other, and that's what I want to see. Jimena proves to be a true Latina as she also wants to see the match.

We take a tour of the center. It's uphill to the main square, Parque Céspedes. We climb up the steep slope of San Basilio Street and pass the balcony of the Conquistador, Cuba's first governor, Diego Velázquez, who bloodily crushed a rebellion by the Indian chief Hatuey in the early 16th century. The Indian, who hid with his warriors in the nearby Sierra Maestra mountains, which we can now see across the bay, and from there waged what we would now call a guerrilla war with bows and arrows, was betrayed by one of his own. The Spaniards captured Hatuey and brought him to be burnt at the stake. Legend has it that before he died, they offered to convert him with the promise that he would go to heaven.

"Are Christians in heaven?" asked the proud chief.

After being assured that they were, he replied that he would rather not go. What remains of him are a few historical memories and the local brewery of the same name. Hemingway, who used to take a few bottles on ice in his boat when he went out to hunt marlin, mentions Hatuey beer approvingly. It's not a bad lager, but I prefer the Cuban brand Cristal, lest anyone think I'm a Hemingway epigone. These days, after all, Ernest is part passé and part non grata. He does not suit the woke because of his alleged machismo, but also because of his complicated sexual orientation, which he hid from the world. Today, the world is not so forgiving, wants to know *everything* and sticks its nose into things that are none of its business.

The Bacardís began brewing Hatuey beer here in Santiago in 1927, the first premium brand in the country, brewed from a recipe by a hired German brewer. Hatuey was a respected historical figure in the Bacardí family. Emilio Bacardí called him "the first martyr who died for Cuba." Beer production boomed in 1948 after the opening of the Modelo brewery in Havana, only to have the family's property stolen by Castro in 1960. They were forced to emigrate. The banner welcoming Fidel and his troops to the capital didn't help. In 1996, the Hatuey brand was revived by Bacardí with the help of brewer Eduardo McCormick, who once worked for Modelo and secretly copied the recipe before fleeing Cuba. The brand was introduced in New York in 2014, after being launched in Florida, and is considered a product of the small brewery category.

Back to Velázquez's balcony, in front of which I now stand sweating and panting. The governor himself didn't enjoy the balcony; it was built by successors for three decades after his death. It is dominated by a stone structure with three arcaded openings, topped by a battlement motif. It serves as an entrance to the balcony, which acted as an observation post for the bay as part of a defensive early warning system against raiders, mainly corsair ships, which could be seen from here during the day. From the balcony I get a majestic view of the city above the harbour and the emerald green of the mountains on the other side of the bay. We are interrupted by a uniformed organizer who tells us that access is free, but if we want to take pictures, we have to pay. I ask if this also applies to taking photos with a mobile phone. It does. I harpagonically let my phone rest in the back pocket of my blue canvas shorts. My wallet rests in my front pocket. The organizer gives me not the least bit of friendly attention, then hisses something that sounds suspiciously close to a sentence:

"It wouldn't do you any harm..."

The woman is young. In the flesh. Black skin. Curious. The conversation is more like an interrogation. Where we're going, where we're from, if we're going to the beach. To the beach! She says we definitely have to go to the beach! I think of my visit to Siboney Beach, and I shudder at the memory. Sand full of sharp stones, water not so clean, body on body, hygiene loose, smell... not Siboney. I tell her I'll go to the beach in Guardalavaca.

"But that's in Holguín. Why?" she remarks with disappointment in her voice.

"Yes, in Holguín," I nod and head out of the balcony towards the square.

From an urban planning point of view, Parque Céspedes is a gem. The square in the middle of the old town has become my favourite place in Cuba, both in terms of atmosphere and aesthetics, and there are many beautiful squares in the historic centres of Cuban cities. I'm thinking of classic, geometrically shaped squares like Parque Agramonte in Camagüey, Plaza de Armas in Havana, or Parque Martí in Cienfuegos, not the sprawling megalomaniacal nothingness of Havana's Plaza de la Revolución. Céspedes Square is intimately quiet, yet the surrounding buildings breathe big city.

It wasn't always as quiet as today, Monday morning, and there were plenty of hustlers and prostitutes around, but the pandemic has dealt them a blow in the form of a significant drop in tourists. There's the stately Hispanic house from which Velázquez, the founder of this eastern metropolis named after St James (Santiago in Spanish), ruled. The luxurious Casa Granda hotel on the corner next to the cathedral has an air of literary pathos, for it was here that Graham Greene got the idea for his pre-revolutionary novel *Our Man in Havana*. In it, Wormold, a vacuum cleaner salesman, is given a responsible assignment by British Intelligence to work secretly for the young Queen Elizabeth, but he can't master the spy craft, so he makes stuff up to justify his side job. He is actually writing fake news, as we would say, which puts him ahead of his time, so that Greene's book can be considered a half-step towards postmodernism. Wormold's fictional agents become increasingly real, entangled in a web of his own lies.

On the south side, the Cathedral Basilica of the Assumption of the Virgin Mary gives the square its characteristic look. Its last appearance in the spirit of Spanish neo-classicism dates back to the early nineteenth century. The original church has been here since the sixteenth century, but its various forms have been destroyed by fires and raids by corsairs, who obviously did not much care for going to the Tabernacle of God. The basilica used to wear a dress of pale yellow façade - I still remember it - but now it is pale blue and perfectly restored, so that in certain light, especially late in the afternoon if it is clear, it looks like candy against the dark blue sky.

On a previous trip I saw part of it under scaffolding, as the cathedral was undergoing renovation. The mixture of pipes and heavy plastic veils took away from the elegance of the square. It is adorned with statues of Bartolomé de las Casas, the priest who was the sixteenth-century protector of the dispossessed and enslaved indigenous islanders, and who also tried to save Chief Hatuey, as well as a statue of Christopher Columbus, whose memorable voyage from the end of the Middle Ages to the dawn of modernity gave birth to the conquista. In the geometric centre of the beautiful basilica, a white marble statue of an angel stands on the triangular relief of the canopy between the two towers. Its long wings have become a symbol of the city's expansion. The angel holds a long golden trumpet in his right hand and a book, probably the Bible, in his left. He looks down on the square with a calm, steady gaze.

Santiago is the centre of Cuban Catholicism. The city has been visited by the last three popes. In January 1998, St John Paul II celebrated Mass here and, true to his legacy, spoke of freedom and justice. He said that the Christian faith is the best path to human development and true freedom, that lay Catholics have the duty and right to participate in public debate and to work for the common good in a peaceful manner. To work properly, John Paul said, the Church needs freedom. To defend religious freedom is to defend the freedoms of individuals and families, to protect human autonomy. It is not known how the Mass appealed to the Castro brothers, who at that time - unlike the country they plundered - were still in full force. John Paul was taken in by then 71-year-old President Fidel Castro in Havana. He exceptionally wore a black suit and tie for the welcoming ceremony. The suit fit him poorly, flapping loosely around his arms and legs like most soldiers accustomed to wearing a uniform. At the Havana airport, Castro towered over the stooped, delicate pope, who leaned on a black cane - a contrast to Francis's visit in 2015. Back then, Castro received the Pope at his Punto Cero residence in September of that year, 14 months before his death. Each man gave the other a book. Castro gave the pope a publication on humor and religion.

One of the two books Francis gave Castro was by Amando Llorente, a Spanish Jesuit who knew Fidel as a teenager and taught at the Jesuit Colegio de Belén in Havana. During the papal visit, the media also reported on Llorente's 2006 interview with the *Miami Herald*, in which the Jesuit recalled his visit to Castro and his rebels in 1958 in the Sierra Maestra. At the time, he spent four days with his former student, trying to find out what the nature of his revolution actually was. In the interview, he mentioned how during Fidel's childhood his father was not involved in his son's life and how the high school student Fidel once told him:

"I have no family other than you. He was probably referring to the Jesuit priests who raised him."

Not everyone was happy with Francis' visit to Cuba. Dissidents complained and contrasted it with John Paul's mission seventeen years before. In his homilies, Francis never once mentioned freedom and justice, instead emphasizing the non-ideological nature of service to one's neighbor. In photos from the meeting, the two men are seated. The Pope clasps the sinewy hands of the dictator, who looks at him with anxious eyes that hold an old man's concern. He is wearing a blue Adidas tracksuit jacket, unbuttoned, and underneath it a white shirt billowing over dark blue trousers. His thinning grey hair and beard are not reminiscent of the wild growth of his youth, and the only thing left of his characteristic decisiveness is the antique profile lent by his long, sharply shaped nose. It would have been interesting to listen to their conversation. From the photographs, their meeting was private. Did they talk about God? About transcendent things? The media said it was an equal debate, unlike Fidel's meeting with Pope Benedict a few years earlier, in which the commander subjected the guest to interrogation.

"So you, Ratzinger, are you saying that God exists?" one hears Fidel's mocking remark at the end and sees the Holy Father's look of consternation. Fidel was still strong enough. A few years have passed and with Francis in the photo he looks as if he is asking for reassurance that he will not go to hell. Chief Hatuey refused the conversion at the last minute. What happened to the shaky, egotistical old man named Fidel Alejandro Castro Ruz, we don't know yet.

Cajun Haiku

It's time for a football battle. We don't know there won't be one yet. I glance up at the angel on the cathedral, who, it turns out, will be chauvinistically protective of Brazilian Catholics, and we head to the bar recommended by the Casa Granda hotel car park attendant. They're guaranteed to have football there, especially when Brazil is playing, he said. And he was right. The bar is on the corner, a few dozen metres from the square behind the cathedral. It's tiny, just a few tables and a counter, a bartender, a waitress and somewhere in the bowels a cook. He occasionally comes out of the kitchen to check on the score, looking happily at the screen and the bartender dryly updates him.

Richarlison. Paquetá.

The "a" at the end is appropriately elongated and proportionately shortens the first two syllables of the Brazilian midfielder's name into bursts from a verbal machine gun: pa-ke-TÁÁ! Richarlison, who is playing in the form of his life in Qatar and whose blonde-bleached hair shines for miles, duly serves the Korean up. Son hides his sadness behind the black face mask he's playing with due to injury, but he's no Zorro the Avenger today.

I'm ordering a sangria, just like Jimena. For a moment I consider sex on the beach, a version of which is wittily called *sesso en Siboney,* and that reminds me that I forgot to mention this Fidel story. Robert Merle mentions it in his book about the attack on Moncada Barracks. The tale is entirely chaste, no sex on Siboney Beach involved, depicting instead a youthful act of heroism. The Castro brothers, Ramón, Fidel and Raúl, studied at a Jesuit boarding school in Santiago. One day, under the supervision of priestly instructors, they went swimming at Siboney. The two students were forbidden to swim by the priests because of some disciplinary infraction. Fidel felt sorry for them, so he suggested to one of the supervising priests at Siboney that he would jump into the water from a height of ten metres if the students were pardoned and allowed into the sea. The priest warned Fidel that it was too high, expressed doubts about venturing the jump, but eventually agreed to the deal. Fidel jumped. His classmates enjoyed swimming in the bay that day. I'd like to make fun of Fidel's jump, but then I recall when I was ten jumping into the Elbe with my friends from the railway bridge. It was barely six metres, but it took me a long time to throw myself from that height into the waves, and that only because I was frightened by an oncoming train. I feel a grudging admiration for young Fidel and probably a little envy. I don't get a *sesso* after all, it's pretty hot out, and with the score 3-0 to the yellows, a fateful haiku runs through my head.

> *Goal hurts Son badly*
> *Richarlison smiles and dances*
> *Football can be cruel*

I'm rooting for the South Koreans, Jimena of course for Brazil. The naive play of the reds is something for the yellows! They'll eat them up like I eat pizza. Normally I don't eat it in Cuba, but here you can't order anything else. I put it carefully in my mouth and find it doesn't make a bad impression. Better than the South Korean defense. Deep, soft, somewhat moist, tastes sharp in a Cajun style, the ham cubes are chopped coarsely and make a good combination with the *queso*. But it's not pizza as we know it from Italy or the United States. Still, within the limited possibilities, I am satisfied and order a second sangria. The final score of the match is 4-1. The Koreans say goodbye to the tournament. The Brazilians are smiling, dancing, and so are the Cubans.

> *Sharp Cuban pizza*
> *with queso as memory*
> *Sangria's sad chill*

I pay and we head up a gentle slope between single-story colonial buildings. In the uneven cobblestone pavement, typical of Santiago's centre, I see here and there the remains of tram tracks, a reference to the city's past glory. We enter a special shop where you pay with dollars. It offers an eclectic assortment, from bottles of whiskey worth two solid months' salary to two kinds of mustard and one kind of pickled olives to cigarettes, mostly Cuban brands. They've adopted the practice of stacking one type of item, or more accurately one brand, the length of the counter to give the impression of abundance. A large can of tuna for $4.95 also winks at me, and I figure it will be cheaper in New York. The shop's clean, the air conditioning is running full blast.

A little further on, I see a depression in the opening of a tall door and an improvised used books shop. Tomes fill every inch of all three walls, on shelves and on strings. A salesman sits on a folding beach chair deep in this slum. I'd like to browse the books in peace, but I can't. He's talking to me and keeps pushing his stuff. As soon as I pick up a collection of Nicolas Guillén's poetry, he immediately recommends several others. My Spanish is pretty lousy, so it might be worth buying some simpler rhymes and wading through them in the evening instead of reading Julian Barnes, which I brought with me and which I always fall asleep at night from exhaustion. I pick up an anthology of revolutionary poetry, a notoriously battered paperback with yellowed pages.

"A true one-off!" says the seller, and probably the owner, enthusiastically. "For you—twenty dollars!"

The price is so breathtaking that I'm putting the book back on the shelf. Our ideas of what bibliophilia is are so far apart that I prefer to leave the shop.

After a few minutes we stand in front of a white building with an ancient facade and Corinthian columns. The Emilio Bacardí Moreau Museum. Entrance is incredibly cheap even by Cuban standards, just a few pesos. The collection was founded by Bacardí in 1899 when he was mayor of the town. The lower floor is dedicated to the history of the city and the struggle for independence in the second half of the 19th century. There is Martí's tailcoat and the hammock in which the dead body of General Antonio Maceo was placed. The upper floor is occupied by a display of sculptures and paintings mostly, but not exclusively, from the 19th and 20th centuries. In the corner sits a black polished stone Aristotle by the

Spaniard Donato Mora, hands clasped philosophically in his lap. He is balding, has short straight hair in the back, is beardless, has a prominent forehead with massive eye arches, and a serious, uncertain gaze. On the other side of the gallery, a large statue of Guevara stands by the window, but to see it properly is an art. It is placed against a light that dazzles anyone looking. Similarly, in Karlštejn, Emperor Charles IV used to sit with the window behind him so that those to whom he granted audience could not see his face. Is his smile rueful or sincere? There is also a good bronze head of Camilo Cienfuegos from the mid-1970s with a sunken face and combed hair. He looks intently ahead, as if he doesn't care that the museum is almost empty.

I spend the longest time in front of a portrait of a black man with disheveled hair and a glassy gaze. It was painted in the mid-19th century by the Cuban classicist José Joaquín Tejada and called *The Head of the Negro Alcoholic*. It is a brilliant painting devoid of mannerisms, it stands out for the realism of its rich colors and breathes one particular human destiny. Like everywhere, the label is just a name and a title. No edifying narratives, no texts about the difficult social situation, criticism of conditions, racism and colonialism, i.e. the propaganda that in our times is attached to every other exhibit in the galleries of the Western world. And this in a country otherwise full of blathering propaganda!

Shortly after this trip to Cuba, I saw the Jean-Michel Basquiat exhibition at the Albertina in Vienna at Christmas. I went from painting to painting and played a private game: I stopped reading the texts next to the paintings whenever I came to the word racism or a variant of it. As a result, I finished reading only a few of the dozens of "informative" texts. Racism was everywhere. New York was a rough place in the 1960s and 1970s. Basquiat encountered racism and had to deal with it. He did it through his work as well, which is evident in several paintings and can be read in others. But his paintings are more than an aesthetic struggle against racism. Such an ideological interpretation of a work of art is always impoverishing. Basquiat excels in his explosion of color and his ability to abstract figures to the point of childlike iconography, his ability to accurately 'describe' and capture the atmosphere of his city. He succeeded in the unheard of, giving a new impetus to Pop Art at a time when it seemed exhausted.

Progressive ideologues do not realize that their heavy-handed tactics are alienating those who, if they used more appropriate methods, would be willing to pause and reflect on their message. Those of us who grew up under communism remember regime propaganda that had the opposite effect on most thinking people, even when it was right. From a young age, the Communists hammered into our heads that the United States was a racist country. As a result, I didn't believe it, and it wasn't until I lived in America that I came to understand that even in the 1960s, racial segregation policies were indeed practiced in many states of the Union, and that the black struggle for equality was not a Communist invention.

American and European *woke* propaganda on systemic racism and the drive to equalize the sexes in galleries, media, universities and corporations is now marching down the same dead end. It will have the same counterproductive effect as Communist propaganda as I experienced it in the 1970s and 1980s. It's sad. Racism has been repugnant to me since I was a child and, unlike many of my peers, it was not a theoretical concept for me, because I grew up in Libeň in Prague and there were many Romani children around me. In football at that time I was rooting for the Brazilians because, among other things, there were bronze and black players among them. Because of their skin color and their dance moves, I considered them aesthetically more beautiful and more perfect people. I still think that today, when I prefer to root for South Korea as the underdog.

I'm looking at Tejada's black man's head, which is all the more impressive without the doctrinaire texts. It gives you room to think. We have a small intimate moment of connection over two centuries, just me and him, long dead. Actually, sadly, no, there's still the attendant, who shadows me all over the gallery and watches me like I'm Maradona. Now she tells me they're closing in ten minutes. I'm supposed to head for the exit. There, another attendant informs me that I should have her mark my ticket and I can come back tomorrow. I politely decline. If I come again, I'll gladly pay, as admission is almost free, but the nice lady insists. I am impressed by her precision, after all, civilization is based on details. We hand her the ticket, curious to see what she will do with it. She pulls a pen from her shirt breast pocket and clicks on it. Simple! The Emilio Bacardí Museum is impressive and sadly under-visited. It's in fact dead. I didn't see a cafe or a bookshop.

The sangria, the heat and the intensity of the artistic experience exhausted us. Afternoon fatigue sets in. But there is no time for a siesta. In the pedestrian zone that rises from the sea, there are colorful one-storey houses with shops and pastry shops offering ice cream and, somewhat unusually, several libraries. Outside the center around Céspedes Square, no one bothers you. People, of which there are many in the streets, go about their business. The streets are lined with palm trees, and there's the famous Matamoros Bar, named after the legendary Trío Matamoros singing group that made Trova famous. Several houses have plaques commemorating the attack on the Moncada barracks. This is where the heroes gathered with their weapons. And elsewhere: Here some of them slept. I climb the hill and get a view of the surrounding mountains. In this part of Santiago, the houses are higher, the offices and other official buildings of the province have been added. On a stone wall behind a large intersection, Fidel's quote is immortalized in gold: ¡Gracias Santiago! All around, greenery and traffic.

We turn left in front of the monumental modernist building of the Palace of Justice, which became an important site of historical drama on July 26, 1953. It was entered by a group of militants under the command of Raúl Castro, who shot the lock of the door on the top floor with a pistol and then fortified himself and his men on the terrace overlooking the buildings of the Santiago Military Garrison, located next to the Palace of Justice. Crossing the boulevard, we see a complex of low ochre-colored buildings decorated with crenellations on the top and surrounded by walls along their entire length. We are in front of the former Moncada barracks. We walk along the wall to the right, towards the top of the hill on which the main buildings stand. There are many children in the young pioneer uniforms with red or blue scarves on their white blouses. The complex is now used for education, the 26th of July Movement School. Turning a military garrison headquarters into a school full of children is an idea worthy of a propaganda genius. The lower part of the complex, called the Polygon in Batista's time, is now a playground. There's dry, trampled

Chapter 4

grass growing and a bunch of boys chasing a ball around it. There's shouting, it's happy and lively. This is where Batista's soldiers executed prisoners just after Castro's putschists attacked. Witnesses described dead bodies with parts of their heads blown off, the lawn stained with fresh blood.

I am standing next to the barrier at the third entrance to the barracks, where two memorial plaques have been placed on a concrete column with text commemorating the morning start of the attack. When I want to walk past the barrier into the building, I am stopped by a doorman with a pistol at his waist. You're not allowed in here. "It's a school," I say, "why not?"

"No trespassing," he tells me, smiling but uncompromising. "Normally, this is the entrance to the 26th of July Museum."

He waves his hand towards the gate a few metres away. A staircase leads up to it where a van is parked. A few metres away from us, behind a barrier under the staircase, a wheelbarrow used to transport mortar on the construction site has been orphaned. It is kept company only by a few discarded shovels.

"But it's closed today," he adds. "Monday."

"Oh, right, Monday. And what time do you open tomorrow?" I ask.

"It's closed tomorrow, too. The museum is under reconstruction. It will be newly opened for the anniversary. In July."

Conversations with Cubans are similar in some ways. The first day I arrive, I ask the owner of my casa particular in Havana how the gasoline is, whether it is there or not.

"Gasoline is complicated," he says, sits down, takes a breath, and begins to explain. He gestures vigorously and articulates with unusual clarity for a Cuban.

"We have two kinds of gasoline in Cuba. Regular, which is cheaper, and special, which is more expensive. As a foreigner with a rental car, you always have to fill up with special. It's impossible to fill up with regular." He holds up a finger. "Out of the question!" I nod and he continues. "It's just that regular isn't available right now."

"Oh. What about the special? Is that available?" I ask.

"Special isn't either."

I remember this gag right here, in front of the former barracks where Batista's soldiers once didn't finish their job.

"So you won't open for six months?" I remark disappointedly, and then put on the most commie smile I can muster.

"Could I take a picture of the entrance? Just a moment."

It's good, he sees me as a foreign revolutionary. He gives permission. I'll go around the barrier. There are authentic bullet holes around the museum entrance, a reminder of the shootout. I take a few pictures, thank the good comrade doing an honorable task here, and walk down along the wall and then to the left. I want to go around the whole building complex. At the bottom of the playground, there's just a wire fence and a hole in it. A black boy of about ten comes running up with a backpack over his shoulder. He's wearing a yellow T-shirt with the number 32 on the chest and green shorts. He stops in front of the hole, takes off his backpack with icy calm, pushes it through the hole and puts it on the pavement. Then he methodically rolls both parts of the hole to the side, deftly slides through the hole onto the sidewalk, and slips the backpack back over his shoulder. In the distance I see the main school building with the big red number 26 on the roof. In the light of the setting sun, its ochre color darkens. Over the fence is a nice view of the Polygon, where seventy years ago the executioner worked. The boy has his movements perfectly rehearsed; he looks like an experienced actor who has practiced the action in advance and visualized all details. He has the nonchalant face of a child movie star. I'm taking a series of close-ups. Like a proper star, he's oblivious to me. What's a paparazzo to him! He throws his backpack on his shoulder and disappears across the street. I shove my phone back in my pocket.

A shorter older guy in a shirt over jeans comes up to me and with a good-natured smile explains that this is where it all started, this is where their journey to freedom, to *real* freedom, began, he says enthusiastically. You can tell he believes what he's saying, so when he asks me where I'm from, I'm a little apprehensive. I might lie that I'm from Canada, for example. After all several times people shout at me on the street, Go Canada Go! Finally, I admit my color. He doesn't respond to the Czech Republic at first. Praga. Then he gets it.

"Checoslovaquia!"

Cubans of a certain age can be counted on. In the United States, nobody knows the Czech Republic. You'll encounter hybrids like "Czecho-Slavia," but you can't blame a nation whose State Department personnel confuse Baltics and Balkans. But Cubans know their Czechoslovakia. *Amigo* gets right to the point.

"We were brothers! We built socialism together. We belonged to the same camp."

I'm waiting, just watching him. He doesn't say it in a reproachful way. He's not bitter. He doesn't seem to be suggesting that we've betrayed them. He simply announces that we were brothers, real brothers, *hermanos verdaderos*. Maybe he doesn't know exactly what real means. Some people confuse words late in life. George W. Bush comes to mind. Then he tells me he remembers our last socialist president, but mutters a name that doesn't resemble Husák, or Svoboda, or even Jakeš, or perhaps Havel. I don't understand him well, I suddenly feel like I'm in an alternate reality. It is as if he is announcing to me that our last Communist president was, for example, Hampl or Košický, and I cannot for the life of me remember. Because I don't want to prolong the meeting, I don't correct him. He smiles again. He's missing a few teeth. The wrinkled, unshaven face refers to a hard fate, but he is clean, well-groomed, and no ill intent emanates from him.

"Once brothers, always brothers," he says, and leaves. Life is complicated much like selling gasoline around here.

We manage to walk around the entire former barracks, named after Guillermo Moncada, the black general, hero of the War of Independence, who was born in this town and made it from a simple carpenter to the conscience of the nation. He died of tuberculosis, exhausted by his Spanish imprisonment, five years before the dawn of the century.

We're going back to the pedestrian zone. It's getting dark. Against the darkening sky, the crowns of the royal palm trees look like something out of a comic book. A red neon sign shines on a one-storey house: Revolución. In the distance beyond the city, the majestic Sierra Maestra and the bay below plunge into darkness. Mopeds race down the main street, along with ladas and moskviches that have survived death in the Caribbean. Long since they were born under the Urals. I'm sure they never thought they'd be enjoying their old age in the warmth of the opposite hemisphere, where they'd be cared for like treasure by swarthy men with their collars up.

Locals rush along the sidewalks, walking to and from work. Probably both. Some of the older women have respirators over their mouths. There's an increasing number of coronavirus cases. We pass a lighted hair salon. The burly black barber has a white beard of fluffy foam on his face. The blacksmith's mare doesn't go barefoot here. He beckons me in through the clean window with a broad smile. I think about it for a few seconds, slow down, I haven't had a Cuban haircut yet. The barbershop looks like a copy-paste from the fifties. A set of razors on display, solid chairs, dark wood paneling. This is where Santo Trafficante or Lucky Luciano would come to chat.

At the beginning of the well-lit pedestrian zone we find a cosy bar. Its door is open to the humid climate, with a few heavy, wooden tables inside. The walls are decorated with Afro-Cuban motifs. We sit down under a masked black man with a cigar in his mouth and a green scarf atop his head. It could be a black woman, gender is fluidly ambiguous. We order coffee. They don't have coffee. My bad, I almost starting to feel normal. But they have beer, Australian import. We settle in and observe the motley company in front of us, engaged in lively conversation.

At the first table near the entrance sits a midget with a New York Yankees baseball cap. He's in his 60s and has the face of a criminal, reflecting a lifetime of experience. He smokes a cigarette and explains something animatedly to his two companions, a young man and an even younger girl with thick make-up. I strain my ears. At the same time, I instruct Jimena to listen discreetly. The man says something in Italian. Or maybe Spanish... we can't hear well and he's talking major league. After a while it becomes clearer. He speaks both Italian and Spanish, switching from one language to the other and back again. He's berating both of his buddies for something. He puts a wad of bills on the table and counts them. He does this several times, taking a drag from his almost-smoked cigarette. He divides the bills into three unevenly thick piles. Is he splitting the loot? He picks up his phone, clings tightly to the girl and takes a selfie. She puts on the most artificial smile she can muster. The runt hums at her, coaxing her into something. The young man just sits across from her, watches the midget for a moment, then stares out the open doorway at the pedestrian zone again. Perhaps he's looking for something. Better times?

The white-coated chef enters the room several times, bringing pizza, the only item that can be eaten here. It's Cuban pizza again, with coarsely chopped cubes of ham and Cuban cheese. When I pay, he walks right past us. Jimena makes small talk. I lower my voice and deploy the "Birán" tactic, but the trio at the table are engrossed in their conversation and the bartender just stares absently at the pedestrian zone. The chef, a short, white, sweating man in his prime, looks up at me impassively and serves me whipped foam:

"State Museum. Castro's home village. No, I wasn't there."

A little further on, the pedestrian zone slopes down to the bay, the local Malecón. We reach the level of Céspedes Square. From here on, the lower part of the pedestrian zone disappears into darkness. Blackout. We turn towards the square, and before we reach it, we have a closed photography studio called Estudio Lídice on our right. It's not the first time I've passed this way, it's an established institution. The name obviously refers to the Czech village burnt down by the Nazis. There were a number of girls born in the world after 1945 with this name, so the most likely scenario is that one of them set up a business here.

Céspedes Square is not affected by the blackout. There are groups of young people sitting around. Some are listening to music, others are just relaxing and enjoying the quiet of the evening. Near the bank, remarkable for its elegant functionalist features, a lone young man sits on a bench, looking at his phone. He is wearing a straw Panama hat, a dark floral short-sleeved shirt, unremarkable jeans, trodden patent shoes and surprisingly thick socks for the local climate. I sit down nearby. After a moment, I introduce myself as a journalist from Europe and ask if he would be willing to chat.

"Yes. But not about politics."

He's tired, his forehead is wrinkled and his Panama hat is pulled up to the back of his head, so that his bald spot is sticking out. He'll be in his early 30s. I promise him anonymity, his name in this story is Juan Panama.

He has a degree in biomedical science. He works part-time as a medical machine technician.

"No, I don't live alone. I live in a house with my mother and brother."

"How is life in Santiago?"

"Santiago is a beautiful city, so I'm happy to be here. But right now, life here is difficult."

"Complicated by a pandemic?"

"Not only. There are more aspects to it. Not just because of the pandemic. Supply is a problem. Electricity is erratic. People don't have money."

"Even less than a few years ago?"

"Much, much less."

"What is it?"

Juan Panama just smiles and it's clear to me that we're not going there together. So I ask him how much he makes a month. His smile turns slightly bitter.

"How much am I taking? In dollars?"

I nod. He unlocks his phone and looks for something for a while, probably today's exchange rate on the black market. Then he looks at me.

"So today I take about seventeen dollars a month."

We speak English together, so he stresses again so I don't overhear:

"Seventeen. Not seventy."

"Is it possible to live on?"

"No, it is not."

"What are you doing then?"

"Here in Cuba, everyone has to do something extra. I trade."

He's pointing to his cell phone. He's trading on the stock market.

"Do you have regular access to the internet?"

"Yes. I need a VPN connection for that. Sometimes the lack of power is a problem."

I hope he's not dealing in cryptocurrencies, but we'll keep the unsolicited advice to ourselves and say goodbye. The cathedral is a little more mysterious in the dim spotlight than it was in the morning, when it was sunning itself unassumingly.

Moments later we are sitting on the brightly lit terrace of the Casa Granda Hotel. I watch the square below me. It's named after Carlos Manuel de Céspedes, a Santiago landowner who led a revolt against the Spanish in the 1860s. The bloody slaughter of the First War of Independence followed, ending in the rebels' defeat ten years later. All Cuban revolts, including Castro's, have their origins here in the Oriente. The people here are rebellious, unruly, and don't like to be dictated to, especially not by the Havanese, who are a long way from here. The East has always been relatively independent. It was only the Communists who managed to pacify it.

At the next table are several young men and women in designer clothes. The boys are wearing Diesel jeans, nicely ripped, obviously not from working in the sugar cane fields. A bleached lady, sitting with her back to me, clutches a Louis Vuitton handbag and sips a cappuccino. We order the same. In places, their conversation reaches us, consisting mainly of them amiably teasing a middle-aged woman in a black dress who sits between them. Jimena is again given the task of listening.

"She's nervous sitting here with so many young people," says a man with a haircut like Richarlison. His back and sides are shaved, and his short top is bleached blond.

"Don't go yet, stay with us," he says to the woman, who is smirking and fidgeting nervously.

"She has to go home. She has to take care of her Castillo," the woman with the purse barks ironically.

"Castillo can take care of himself. Anyway, let's call him! He can come too," Richarlison suggests.

"No, no, she has to go home, she has to cook for Castillo and take care of him," says the young woman. I can't see her face, but I bet she winks meaningfully, because her innuendo evokes mirth. The middle-aged woman, who is being teased in a friendly manner, looks embarrassed. She doesn't like being the center of attention. In comes another young man who looks like the Brazilian footballer Neymar. Everyone says hello. Smiles sparkle. Jewellery clinking. Neymar, too, has a Louis Vuitton handbag, the male version, and a silver chain on his jeans. I'm not the fashion police, but I had no idea they still wore that. Neymar gives some sort of story to go with it, which again triggers a wave of hilarious reactions. From what I pick up, I hear them talking about parties, about who got drunk and had impossible conversations. A young woman mentions visiting her cousin in Zaragoza, Spain, and all the things she brought back. She opens a wooden box of jewels and lets them circulate. She also says she bought a lot of clothes from Zara. A person who prides herself on Louis Vuitton probably despises brands like Zara, which leads me to the amateur hypothesis that their more expensive cloths will be copies. Jimena agrees with my conjecture.

I lean out from the terrace, above which red and white canvas awnings are extended into the square. I wonder if they adorned the square when Graham Greene stayed here, in an era of borsalinos, shiny clicking patent shoes, understated suits and cocktail dresses? Later, I look at photos I took here ten years ago. In them, the awnings of the hotel are dark. At the end of the terrace is a wooden antique bar with a polished counter and meticulously crafted furniture. It's besieged by four waiters. The conversation next door begins to cycle. I'm paying. A cappuccino is a dollar seventy. I turn my head into the plaza toward the Bank. Juan Panama is still sitting there, looking at his cell phone. For his monthly salary as a skilled professional, he could have ten cups here.

We walk through the darkness on big cobble stones to Velázquez's balcony. Behind the bars of the low fence lies a tired dog. He has a brown, matted fur coat and lies on the black-and-white tiles in front of the house, watching me amiably and closing his eyes. He should be guarding, but he doesn't want to. I guess he knows there's nothing inside to steal. At the corner, the taller, slender figure of a parking attendant from the Casa Granda Hotel emerges from the darkness, his shift over. We say hello and thank him for recommending the bar for a Brazilian whipping. He's a retired man in his seventies, with a thick mane of silver hair, a kindly, weathered face, and a long-sleeved blue shirt. After his shift, he keeps them unbuttoned, the cuffs turned up in a dandy way. We ask about our street, San Basilio, which we must have missed. The guard gesticulates, points in the direction, and even though it's exactly the opposite way from where he was going before, he jogs a few meters in our direction. It occurs to me to try the "Birán" tactic on him. We stand under the dim light of a streetlamp, surrounded by the low houses of old Santiago. At the mention of the name of the fateful village, he pauses. I hold my breath. It's here! He dreams, puts an H.Upmann cigarette to his lips, and inhales the smoke deep into his lungs. He lets it out, looks out into the dark behind me and says excitedly:

"Birán! I mean... wait."

I am barely breathing.

"You have to see it there. It's a beautiful farm, there's a museum. Fidel's birthplace, a villa, the whole estate…it's so charming. Listen, you've got to go there. You have to see it!"

The ingenious conversational trap has failed. In my room tonight, I open *Flaubert's Parrot* by Barnes. I didn't buy the revolutionary verses. Nothing will come of practicing Spanish.

"History Will Absolve Me!"

The idea to attack Moncada's barracks originated in Castro's head for a simple reason. His militant youth group was determined to take on Batista through armed rebellion but lacked weapons. The barracks was a welcome arsenal for them, some of which they intended to seize in a lightning-fast attack. To be successful in attacking a much larger garrison full of soldiers, the radicals needed at least some firearms. Castro decided to solve the *Catch-22-style* problem one step at a time. Over the course of less than a year before the attack, his movement slowly grew with new and new conspiracy cells coordinated by a central staff of just a few people. Only they knew about all of them; the members of each cell did not know each other because of the secrecy. They bought weapons, mainly hunting rifles and pistols from the military's scavenged supplies, and military uniforms. To confuse the enemy, they needed the same military camouflage as the soldiers in the garrison, only they still didn't have enough of it. How to resolve this conundrum? The wives and girlfriends sat down at their sewing machines and dozens of uniforms were created by their efforts.

The date of the attack was clear from the beginning. The fact that it coincided with the Santiago Carnival, which began on July 25, should have added to the surprise. In the meantime, the rebels had been practicing shooting in small groups, both at Havana's shooting ranges and in a windowless university room under the iconic long staircase of the University of Havana in the San Lázaro neighborhood. They didn't shoot there, of course, just learned corps and disassembly, gun care and proper aiming technique. Castro was also careful to improve the rebels' fitness. The core of the group was made up of members and sympathisers of the youth wing of the Orthodox Party, but it was not an official party event and there were quite a few left-wing radicals among the putschists. Lenin's and Marx's writings passed from hand to hand among them. The Jesuit-raised Raúl Castro became a young Communist at that very time. A minority of the attackers were students and intellectuals, while the majority were young workers, peasants and farm labourers, as well as waiters, mechanics and the unemployed. They were united by their hatred of the military dictatorship and their desire to do something about the social conditions in the poor countryside.

The military garrison in Santiago was chosen by Castro himself. Compared to the Havana Columbia barracks, it was noticeably smaller. Santiago, some eight hundred kilometres from the capital, offered the possibility of creating an alternative power centre, and it would have taken some time for the regime to organise itself over such a distance and respond effectively to the rebels if they had succeeded in taking control of the entire eastern metropolis, which had been the capital of the colony. Castro reckoned that if he took over the quarters, seized the local arsenal of weapons and broadcast his political statement on the radio, the people would join him and overthrow the dictatorship. He originally intended to join in the coup with Raúl Chibás, the brother of Eduardo Chibás, the founder of the Orthodox Party, whom he greatly admired.

This politician was popular in Cuba during the democratic republic in the 1940s and 1950s, when he also ran - unsuccessfully - for president. Eduardo Chibás was known for his anti-corruption views and speeches. He was an emotive, charismatic figure with a penchant for histrionics. In 1951, he committed an eccentric suicide when he shot himself in the stomach at the end of his regular half-hour radio address in which he criticised the corruption of President Príos. But he did it clumsily, and twice at that. Firstly, he planned the shot for the very end of his speech, but he miscalculated the time, so that he was no longer on air when he pulled the trigger. Moreover, he aimed so unfortunately that he did not die immediately, but only a few days later. His slow death became a national political gesture against corruption, and Fidel then held a guard of honour at his coffin. Brother Raúl Chibás, however, disappointed the young putschist when he refused to join his action on the other side of the island, even symbolically.

The main problem with Castro's coup was its lack of preparedness. Because of the secrecy, most of the 150 or so rebels only learned of the target and the execution of the attack after they had moved a day or two beforehand to a rented farm near Santiago in the village of Siboney near the famous beach, a place seventeen kilometres from the city centre. Raúl Castro learned on the train to Santiago that the military quarters were to be attacked. He immediately thought it was a suicide mission. Groups of rebels were moving to the Siboney farm in private cars, by bus and last-minute trains. Many of them arrived the night before. They'd made a tiring, hours-long journey. At least two drivers drove into a ditch, overcome by microsleep from exhaustion on the way.

Castro wanted the strike to have maximum effect, so he decided that thirty rebels would raid a small barracks in Bayamo, a small town about 100 kilometres away, which is now the capital of the Granma province. Moncada was to be attacked by 120 fighters, Bayamo by 30. Because the leaders met resistance from about a dozen university students after announcing what it was actually going to be, they decided that those who did not want to participate did not have to. As a result, fewer than 110 putschists participated in the Santiago ambush, and even then only in theory, since during the morning raid in private cars many of them wandered off in search of the barracks while the gunfight was already raging. The extent to which stragglers participated in the fighting is unclear. In fact, cars carrying students on their way back to Havana joined the convoy of fighters heading into the city center toward the Carretera Central exit in the morning, confusing some drivers into following them out of town instead of toward Moncada.

The fortress of Santiago housed about a thousand soldiers at the time. A hundred raiders could therefore have stood a chance under only two assumptions: the attack would have been lightning-fast, taking advantage of the element of surprise, and the barracks commanders would have surrendered quickly. Castro therefore set the attack for Carnival week. Groups of fighters would be lost to the eyes of the police in a riot of merriment on arrival from Havana, and then, as Fidel hoped, the morale of the troops would be loosened. Fidel estimated that after the first night of Carnival, the soldiers would be asleep. For this reason, the column left the farm before 5:00 a.m. and arrived at its destination at 5:15. Poor preparation and poor coordination, which must be attributed to an excessive effort to conceal the action until the last moment, was evident right from the start. The plan was that the first group, under Fidel's leadership, would arrive at the third entrance to the barracks, get inside quickly and disarm the commander. He would be supported by a group under the command of his deputy, Abel Santamaría, which was to occupy the hospital on the main avenue opposite the barracks. There, the putschists were to take up a strategic position and open fire on the barracks from behind. At the same time, a group led by Raúl Castro was to take up residence on the terrace of the Palace of Justice and from there, from a height and distance of 80 metres, cover Fidel's troops with fire.

The attempt to surprise quickly failed right from the start. At the third entrance to the barracks, at the place where the porter with the pistol had stopped me, there were more soldiers than Castro expected. In front of the entrance, the driver of the car in which Fidel, cleanly shaved with short curly hair, dressed in the military uniform of the regime, was sitting, wanted to drive onto the sidewalk, but he hadn't taken into account the height of the curb. The car hit the curb hard, and the engine cut out. Fidel's group and the group in front of him stumbled clumsily out of the cars. The young men stumbled over each other. The attempted coup took on a tragicomic quality. There was a shootout, followed by a deafening siren from the barracks, alerting government troops to the alarm. The rebels took cover as best they could behind curbs, walls, cars, buses, carnival floats, behind fences and windows of nearby bungalows, in the Palace of Justice and in the hospital. But a thousand well-armed and well-trained soldiers will have a decisive advantage in any reality, even the most alternative, against a hundred poorly armed and ill-prepared attackers. It was a bloody massacre that lasted just over two hours. At the end of it, about a dozen militants lay dead. More than half of them, however, lost their lives that day because the soldiers did not spare them. They executed them immediately and wherever they could, especially on the grassy area of the Moncada Polygon, from where I watched the boy with his backpack.

The attack by thirty Castro putschists in Bayamo was similar. Two-thirds of them lost their lives there. There were no surprises there either. Doors that should have been open turned out to be locked. In the courtyard, the attackers tripped over discarded cans, waking the horses in the stables and their neighing woke the soldiers. It is not easy to get reliable casualty statistics. The Castro regime has made 26th July a sacred day and turned the events into a legend. The leader's "memories" occupy a central position in it. Thus we read of heroic stunts, such as how Fidel was fleeing the fighting when he saw a lone comrade in the street, to whom he immediately gave up his seat in a crowded car. He stepped out onto the boulevard, where the shooting was still going on, and so he put himself in danger of losing his life rather than lose his comrade. Another tall tale relates to a situation a few days later when Fidel was caught and arrested near the Gran Piedra mountain. There, a Batista corporal allegedly refused to shoot him, despite the wishes of his superiors, with the remark: Ideas are not killed.

Unfortunately, Castro's tales has been taken over by other sources, so that wading through the literature of Moncadiana is like hacking your way through jungles of poisonous vegetation with a machete. Both Raúl and Fidel were captured by soldiers after days on the run. Raúl went to his home village of Birán. There he was recognized and picked up. Fidel's arrest was probably negotiated by his then-wife Mirta. The Archbishop of Santiago, who had been instrumental in the efforts to preserve the lives of the two brothers, played an important role. Fidel probably surrendered voluntarily.

The attack on the barracks gave Castro a national identity. Day by day, the dictatorship was losing popularity. After his first democratic mandate during the Second World War, Fulgencio Batista returned to the presidency after eight years, not as an elected president, but as the leader and organiser of a military coup. His secret police, the SIM, acted brutally against potential opposition, torturing and killing political enemies and suppressing civil liberties. When Petty Officer Batista took control of the army during the barracks coup in the first half of the 1930s, he was an intelligent, charismatic and hard-working man from humble circumstances. He came from the port town of Banes here in the north of the Oriente. Like many of his fellow citizens, he was of Afro-Cuban-Asian descent. His life story was one of social mobility and overcoming racial prejudice. Cuba was gradually becoming a modern state. Batista was elected president of the democratic republic and ruled as a civilian

In December 1946, after the end of his term, when he was out of politics, Charlie "Lucky" Luciano and "Accountant" Meyer Lansky called a meeting of mob bosses in Havana. All the major figures in American organized crime attended. They met for several days of negotiations in the elegant rooms of the Hotel Nacional de Cuba on the Malecón, with Frank Sinatra singing for them. The meeting was recreated in The Godfather, Part Two. Unfortunately, director Francis Ford Coppola's crew was not filming in Havana, but in Santo Domingo, Dominican Republic. The hotel there, the Occidental El Ambajador, is a far cry from the glamour of the Nacional. The result of the meeting was to divide the influence of the families present into territories and industries. Lansky became the boss over the Cuban gaming industry and in 1952 he wrapped Batista, who had since seized power that year, around his finger in such a way that it was rumored that he was a kind of unofficial minister for the gaming industry in his government. It was, of course, an exaggeration.

During Moncada, Castro was just under 27. He looked youthful, he was tall, handsome, he was an articulate radical, and the fact that he confronted Batista with a gun was appreciated by the people. His popularity grew even more wings when, in the autumn of 1953, the text *La historia me absolverá* (History Will Absolve Me), based on Castro's defence at the trial, began to circulate around the island. The young lawyer took advantage of the situation to defend himself. It was a clear political gesture, and it is astonishing that the Batista dictatorship allowed such a thing to happen. It is hardly conceivable that the dictator Castro would have allowed such a thing to happen to, say, José Daniel Ferrer or Dagoberto Valdés, the current anti-Castro dissidents. *La historia*'s speech is obviously an artfully created myth. Castro is said to have spoken for four hours in the courtroom, which is hard to believe, even though, as we have already noted, the long speeches were his signature.

The trial itself did not take place in Santiago's Palace of Justice, but a few dozen metres away in the hospital, the place where Santamaría and his men had fortified themselves and where they lost their lives. Although Fidel had carefully drafted the speech over several months in detention, he had not written the text in advance. As was his custom, he spoke from notes. Several journalists sat in the room taking notes, but there is no audio or film. The famous sentences with which Castro was to end the exhaustive speech - "Condemn me. It doesn't matter. History will absolve me." -were almost certainly not heard in the hospital conference room that day. According to one apocryphal account, he concluded with something like, "History will show us how it was."

The essay, with its powerful ending, was loosely based on his defense and composed while he was in prison on Isla de Pinos, where he was sent for 15 years. Castro's accomplices smuggled the text out, gradually compiled it into its final form and expanded it. The content of the essay is partly devoted to the details of the action as Castro presents them for belief, mainly the cruel treatment of his comrades by the soldiers, about half of whom, unlike him, paid with their lives. At the heart of the pamphlet is a critique of regime corruption, poverty and social conditions. Fidel positions himself as an advocate not just for his own person, but for all the weak and oppressed people on the island.

He was already free in 1955. He went to Mexico, where he met Guevara. Twenty-sixth July 1953 is considered the beginning of his long revolution, and for orthodox Marxists it is the start of the road to "real" freedom. The red-and-black visual identity of the 26th of July Movement is exclusively associated with Fidel until his identity as a Communist comes to a head in the 1960s, but it never completely disappears.

Despite the dismal outcome, Castro was proud of Moncada. Even before 1959, he jealously guarded her legacy. His reaction to the attack on the presidential palace in 1957 is testament to that. This was the failed assassination attempt on Batista on 13 March that year, carried out by the student opposition group Directorio Revolucionario Estudiantil. On the same day, another section of rebels attacked the editorial office and studio of the Radio Reloj radio station in the Radiocentro CMQ building in Vedado. Both actions posed a greater threat to the regime than Castro's attacks in Santiago and Bayamo. Batista had to fortify himself in a suite on the top floor of the palace because a fierce battle was taking place outside and inside the building. The soldiers eventually managed to call in reinforcements, including tanks, in time, and shot the attackers and captured them.

Castro said he did not approve of the Directorio efforts to kill Batista. By then he must have been influenced by Marxist-Leninist literature, for his main argument against the March attack is like something cut out of the textbook of the international labour movement. Trying to kill Batista would solve nothing, he said at the time, because the enemy is not one man, the dictator, but the whole system. The words echo those of Lenin, who said the Bolsheviks were not fighting the Tsar, but Tsarism. Since we know so much about Castro and his policies decades later, it is clear that his reaction at the time was impulsive. He purposely sought justification, but in my opinion, he was motivated mainly by jealousy. The March attack took place four months after Castro's landing in the south-west of the country, where he and eighty companions had landed after a few days' sailing from Mexico on the yacht Granma. Another disaster awaited him there. The army killed dozens of guerrillas. Fidel and Raúl managed to escape with a small group and set up a base in the nearby mountains.

5.

Sword of the Liberator.

Holguín

In the morning I get advice at the house on San Basilio to refuel in Santiago, as it could be an adventure outside the city. Driving out of the historic centre we pass the Palace of Justice on our right, then the former Moncada barracks and the hospital where Santamaría was shot, and just a few hundred metres further down the main road we actually find a petrol station, surrounded by cars and motorcycles. They have special and normal. In the heat, I inhale petrol fumes and try to read the display at the station the clerk has designated for me. It's so faded that the amount or number of litres is not visible in the sunlight. I fill up blindly and wait for the click to signal the lock. But it doesn't come. I've paid more than I can fit in the tank. Fortunately, the salesman is honest, gives me a refund and an official receipt.

We were on our way to the cemetery of Santa Ifigenia, where I wanted to see the grave of the bearded man. It's soon on my left, but I can't find the turnoff and I can't get to it. It covers a huge area, so I try to go around the back, but there we get caught in the shantytown that sticks to the back wall of the necropolis like worn Play-Doh to Meissen porcelain. We drive through streets of choked dirt. It rained during the night and the streets are muddy and full of huge puddles. The ghetto residents look at us in disbelief. We pass tiny shacks with clotheslines strung between them. Dogs roam around. The ghetto is full of squalid, depressing dwellings. It occurs to me that they have a fraction of the market value of the whitewashed tombs under the palm trees just a few dozen yards outside the wall. It's not a pretty picture, but somehow I can't shake it. Then, for a brief moment, I see a huge wild cat with sinister eyes, ruffled fur, and huge paws behind the gate. It's an awesome sight, even more surprising since normal cats here tend to be malnourished. What's he doing here? Could someone be breeding a puma right here? What would he be feeding it? I don't have time to investigate, so the disturbing sight vanishes in a flash into the surreal, the realm of hallucinations. I try with all my might to get out of the narrow alleys and onto the main road.

In the end, the effort pays off and this time I don't miss the path to the parking lot in front of the cemetery entrance. There is no one there, just a parking lot attendant who tells me where I can buy a ticket. He also says that I can give him whatever I think is appropriate for watching my car. I pull out two hundred pesos, a little more than a dollar in conversion, hand him the bill and walk to the cemetery's majestic entrance, built in the 19th century style. Santa Ifigenia is the equivalent of Prague's Slavín Cemetery, where famous figures of history rest. We reach a wide tarmac avenue separating the parking lot from the cemetery itself. At first glance, it's an American-style cemetery. From here I can see white tombstones glowing in the sun, a palm tree here and there, Cuban flags, blue sky and green mountains in the distance. Light, warmth, sunshine, not a trace of the gloom, darkness and mystery of Central European final resting places.

The front part of the cemetery is dominated by a generous cairn built in Martí's honour. Just as we are about to cross the wide tarmac road, a chubby female guard in uniform starts calling out to us. We're told to wait. From a white house with arched windows and a single arched entrance, a group of servicemen and women in olive drab uniforms come out in a solemn column, and a funeral march is heard over the loudspeakers. The ceremony of changing the guard at the graves of the heroes is repeated every half hour and lasts about five minutes, during which it is impossible to enter through the main gate. The soldiers raise their straight legs to the sky, bayonets in their left hands, golden cords bouncing on the ironed skirts of their uniforms, shaking to the rhythm. The female soldier's long black hair covers half her back. She leads three other guards to the ornate tombstone of Mariana Grajales, mother of General Antonio Maceo, a hero of the War of Independence, revered by Cubans as the Mother of the Nation.

A group of tourists, elderly, well-to-do looking men and women, came up to us. They are dressed in designer shorts and golf shirts with their collars turned up, wearing sneakers or sandals. The ceremony is over. We are given permission to cross the road. With a determined stride, we walk to Castro's grave, which is located between Martí's cairn and the white house, where the soldiers whose service has ended have taken refuge. I don't really know what to expect, but what I see takes my breath away. In front of me is a two-metre-high boulder with only a memorial plaque with a gilded inscription: 'Fidel.' That's all. There are no quotes or revolutionary symbols, not even his surname, just a simple stone bench in front of the boulder and a few low green bushes tickling the boulder from below. When he got it right, Fidel was a public relations genius. Behind his grave, however, looms a large, conventional monument to the 26th of July martyrs, and to the right of it a monument to the "internationalists" or Cuban soldiers sent by Castro to die in Angola for the eternal glory of the socialist revolution. There is, after all, a long quotation from Fidel's speech.

We are standing with tourists in front of Fidel's boulder. A uniformed guard watches us closely. At one point, a pensioner in a blue T-shirt with a raised, canary-yellow collar trips under my feet, so I cut my way to the entrance across a metre of trimmed green grass. The soldier rolls his eyes, opens his mouth, and holds up a finger to let me know that trampling grass is not allowed! He almost faints at my audacity to stray from the marked path. Nice symbol for the whole country. A shepherd dog making sure the sheep in his care don't run away.

I walk among the graves, palm leaves rustling high overhead and the red and black flag of the 26th of July Movement fluttering on some of the stones. There are poets, artists, Revolutionary War heroes and the tombs of wealthy 19th-century families. Even the singer Compay Segundo, who achieved global fame in his old age thanks to Ry Cooder and the movie *Buena Vista Social Club*, rests here. In its layout and atmosphere, Santa Ifigenia Park is reminiscent of Arlington National Cemetery in Virginia near the United States capital. The difference is that the cemetery here is a more fitting picture of life, where you'll also meet real heroes and villains in close proximity, as well as a number of quite normal people, both talented and those who have bought notoriety.

What happens when the dictatorship falls and Cuba becomes a democracy? Will anything change here? Would they abolish the grotesque North Korea-like ceremony that is repeated every half hour? Would they exhume Fidel and remove his stone from its place of honour? Or would everything remain as it is, in Catholic reconciliation and stoic silence? Martí and Maceo, heroes who sacrificed themselves for the nation. Narcissus Castro, who lent his undoubted talents to an ideology that destroyed the lives of two generations. In such a case, is generosity or justice in order?

From the cemetery, I drive uphill towards Palma Soriano with a full tank of thoughts and then turn towards Holguín. The road is surrounded by tropical vegetation the color of malachite. Strings of sunlight shine through it.

Birán

In the second half of the 20th century, Castro became a planetary icon. In the midst of the missile crisis in October 1962, he urged the Russians to launch a frontal nuclear attack on America. It was nine years after the failed Moncada coup, and three and three-quarters years after he had seized unlimited power in Havana. Was he serious? Maybe he was. It is equally possible that he knew Khrushchev would not commit to nuclear war, and he was building a brand of a certain type in front of him, in the inner circle. The image of a tough guy in an olive-green uniform who is *different*, unpredictable, who is better to have on your side. As the Americans say, some people are better inside the tent because then they piss out. If you leave them outside, they will urinate inside.

We go to see the place where fate has decided, Birán, the birthplace of Fidel, Raúl and his siblings. Our Santiago landlord was right, it's only eight kilometers from the main road, but they'll make up for some thirty. Even by Oriente standards, the road is in tragic condition. The first few kilometres look like leftover asphalt, then pothole after pothole, with dry fields and wasteland all around. You would think that the regime would want to show off and build a golden road to the sanctuary.

Birán is the village to pass through, and then you look for the estate of the late Ángel Castro, Las Manacas, which is a few hundred meters away. It's a vast area with many buildings far from civilization and feels like an alternative world compared to the poor neighboring settlement.

Ángel came to Cuba in the late nineteenth century from Galicia in the north of the Iberian Peninsula in search of better luck and found it. He made his fortune in sugar cane and cattle ranching. He had five children with his first wife. Then he wooed a domestic servant twenty-seven years his junior, Lina Ruz, who had served on the latifundia since she was fifteen. She gave him seven more children, including Fidel and Raúl, two future putschists and presidents. With another maid, Ángel fathered at least one more child. He did not formally marry Lina until during World War II, after all the children had been born. According to the available sources, he was peculiar, tough, and not very present in the lives of his offspring, at least no more than he himself thought necessary. The news of his death at the age of eighty was received with equanimity by the otherwise emotional Fidel. In general, Fidel's emotions were more evident in politics than in private. Fidel's relationship with his own nine children was similarly distant as Ángel's relationship with his brood.

We drive into the open gates of the estate, where a soldier stares at us in surprise on the grassy area. He recovers quickly and calls out to the wooden house:

"Tourists!"

The janitor appears in the doorway, wearing a red baseball cap, light-colored short-sleeved shirt and dark blue trousers that billow over him. He's a shorter, middle-aged man with earthy eyes. The area is empty, no visitors, so we ask if it's open. He nods. We immediately begin our tour, and interestingly, he doesn't ask us to pay admission. We walk through a wide-open space between trees and several large wooden buildings to the manor house, built between 1915 and 1917. In fact, this house is not original, as the first structure lay in ashes after Ángel fell asleep with a lit cigar in his bed. Fidel then had an exact replica built in the mid-1970s and turned the grounds into a museum. They moved what was left of the furniture into the wooden manor house. It is a two-storey yellow building with white windows, a sloping brown roof and a large terrace, built on wooden pylons to protect the ground floor from rising water during tropical rains. The space under the house also served as storage for various machines and tools, and as an improvised garage. Parked here is a beautiful ford, a van from the First World War.

We're entering the ground floor. The closed shutters and blinds don't let in much light, and as a result it is mysterious, but also somewhat sterile dark. A long, narrow corridor runs the length of the floor plan and gives a view of the rooms to the right and left. There are beautiful leather saddles hanging on the wall, riding crops next to them, a little further on the other side is a room with a bed, fitted with a metal hospital frame, where Lina gave birth, and a large living room with an ancient television and armchairs made of polished dark wood. It's a typically unoccupied house, and indeed no one has ever lived in this version. We walk across the grassy area to the opposite building.

"Ángel built this house for Fidel," says the guide in a disinterested voice. "But Fidel never lived here. He went to schools in Santiago and Havana and stayed there. Instead, the family moved here after the mansion burned down."

I'm looking at a large yellow and blue building with a red tiled roof. It's also made of wood, like all the buildings on the latifundium. It doesn't look to me like Ángel built this house just for Fidel. Why is that? Well, he had five children with his first wife. Fidel was only the second son with Lina, after his brother Ramón, who had a lifelong interest in agriculture. Fidel was also a farmer, and ranching was his hobby. Even as dictator, he tried and failed to breed record-breaking Scottish dairy cattle. Perhaps Ángel saw the talented Fidel as a strategist and hoped to multiply the family's wealth? I'm suspicious of everything the guide tells us. His information should be taken with a grain of salt. He's not an independent researcher, he just repeats what he's told upstairs. "Fidel's" house is cozy. You can tell that the family really lived here. We go upstairs to a large white tiled kitchen. I see a big American refrigerator. Despite some closed shutters, the room is bright, spacious and pleasant. The wooden walls upstairs are painted a cheerful blue, pink and turquoise. Crosses and Catholic-themed objects fill Lina's room.

In the living room there is a boxy television set on the coffee table and a framed black and white family photograph hanging above it. It shows Fidel as *Líder Máximo* in camouflage. The guide stops in front of it, conjures a pointer from somewhere and uses it to explain who is immortalised. The photo is from Fidel's sister's wedding, and we also see Lina, Ramón and a still quite young Raúl. Ángel was already dead at the time. I walk past the door leading to Fidel's room, which has a wooden closet against the opposite wall. One wing of the door is ajar. Inside, several outerwear items hang including a white baseball jersey with the number 15 on the back and the name F. Castro written in blue. Again, I wonder if it's an authentic shirt. Did Cuban baseball players in the 1940s have their names on their backs? Looking at old photos of American pros in the 40s and 50s, you usually don't see names on the back at all, just numbers. Maybe it's a gift from an aspiring ambassador that Fidel had hung up here. But who knows?

In any case, the information that Fidel didn't live here much is amply substantiated. He settled in Havana while studying law in college and has remained there ever since, except for the imprisonment on Isla de Pinos, Mexican exile and adventures in the Sierra Maestra. There is a story from his college days Fidel used to tell around the campfire while drinking with his guards, as Sánchez recorded. The young law student received a solid monthly allowance from his father, but decided to "save." He paid each landlord two months' rent in advance, even though they didn't ask him to. The enthusiastic landlords wrung their hands that they had caught the son of a good family. But this son had a plan. He always stayed with them for four months without paying for more than two, and then he disappeared. He did this several times.

"There must be quite a few people in Havana who are still looking for me," Fidel told his cronies, laughing loudly all the way round.

The largest and most generous room on the upper floor is the darkly decorated Ángel's bedroom. On the wall hangs his portrait, a black and white photograph in a dark frame. He could have been well into his seventies at the time. He is looking directly into the lens, wearing a light jacket and dark shirt, his round, bare skull shining into the gloom of the room. Ángel's gaze is fierce, and this impression is accentuated by his narrow lips, for which smiling was apparently an unnatural pose that was not wasted even in the photo studio. The massive chin with its unshaven stubble completes the impression of a strong personality, a man who was good to avoid. Did he have this portrait here in his lifetime? Did he look at himself every morning? Unlike his son, Ángel does not give the impression of self-absorbtion.

A surprise awaits us in the corner in the form of a massive iron vault. It's got double doors forced open. There's a hole in the middle that must have been blown with a detonator after Ángel's death. *Padron* never told anyone the combination to open the safe.

"So they had to force it open," the guide says.

He no longer has the pointer in his hand, which he has placed on the small wooden box of a 1950s television. He looks straight at me and for the first time his eyes flash something like participation, or even interest.

"And imagine! They only found some documents in the safe. No money!"

Every one of us on this planet will eventually find something of interest. On my way down the staircase, I see a large automatic rifle in a glass case. It's got a clip on it and a spare magazine laid underneath; just in case, I guess. I stop at it and look it over carefully.

"This is Raúl's gift to Lina," says the guide.

"Did he give his mother a rifle?"

"Yes, during the revolution, when the police went after him."

One would think that when the police are after you, a gun like that would come in handy, but what do I know? We'll go around the back of the house. There's a separate entrance to the bar and gambling room where they used to go for *un whiskycito*, *cohibas* and a bit of man talk.

"There were deals being made in the bar. Fidel played pool there," I learn.

The low building next door served as a post and telegraph office. About a hundred yards away I can see a larger two-story building with a terrace all around and a sloping red roof among the trees.

"It was a hotel. After her wedding, Fidel's sister and her family moved into the entire top floor."

Chapter 5

A few dozen metres from the building, two cows, a brown and a black one, graze near a sparse forest of palm trees and eucalyptus. From time to time a worker passes through the estate, tending to the upkeep of the grounds, but otherwise it is almost completely deserted.

"Don't tourists come here?" I ask.

"Not so much now," says the guide evasively, as if asked about state secrets.

"How many arrive in a day?"

"One or two," he says carefully, and it's clear he's probably referring to Jimena and me.

"The road here is bad. You have seen. It puts people off."

"Will it be repaired?"

"Yes, yes," he nods eagerly. "The repairs will begin soon."

We walk to a low, gray-painted house. It's a one-room schoolhouse, where the Castro siblings attended their first years of primary school. Rows of thickly painted wooden desks gleam in the light of dim lamps. In the middle of the first row, one chair bears a sign - this is where Fidel used to sit. It's odd because the benches are designed so that a surface slides out from the back of the front bench to serve as a desk. Naturally there are no front bench backs in the front row. I'm asking how this is possible. Fidel wouldn't have anything to write on, would he? My guide thinks for a second or two.

"Fidel was a gifted child, he went to school early. These younger kids just sat and paid attention. Nobody asked them to write."

He looks serious. Fidelito was sitting in the front row, and while the other kids were learning to write, he was just "paying attention"? He attended this school from 1931 to 1933, according to official records. He sat in the front row for two years without a desk? It's easier to imagine the restless son not in the premiership first row, but in the rebellious last, interrupting, pinching his classmates' backs and pulling their braids. The walls are decorated with photographs of Fidel and Raúl from their childhood and youth. Hanging there is Fidel's high school diploma, which also bears one of the names he didn't use much, Casiano. Fidel Casiano Castro Ruz, registered in the district of Cueto in the province of Oriente. So far the longest name of Fidel's that I have come across in my research is Fidel Casiano Hippolito Alejandro Castro Ruz González. But perhaps other names will emerge from the darkness of history.

A few tens of meters further we can see an arena for cockfighting, a covered circular barn with raised galleries.

"The whole village came to watch them," says the guide. His tone has returned to nonchalance. The excitement of the vault story had faded.

"Ángel sold alcohol in this wooden stall. Tickets for the cockfights were based on the distance to the battlefield. The richest people sat in the front row."

Like front row tickets to a professional hockey game, $1,000 for the front row. Same principle. If you want to smell the sweat and see the blood, you pay extra.

The last group of buildings to which the guide has something to say are the dwellings for Haitian workers. They came here for seasonal work and Ángel housed them in wooden huts under palm leaf roofs. He maintained good relations with the Haitian consul in Santiago. I'm entering the shack. It's an empty, leaky hut with a smothered floor. Dozens of wage laborers lived here and had their lodging deducted from their wages. Families could rent smaller huts and have a little more privacy.

Excalibur

From 15 to 17 January 1974, advertisements with mysterious contents appeared in the main Colombian newspapers. A surprised reader saw the following message:

"Parasites? Worms? Memory loss? Lack of activity? Here comes M19!"

Before the elite had time to recover what this actually meant, Jaime Bateman Cayón, founder of the urban guerrilla M19, ordered a spectacular operation. On the evening of 17 January, terrorists from his group broke into the Quinta de Bolívar museum near the capital Bogotá and stole the sword of the liberator.

Let us pause for a moment with this historical figure. In Europe, most of us do not understand the true depth of Simón Bolívar's legacy, especially after various unsavory regimes have tried to appropriate it, most notably the leader of "Bolivarian" Venezuela, Hugo Chávez Frías. This does not change the fact that Bolívar was indeed an authentic hero worthy of respect. This George Washington of Latin America, Venezuelan soldier and politician, played a fundamental role in the first third of the 19th century in establishing several South American countries as sovereign states, independent of Spanish rule. He was at the forefront of the campaigns that led to the independence of Venezuela, Colombia, Ecuador, Peru, and Bolivia, and is rightly considered one of the most influential politicians in the history of the Americas. He died in December 1830, and almost until his death in April of that year, he was the first president of independent Colombia.

There are more swords that are said to have belonged to him, and it is difficult to verify their authenticity. Some have been handed down from generation to generation in the attics of private chateaus, while others have been discovered out of the blue in a variety of locations or have been donated or sold to various interested organizations. They are now on display in museums and institutions of historical memory, such as the Museum of the Revolution in Caracas, the Bolívar Museum in Bogotá and the Bolívar Museum in Quito. Others are owned by private collectors. Certainly not all of them are authentic. They may be replicas or swords used by other generals of the time. So the question is whether Bateman really stole Excalibur of the Liberator.

But there is no doubt that Fidel considered it genuine. As Sánchez writes, on a beautiful day in 1980, Bateman suddenly announced himself in the presidential palace in Havana, which by then had a new name, the Palace of the Revolution, and handed the relic to an impressed Castro for safekeeping.

"Commander, here is the sword of the Liberator, which we took from the museum to put it in better hands," said Bateman, greatly moved, adding: "that you take care of it until it can be returned."

"Comrade," Sánchez quotes Castro, "I am now the keeper of the sword!"

He kept the sword with him for twelve years, and then returned it to Colombia, where it was needed as a condition of peace.

Let's reflect on the scene in the president's office. We can take an ironic Central European attitude to it. After all, there stood a Bolshevik satrap and a dreamer who had done more harm than good, pathetically passing a piece of iron whose authenticity may be in doubt. And yet the scene expresses something of the core Latin American political essence. Freedom and independence in the Bolivarian sense was national freedom, a point Bateman himself gradually came to. Just as the liberator stood up to the Spanish, Castro stood up to the Americans. That is why he grew up to be a great leader in the eyes of multitudes of intellectuals and politicians, and not only in Latin America. They looked up to him and he saw himself as carrying on the best traditions of the continent. His actions were guided by a claim to power, an irrepressible will of which, without defining it precisely, the old metaphorician Nietzsche writes. But that was not the only arrow in Castro's quiver.

More than anywhere else, the ability to create a public image is useful in politics. Fidel's efforts at self-portraiture were on my mind as I walked through the deserted Las Manacas estate. The sky had clouded over, the clear gave way to a half-light. It must have been a beautiful property once. Why did Fidel leave here? He could have been a wealthy latifundista, but he refused. Did his relationship with Ángel play a part in his choice? Or was it the big world of stage and TV cameras that attracted him so much? A world of acrid gunpowder and the sweet smell of blood. Birán wasn't enough. In the morning, I had seen his final resting place in Santiago, and now, in the afternoon, his birthplace. Two points on the line of life, the end and the beginning. I traveled against time, with the hindsight of a match whose outcome is known. Unlike the footage of a sports game, the view is still thrilling, especially when we consider what was at stake. In the span of nine years, from the Moncada coup to the missile crisis, Fidel raised the stakes from his own fate to the fate of a country, and ultimately to the fate of the planet. The boy, raised by Jesuits, made Cuba the playground of the superpowers, the stage on which the world's drama was played out. In the process, he himself went from being a district formar to a Shakespearean actor. His teachers, the clergy at Havana's Colegio de Belén, recognized his talent. At his high school graduation, they issued a glowing report:

"Fidel always excelled in all literary disciplines. He has excellent qualities. He is a true athlete who has always bravely and proudly defended the school banner. He has won the admiration and affection of all. He intends to devote himself to law, and we have no doubt that he will write dazzling pages in the book of his life. Fidel is made of good stuff, and there is no lack of the artist in him."

Artist. One who has created a new life for himself and his country, one who has learned to paint his own portrait. The evaluation shows the pedagogical interest and Christian love with which the teachers attended to the children, and one wonders how wasted Fidel's talent ended up, how unfulfilled and misdirected.

Politics is not an easy discipline, and in Latin America this is doubly true. It is supposed to be a space for resolving disputes, a substitute for violence. Its problem is the problem of life itself. It differs from chess to which it is often compared, in the absence of clear rules, or rather in the preference for one rule: the end justifies the means. I recall another Fidel story. It concerns his time at a boarding high school in Santiago before he moved to the capital. He stayed with his father's friend and his godfather, the aforementioned Haitian consul. For the sake of the pocket money for the cinema, which he received only for good grades, Castro pretended to have lost his report card, so when he got a new one, he had two. He only kept his As in one and then showed it at home. The godfather was delighted—Fidelito was the premier student! At the end of the year, he went to see the annual awards ceremony, convinced that the godson would take home several diplomas with honorable mentions. As the excited students took turns on the stage and Castro's name would not come up, the godfather became restless. Fidel was sweating and wondering how to slip away. Then he remembered he'd missed a lot of days due to illness. So, he explained to his "uncle" that this was the reason he was not included in the competition for the best students in each discipline. It was a close call! Like the story about the unpaid rent, Fidel repeated this one often and had a good time doing it. It should be noted that neither story made it into the official *Granma* newspaper.

Fidel is a particularly good example to discuss another fundamental theme of politics, the difference between reality and image. It is naturally easier to cultivate an image in a dictatorship, in which the politician can control outcomes more and create a cult around him. In Cuba and elsewhere in the world today, after his death, many people are still in thrall to the cult of Fidel. As a child, I remember Castro from television footage of him hugging Czechoslovakian Communists. It was always a bit slobbery and smelly, like taking your feet out of military boots after a long day. I pigeonholed him, and only much later did I gradually realize that he was not one of the Husáks, Honeckers, and Zhivkovs. He sold himself to them, but secretly despised them. He had a cold relationship with Brezhnev and other Soviet leaders, he did not consider them his intellectual equals, but that did not prevent him from being financed by them. During the war in Angola, in which the Cuban army had to coordinate with the Russians, Castro was highly critical of the Soviet advance within his inner circle. He disliked their ill-considered moves, their poor logistics, and their conquest of trenches that they had to abandon because of inadequate security.

Former Czech Senate President Petr Pithart, who met with Castro and others in his entourage, recalled his surprise at how different these people were from the Czechoslovak "normalizers," the top Communists who came to dominate the hierarchy after the Soviet invasion in 1968. Most of these people were deeply mediocre at best. They replaced the reformers who were the real brains of the party. As Pithart noted, the Cubans surpassed them in skill and intelligence. They were still Communists, convinced of their truth, tough and relentless, but not mediocre.

Castro's way of life demonstrates an eye for detail and a sense of purpose. He didn't overindulge in alcohol like Raúl. He had the occasional glass of whiskey, ate healthily, played sports and read everything he denied his subjects to read. Sánchez, the bodyguard, writes that as an intellectual, Castro did not pay attention to clothing, and therefore usually wore a uniform so that he would not have to dwell on thoughts about the appropriateness or inappropriateness of clothing for different occasions. Also, the beard, his iconic feature, was an expression of Fidel's reluctance to shave daily rather than a matter of fashion. His extensive personal apparatus, however, ensured that he wore a clean, pressed uniform every day. Personal meticulousness is evidence of the right kind of aspiration.

And then there is the subject of the already constructed political image and its acceptance by those for whom it is intended. I have been close to

Chapter 5

several top politicians whom people admired. Whenever I witnessed their cowardice, mendacity, deceit, and calculations, I thought that their admirers would probably be surprised if they had the opportunity to see it too, that their popularity would rapidly decline. But then Trump came along and made such behavior a matter of public record. He did on camera what many do only in private, and it didn't hurt his popularity one bit. A similar pattern of perception applies to Castro's many admirers. Ivan Pilip told me how Chilean socialist politician Juan Pablo Letelier, son of Allende's defense minister, Orlando Letelier, who was assassinated by Pinochet's secret police in the U.S. in the 1970s, was involved in the negotiations over Jan Bubeník's and his release from the Villa Marista State Security prison.

"Letelier greeted and hugged the Cubans like best friends. Even though he flew to Havana as a representative of an inter-parliamentary organization, i.e., in the role of a neutral mediator with the ostentatious goal of getting us to freedom, it was actually quite unpleasant to watch. Apparently, he was attending the negotiations for our release mainly to spare Castro PR problems. He didn't care who we were or what we were doing in Cuba. Or at least that was my impression at the time," Pilip remarked more than two decades after his imprisonment.

People like Letelier enjoy the benefits of democracy, which does not prevent them from admiring the Cuban dictator, probably sincerely. The Colombian writer Gabriel García Márquez, called Gabo, one of Castro's few true friends, whom *El Comandante* called *hermano*, brother, was a chapter unto himself in this regard. García Márquez arrived in Cuba in the 1960s as a young Colombian reporter and worked for the Prensa Latina news agency. A group of Latin American journalists founded the agency in the first year after the coup, 1959, with the ambition of being the authoritative 'voice of the revolution'. The agency's strategy replicated Castro's efforts, combining ideas of the extreme left and pan-Latin American unification. The policy received a massive boost after the failed invasion of Cuban exile troops in April 1961 in the Bay of Pigs. Castro was able to cast himself in the role of 'victor over the United States'.

Later, García Márquez moved away from propaganda journalism and became a world-famous novelist and Nobel Prize winner. His friendship

138   Cuba: A Brief History of the End

with Castro endured. The latter gave him a villa with a swimming pool in Havana's Playa district, full of the homes of regime notables, and often took him to his private island of Cayo Piedra, where Gabo had a guest house. Fidel had him as a companion in the presidential office, hosted him in his home, went fishing with him, and took him on some president's trips, such as his triumphant visit to Managua, Nicaragua, after the Sandinista takeover. It would be interesting to know the true nature of their friendship. Did they talk to each other as equals? Was Gabo willing to argue with Fidel and send him to the woodshed? Or did he just skillfully maneuver around him his whole life for the advantages he got out of it? Fidel hated being contradicted, and would obsessively attempt to convince everyone of his truth, usually by repeating the same arguments over and over again until his partners decided there was no point in resisting. Was it different with Gabo? Was he the one telling the leader what he really thought? Why Fidel cultivated Gabo is no secret. It certainly did him good to have a world-famous writer in his circle. Conversations with him were enriching for the dictator.

And *the Líder Máximo* could count on García Márquez to let him win every time. One tropical night, Gabo found himself with Fidel on a fishing boat about a nautical mile from Cayo Piedra. On board with them was a businessman whose name Sánchez (who recounts this story in his book) did not remember. It was around midnight when Fidel the night owl, accustomed to staying up late and getting up around 11 a.m., decided to hold a contest to see who could catch the most fish. But alas, from the start, the businessman was more successful. He pulled one fish after another out of the dark Caribbean night and soon had a solid lead. He was elated and didn't even notice that with each fish he pulled in, the face of the Commander-in-Chief of the Revolution was getting more and more sullen. The otherwise articulate Castro remained stubbornly silent. The one who knew how to play such games was Gabo. He would yawn, yearning to sleep already. At the same time, it was clear to him that unless Fidel had at least one more fish, the fight would not end if it were to last a week. Gabo then casually walked over to Sánchez and motioned for him to do something about it. The latter passed the message on to the businessman, so that he, too, got the light. As if by magic, his luck had left him. Fidel took the lead, happily announced the end of the fight, and went to bed.

He didn't know how to lose, whether it was basketball, fishing or politics. We enjoy poking fun at those who flatter their bosses, as well as at the bosses who expect any game they play to be rigged in their favour. It becomes the butt of jokes and movie gags. In politics, unfortunately, it is more widespread than one would expect. Fidel, for example, during his frequent basketball games with members of his security detail, demanded that he be constantly passed into positions from which he could score. Woe betide anyone who dared not pass to him and go to the basket himself. Another avid amateur basketball player, Barack Obama, did the exact opposite. He had a steady group of friends who played with him on the weekend and whom he required to be completely normal on the court and not spare him in any way. Anyone who disobeyed was in danger of not being invited to play next time.

The attempt to fix the outcome of the competition in advance has always been part of the manipulation of the political context. In democracies, politicians have limited opportunities to succeed in such efforts, but in dictatorships the only obstacle is the courage of potential rivals, a rare phenomenon. A psychological study of figures like Castro to determine the extent to which they believed in their athletic achievements would be useful. The tendency to win at all costs is undoubtedly good for the construction of a political persona. A dose of self-deception is useful in all circumstances and regimes, without which it is impossible to lead convincingly. People who can critically reflect on this self-deception and thus maintain their sanity are rare in politics.

Leaders' self-deception is not the only illusion needed to constitute and sustain the political game. For much of the world, Castro was a take-no-prisoners hero, the standard-bearer of the "anti-imperialist" forces. The empire kept him? So what? The Leteliers and García Márquezes of the world had a hand in this, they had a stake in spreading the myth, whether through political careers, the admiration of their peers, or a villa with a swimming pool. Rarely could they say no to the Commander, either to his face or indirectly. Gabo did it once on a very important matter. In the 1980s, Castro tried to get him to run for president in Colombia. It was shortly after the Cuban-funded coup in Nicaragua, and Fidel promised to help. But that was a bridge the writer was unwilling to cross. Castro's efforts are indicative of how much he saw himself as a director of events behind the scenes, of politics on an international scale. Rhetorical exercises at conferences of the Non-Aligned Movement were not enough for him. That's why thousands of Cuban boys had to die in the senseless Angolan expedition. García Márquez and other admirers, including Western democratic politicians like the later assassinated Swedish Prime Minister Olof Palme, served as a kind of snowman builders. Their balls were gradually rolled by many others.

For me personally, the bottom of the disillusionment came in 1995. Castro flew to New York for a UN meeting held in the anniversary year, half a century since the founding of the World Organisation. He went about his duties and then, out of the blue, as was typical of him, stopped to talk to the staff of America's most important newspaper, *The New York Times*. The information got around, so that when he entered the building, hundreds of people came out into the corridor and gave a rousing round of applause. I was living in the United States at the time, and I still remember the feeling that gripped me when I learned of their spontaneous welcome. I felt almost physical pain. Ours is a time of public apologies, not infrequently for the injustices perpetrated by our ancestors against the ancestors of other races in the name of colonialism. I think *The New York Times* owes a collective apology to Cuban political prisoners and their families for this.

"I Lived in a Monster."

To the will to power and the construction of a planetary persona, let us add the third ingredient of Castro's fame, namely the expansion of Marxist ideology and its subsequent derivations. The influence of Marxism on how elites have perceived the world over the last hundred plus years is enormous. Marxism has given a sophisticated conceptual apparatus to our need to see social events as a contest between good and evil. There is capital and capitalism, surplus value and exploitation, base and superstructure, there are social classes, and then there is the fiction that there are iron laws of history. In Marxism and its later derivatives, people are divided into progressive and reactionary, and they can be known not by a close study of their work and the impact of that work on other people, but by pre-determined abstract patterns. It is not the ordinary actions of people under moral scrutiny but their membership in a predefined group that determines their value and role.

At the same time, Marxism pretends to be a tool to unmask the real truth. It explains the world as a conspiracy of the powerful and puts itself in the role of the one who exposes reality. It thus gives people the illusion that on the basis of a few precepts they can understand very complex processes, that they can explain phenomena and realities of which they know little in reality. We have no problem condemning such generalizations on the extreme right as racism and anti-Semitism. We have much more trouble condemning them on the left. One hundred-year-old Soviet posters are now a valuable commodity for art collectors. Not so posters from Nazi Germany. That's why it's still good to be reminded that Stalin and Mao murdered far more innocent people than Hitler and Mussolini. In the Caribbean, Castro carried the banner of Stalinism. His gift for public relations endeared him to the press, especially the American press, published in a country that, although synonymous with the inferno for many South American intellectuals and rebels, is where they like to retreat to for exile and rest. Let us remember Martí. He lived in New York, a city that gave him freedom of expression and the opportunity to prepare for the fight against the Spanish crown. And what did Martí write about his time in the US?

"I've lived in the monster, and I know its innards."

Besides, it has always been possible to find allies in the United States, a country that guarantees freedom of thought, in the struggle against "capitalism," "exploitation" and "neo-colonialism." The US media served the South American rebels as a useful mouthpiece with which to trumpet their message to the world, and Castro proved to be one of their most successful manipulators.

On Sunday, February 24, 1957, *The New York Times* carried on its front page the first of a series of three extensive reports from the Sierra Maestra with the headline "Cuban Rebel Visits His Hideout" and the subtitle "Castro Still Alive and Still Fighting in the Mountains." There was an end to doubts about whether Fidel had perished like dozens of his guerrillas after the landing of Granma. The report was written by correspondent Herbert Matthews, who describes the rebels sympathetically as a group of young people, democrats fighting a dictatorship. The report was orchestrated by Castro who later recalled, among other things during a visit to *The New York Times* office in the 1990s, how he tried to influence Matthews' writing in his favour. For example, he instructed his men to move from one side to the other and back again in groups as they talked, to give the impression that there were more men in the jungle than there actually were.

The next hit on the PR target took place exactly one year later in Havana. Before the Cuban Grand Prix in February, Castro's soldiers kidnapped the phenomenal Formula One driver Juan-Manuel Fangio from the Lincoln Hotel. The militants also wanted to kidnap Fangio's teammate Stirling Moss, but the Argentine managed to talk them out of the idea by pointing out that there were enough cops around to increase the chances of capture by the minute. To play on their emotions, the spirited Fangio tipped them off that Moss was in Havana on his honeymoon, which was not true. The rebels put Fangio up in a pre-arranged apartment near the hotel, treated him to a solid steak in the spirit of good Argentine tradition, and had him sign a statement that he had been treated decently. After the Grand Prix, they returned him to the front of the Argentine Embassy.

In keeping with the Stockholm Syndrome, Fangio spoke sympathetically about his captors in the media. The world press interpreted the kidnapping as a humiliation of Batista's government. Even today, you will find articles in this vein on the web. They are full of stock expressions; there is the corrupt Batista and his mafia connections; there are the young, bearded rebels who have won the sympathy of the people. That was part of the truth. The other part of it is the fact that the standard of living of the average Havanese in the 1950s was infinitely higher than after 60 years of rule by young rebels who have since aged, lost the sympathy of the Cuban people, raised successors and died in luxury. The mainstream narrative of the Cuban situation, in which *The New York Times* and hundreds of other Western media outlets participated in the late 1950s, took hold perfectly, and survives to this day.

Castro publicly embraced the world socialist movement. Among the superpowers, he chose as protector the more distant one, the one that Latin American intellectuals did not oppose, indeed many were sympathetic to and supported. Castro took the outcome of the missile crisis of autumn 1962 as a personal humiliation, but he had no choice but to continue the game. The door to Washington was closed; indeed, the US intelligence was trying to kill him, and he knew it. The most famous was the alleged attempt to poison him in the Havana Hilton, an imposing tower on the edge of Vedado, not far from the Malecón. There, the leader had met his mistress, the German Marita Lorenz, and she was supposed to have slipped poison into his food, allegedly passed on by CIA agents. Lorenz is said to have failed to kill her revolutionary lover. According to her later account, she got rid of the poison at the last moment in a panic.

The story, later told in different versions, must be evaluated with caution, and what exactly is true and what is fiction will probably remain shrouded in a veil of uncertainty. Lorenz was known for spreading wild tales. One, which she told in 1977, was that on the eve of the Kennedy assassination, she traveled with Lee Harvey Oswald and Frank Sturgis (later implicated in the Watergate affair) by car to Dallas, where CIA operative E. Howard Hunt (also later implicated in the Watergate scandal) and Dallas nightclub owner Jack Ruby were waiting for them. A House of Representatives investigating committee concluded that the story was not credible. Oswald, a Communist who had lived for several years in the Soviet Union, shot Kennedy in Dallas in November 1963, and Ruby then shot Oswald there. Castro and his regime later boasted that Fidel had survived "hundreds" of assassination attempts by Americans, which is obviously nonsense, but there were several; at what stage they ended is unclear, but naturally none were followed through.

Either way, Castro survived, and was therefore able to introduce economic control, censorship and ideological indoctrination of the education system in the 1960s. He boasted to the world of the investment in health care and the generous social support he had given to the poorest classes. He stunned with statistics on the reduction of illiteracy. Strictly factually, this was true. In the late 1950s, less than 24 per cent of the adult population in Cuba was illiterate, but this was one of the best results in

South America at the time. After Castro's campaign, that figure was reduced to 4 percent in a few years. People who cite these figures approvingly, such as leftist Senator Bernie Sanders, forget that the primary goal of the campaign was not to increase educational attainment, but to consolidate control over the enslaved population through the Marxist-Leninist brainwashing that permeated the entire educational system. People can be controlled in several ways. Either you keep them illiterate and systematically oppress them by force, or you teach them to read and write to enable brainwashing. They called it creating the new socialist man.

Other real or imagined reforms of Castrism were of similar value. The independent American Association for Cuban Economics debunks the mantra that Cuba was socially and economically backward in the 1950s and that its development, especially in health and education, was only possible because of Castro's socialism. Despite the widespread acceptance of this view, the available data show that Cuba was a relatively advanced country in 1958, at least compared to other Latin American countries and, in some respects, to the world. The data show that Cuba maintained solid levels of health and education between 1959 and 1996, but that in other areas it paid the price for Castro's totalitarianism and economic policies. Cuba's position among Latin American countries is worse today than it was in 1958 in almost all indicators of socioeconomic development, with the possible exception of education and health, both of which have declined significantly in the last twenty years due to Cuba's isolation from modern trends and lack of technology.

One of the first campaigns Castro unleashed in the 1960s was an attack on freedom of conscience. The government systematically suppressed organised religion, promoted atheism, arrested priests, monks and nuns, harassed them and forced them to turn away from their faith. Churches and institutions were seized or closed and religious education in schools was banned. Reinaldo Arenas recalled how the little ones were turned away from Jesus. A comrade came into a school classroom and asked the first graders:

'Do you believe in the Lord Jesus Christ, children?'

Most of the children agreed.

'And you like ice cream?'

All hands flew up to the ceiling.

'Then close your eyes and ask God to bring you ice cream.'

The children did so, opened their eyes, but the ice cream was nowhere to be found. The good uncle was standing there, explaining to them what miracles comrade Fidel was performing. And then he said:

'Now close your eyes and ask comrade Fidel for ice cream.'

And when the children opened their eyes, there were ice cream bars on their desks.

At that time, each of the countries of the Soviet bloc pledged to help Cuba. In Czechoslovakia, where state television began broadcasting in 1953, a few television enthusiasts came up with the idea of advising the Cubans on how to do it. A delegation of comrades from Czechoslovak TV travelled to Havana and visited the television studios there. What was their surprise when the comrades-pioneers of socialist television found in them modern American equipment they didn't even know existed, including cameras for broadcasting in color! No socialist help materialized, for the technology in the Prague studios was primitive compared to the Cuban equipment. A few decades later, everything was socialistically straightened out. It comes to mind whenever I watch baseball on TV on the island - the great quality of the game contrasts with the backward way Cuban TV captures it.

Television was not the only sector of international aid in which Prague was involved. The comrades had Czech apples loaded onto a Czechoslovakian shipping vessel and taken to Havana. The apples were unloaded and distributed to stores. However, at that time Californian apples were still available there and the ungrateful islanders, in complete contradiction to the anti-imperialist policy of their government, despised the Czech varieties and preferred American imports. One naval worker got his satisfaction after all. According to the account of a witness, Castro himself gave him a palm tree as a token of gratitude. The comrade brought it home and planted it in a pot in his living room in Prague. There the palm grew for several years and after a while, when the apartment in the housing estate was too small, it was moved to a larger apartment, then to the hall of a villa near Prague and finally, after the Velvet Revolution, to the atrium of the Catholic Theological Faculty of Charles University in Dejvice. The story was told to me by a friend in whose living room in Prague's Old Town the palm tree by Fidel grew for several years. It has no happy ending. The palm tree died in the atrium of the Dejvice school. It is not clear whether its demise was related to the anti-Communist climate after 1989, which Fidel's tree could not stand, or whether it may even have been a punishment from God on the grounds of the Christian-oriented school. The people who lack imagination claim that the school's maintenance simply didn't water it.

Today, Cubans would be grateful for any apple. I didn't see one in the store on my last trip. Older people remember the '60s and '70s as a golden age. The regime's social policies helped the poorest of the poor out of the worst poverty. Literacy rates skyrocketed and early investments increased access to health care, which was suddenly "free." The Cuban economy joined the exchange system of Communist countries, among which goods circulated. It was of inferior quality, but available. The Soviet Union provided cheap oil and natural gas. Compared to today, the regime was able to keep the shops solidly supplied, although the quality and quantity of goods were not comparable to market economies. The cities did not flourish, but the houses still held together. They would turn into ruins only later. For the system, those years were a time of expansion, energy and boom. In the 1970s, the government decided to build a network of highways. We know how that turned out. As in all socialist states, Cuba was incompetent in economic management. An example of this is the "support for agriculture" campaigns of the 1960s, which in the Cuban case meant concentrating efforts on sugar cane cultivation at the expense of everything else. The impossible sugar cane quotas were not reached, while the rest of the economy was irreparably damaged.

It would therefore be wise to be skeptical about the talk of the good life at that time. Indeed, at the first opportunity, tens of thousands of Havanese decided to flee the island paradise. I refer to the crisis known as the Mariel boat lift, the largest exodus from the island up to that time. Between April and October 1980, more than 125,000 Cubans left for the United States. The emigration was ultimately made possible by Castro himself, who declared that whoever wanted to go could go. The United States had to hastily organise the arrival of large numbers of refugees, whom it housed in military bases and refugee camps. Most were granted permanent residency by the government. The crisis began in Havana when, in the spring of that year, people took refuge in the Peruvian embassy. Word spread around the city that the Peruvians were not only allowing access to the embassy premises, but also preventing Cuban police from intervening. The people took the embassy by storm. It's reminiscent of the events in Prague in the summer of 1989. At that time, thousands of East Germans took refuge in the West German embassy in the hope of emigrating.

Around ten thousand Cubans camped in the garden of the Peruvian embassy demanding to leave, which Castro at first refused, but even he realised that the situation was humiliating. To avoid deepening the international embarrassment, he turned around and on 20 April declared that those who wanted could leave from the port of Mariel near Havana. The announcement mobilized thousands of Cubans in Florida who sailed to Mariel to pick up relatives and friends. Officially, the ferrying ended in the fall, but in the years that followed, people continued to leave Cuba in smaller numbers and over the resistance of the Coast Guard in boats, rafts, and improvised vessels - hence they came to be called *balseros*.

The cunning Castro had a surprise in store for the Americans at the time of Mariel's transfer. He opened prisons and insane asylums and herded the population onto ships. Among the refugees were murderers, robbers and the mentally ill, often dangerous to their surroundings. When he became the target of public criticism, he claimed that he had long ago told everyone that there were no political prisoners in Cuba, only criminals... After the immigration wave, therefore, crime increased in South Florida. The motif was used by film director Brian De Palma in *Scarface*. The Mariel crisis served as the context for a plot about a Cuban refugee who becomes a drug lord in America. "Mariel" only surpassed 2022, when approximately 300,000 people emigrated from Cuba.

But even the continuing waves of emigration have not opened the eyes of Castro's sympathisers on the left. During my stay in the US in the 1990s, I was constantly baffled at what people defending Castro could say with a seemingly authoritative emphasis in their voices. The most common argument was free education and health care. At that time, I did not yet know the situation in Cuba by direct observation, but I could imagine "free health care" in practice, because that is exactly what we used to have in Czechoslovakia, and everyone who experienced it remembers its inferior quality. Because of the isolation from the world, the inability to go on fellowships and travel to congresses, doctors did not have timely access to the latest knowledge and procedures, which, with rare exceptions, were not created in the ecosystem of "free" healthcare, but in free countries with free market economies. There was no money for quality drugs and devices. Doctors' approach to patients was similar to that of commanders to basic service soldiers. The patient was not a client, but a poor wretch who had to obey his titular master. Anything slightly above standard had to be bribed. When I spoke to Filiberto in Havana, I asked him about the quality of care in the hospitals. His wife is a doctor with many years of experience.

"It's terrible. There's no medicine. There are no machines. Sometimes there are not even basic necessities like bed sheets or toilet paper. Hygiene in hospitals is at a low level. Even the quality of medical education has fallen far behind the world. Students do not have access to quality literature. It has improved a little with the introduction of the internet, but only slightly," Filiberto told me. He had the opportunity to compare, having worked in Portugal for several years. Most Cubans have no comparison. I looked into several Cuban clinics. Talk of quality care is empty propaganda. In San Germán, I saw dirty rooms and beds without sheets that the patient had to bring in himself. After several conversations with locals, I found out that they had a shortage of doctors, so the clinic was staffed mainly by interns and nurses. The doctors at the time were on "international solidarity mission" in Venezuela, where the regime was collecting hard currency, oil and gas for them. Yes, there is a solidly equipped clinic for foreigners and top apparatchiks at Varadero. In recent years, the government has been luring visitors for medical tourism. You can pay to stay by the sea and get your teeth fixed and it will work out cheap. But for the average Cuban, the prices are astronomical.

Every time a talking head on U.S. television starts ranting about Cuban health care, I wonder if he believes it or if it is just "talking points" designed to fight an ideological opponent. For some, it may be naivete and lack of information. But there are others I would call conscious manipulators, such as the creator of the 2007 propaganda film Sicko, left-wing activist Michael Moore. He took a group of Americans who couldn't afford health insurance in the U.S. to Cuba to prove that socialist health care was superior to American health care. The problem was that Moore took his people to an institution for privileged Communists, though he passed it off as ordinary, and the Cubans had plenty of time to prepare for the film. He served up a Potemkin village to the US audience. I wish no one ill and hope that Moore lives to a respectable age in good health. But if he does have health problems, perhaps because of his obesity, I certainly wouldn't recommend that he check himself into your average Cuban hospital.

Ideology is a powerful mobilizing method, and the Marxist narrative of Cuba, far from being dead, allowed Castro to play the role of protector of the weak, the oppressed and the exploited until the end of his long life.

Life in Luxury

Castro possessed an attention to detail unusual in the Caribbean. He crafted his public image carefully. For example, for a long time, people knew almost nothing about his private life. They didn't know that he was married to a teacher, a blonde named Dalia Soto del Valle, that he had five sons with her, or that their names, somewhat Old Testament-style, began with A: Alexis, Alex, Alejandro, Antonio and Ángelito. The first three names are variations of Alexander, the name Fidel used as a pseudonym in reference to Alexander the Great. He met Dalia in the early 1960s. They lived together since then, but he did not officially marry her until the early 1980s. Information about the First Lady remained a secret to most Cubans. They did not even know that Fidel had at least nine children and that Fidelito was not the oldest of his marriage to Mirta Díaz-Balart - his illegitimate son Jorge Ángel was born a few months before him. Castro never claimed him.

Few Cubans knew that Alina Fernández Revuelta, a model and the result of a love affair with the famous Havana beauty Natalia Revuelta, who participated in the preparations for the Moncada coup, had fled to the

United States and was critical of her father's dictatorship. Fidel made sure that his people saw him as totally committed to the revolution, as a leader who worked for it 24/7, as a Commander-in-Chief with no time for private life, let alone pleasure. In fact, his chauffeur drove him almost every day in his official Alfa Romeo and later in a Mercedes to an inner-city building called El Once, Eleven, a block of buildings in Vedado on Eleventh Street a few streets from the sea. In one of the buildings there, on the fourth floor, lived Celia Sánchez, secretary of the Council of State and former member of the Resistance, who in the fifties worked as a courier for the guerrillas in the Sierra Maestra. Sánchez was also Fidel's longtime mistress. According to Sánchez, the bodyguard (they were not related), Fidel trusted Celia, consulted with her and, with her in mind, married Dalia, who was unaware of her existence in Fidel's life, only after Celia died of lung cancer.

Fidel had a legion of other mistresses, including interpreters and a flight attendant, and even otherwise behaved more like an ordinary dictator than a tireless revolutionary breathing for the country. He spent many weekends and practically all summer on his private island of Cayo Piedra, with its white sand beaches. He would occasionally hop a helicopter to Havana to greet foreign delegations. In addition, he had about twenty other houses around the island, one more luxurious than the other. In Havana, his family lived in a place called Punto Cero in the Siboney district. It is a large, heavily guarded property on which vegetables and fruit are grown and domestic animals are kept strictly for the use of the Castros and a few other prominent families. His wife Dalia has set up a selective school there for her children and the children of members of the high nomenklatura. She kept the teachers under strict methodical supervision.

Bodyguard Sánchez states another curious fact. Castro, who was obsessed with cattle genetics, had a small barn built on the roof of a building in El Once. He had four cows pulled in by crane and tried to breed record milk yields. Something of the son of latifundia remained in him. Very few people knew of the existence of the barn on the roof of a building almost in the centre of the city.

Interestingly, although the Castro brothers lived not far from each other in Punto Cero, their families barely interacted. Fidel's family lived in almost complete isolation. Even contact between Fidel and Raúl was limited to the most basic state business matters. Fidel's sons with Dalia first met their older cousins by chance at a party when they were in their teens. When Raúl heard the news, he gleefully opened a bottle of something good to drink to the ununusual event. Unlike Fidel, Raúl was said to have a sense of family. It was probably he who arranged for Mirta Díaz-Balart to travel from her Spanish exile to visit her son Fidelito. Fidel was no stranger to various foibles, but he cared little for his children and extended family. He only took an interest in Alina when scandal threatened, as when he discovered that she had posed in a bikini for a magazine. He had her summoned to the president's office to talk her down, but he hadn't counted on Alina defending herself forcefully. A shouting match ensued, whereupon Alina left the room, slamming the door behind her.

All of this, including the existence of Dalia, has only become more widely known in the last twenty years or so, a time when the mainstream world narrative on Fidel Castro was already well established. You will still see claims today that the Cuban elite, unlike some of their ilk, did not live in luxury. This is not true. It's just that a private yacht, a private island, beautiful villas, mistresses and illegitimate children don't fit into tales of an ascetic revolutionary. If we want to see the world as a simple struggle between good and evil, based not on field research but on textbook formulas, we have to rely on myths, and the one about Castro and his generation of *barbudos* has great staying power. It fits in with today's ethos of progressives and their struggle against 'capitalism,' 'corporations' and 'neo-colonialism' - whatever we imagine behind these poster slogans.

I believe that reality will eventually find its way through the cracks of ideology and come out into the light and claim a voice. No myth, not even Castro's, can reach the sky. Policies must be measured by results, not rhetoric. After all, as news of Cuba's misery became more widely known with the rise of the internet and social media, the narrative of a progressive Cuba became increasingly difficult to sustain. In this context, I got into arguments with friends on the Western European and American left. They had, and some still have, a tendency to repeat, in various forms, the regime's propaganda about the harmfulness of the US embargo and the collapse of the Soviet Union that damaged the Cuban economy. However, it is becoming increasingly difficult to repeat these seemingly convincing claims with a straight face. Even the Czechoslovak economy was hit hard by the collapse of the Soviet empire. Today, Czechs are on average four times richer than they were thirty years ago. Cuba may not be able to trade with the United States, but it has the rest of the world at its disposal. Canadian and Spanish hotels operate on Varadero.

The problem is not the embargo, it is that it produces nothing of value. It is broke as a result of decades of socialist devastation. During my visits to the island over the past decade, I have driven across several times, thousands and thousands of miles. I've only seen a freight train cross the road twice with my own eyes, and the last one, near Santiago in December 2022, had three whole cars. The Cuban economy is virtually nonexistent. The once expansive claims of leftist friends defending Castro usually boil down to the argument that poverty is even worse elsewhere in Latin America. Even that is questionable, since very few countries in the region are poorer. But let's say, for the sake of argument, that they are right. If this is the main argument in favor of the Castro dictatorship, which has lasted more than sixty years, that *it is even worse elsewhere*, then that is all I wanted to say, ladies and gentlemen of the jury. I conclude my statement.

I look at the cows grazing happily in the meadow of Ángel's latifundia. It gives you an idea of how beautiful Las Manacas used to be, until it became a well-kept but abandoned museum. It has enormous potential for institutions of historical memory. It could be the Cuban version of the Czech Post Bellum, the NGO that keeps alive the memory of totalitarianism and its crimes. Perhaps one day it will become one, when the "Island of Freedom," as the Communists called it, is finally liberated. There's plenty of room for a library, classrooms, international conferences, art festivals and school trips.

From the huts of the Haitian farm workers, we walk through the greenery of the estate and our visit comes to an end. A light shower drenches us from above, then the rain stops without the sky clearing. We pause at a plaque commemorating the historic Camino Real, the royal road across Cuba, which ran through this property. It was built from east to west, from La Punta de Maisí to El Cabo de San Antonio, and covered 1,591 kilometers and 696 meters.

"Passengers described it as a hell of mud and dust, due to the constant changes in weather that brought rain and drought," reads the information sign.

The guide looks at me intently. I ask him how much he values his service.

"You can give me whatever you want," he says.

It's the second time I've heard that sentence that day.

6.

Leodán.

Jamaica

The right rear fender of the Hyundai is holding up so far, although the car is jumping wildly on the rough road north. Some sections, where the road is indistinguishable from the bed of a dry river, I sprint through at a turtle's pace. I take the route from Cueto to Banes, recommended to me by our Snatiago landlord, and wonder what the one he discouraged me from would look like. The countryside undulates around the road, the soil a brick red, low plantane trees growing with large leaves shooting up like tattered umbrellas, glistening in the late afternoon sun after the rain. The light is perfect for landscape photography. We're on our way to Guardalavaca. Then a light shower again, but the sun is shining; I look around for a rainbow. Unmarked villages with huts, surrounded by fences of slender, green-yellow cacti, look as if it were December 1822. The 19th century illusion is broken by loudspeakers at stalls selling mangoes, plantanes, and yucca root. Music blares from boxes. Houses are covered with clumps of roofs made of dried palm leaves.

The road surface requires a deliberate pace. At unexpected places along the way, people in agricultural clothing will appear from time to time. A yellow excavator on the side of the road scoops up red soil. A Russian Kamaz truck, a monster from the 1980s, sits a little further on, with a crew of workers working in front of it. They have no protective gear or reflective vests and are not protected by roadblocks. They are part of the ecosystem of the local traffic, which at the moment consists of my dirty Korean friend and an oncoming ox-drawn cart. I reach the highest point above the valley, which I leave behind me, and step on the gas. The car windows are open, gravel is bouncing off the wheels and my private Monte

Carlo Rally is banishing thoughts of the fear of a puncture as there is no spare in the boot. In the car's catalogue I have a phone number for an emergency service that supposedly operates around the island 24 hours a day, but there is no signal. It only takes a few minutes to get up to speed, then the brakes again and a herd of cows. First I just stop, but since the cows don't want to go anywhere, I turn off the engine. I look at their happy expressions and dusty white skin, which you never see in the movies. Hollywood always and everywhere has cows with Milka's clean skin. Then something moves up front. I see a rider in a hat and a brown Adidas shirt. *Vaquero*. His dark skin is taut across his cheekbones, like he's drying it after a tropical downpour. He holds a riding crop and whips the reluctant brown horse in the side. Jimena doesn't like it one bit.

"Asshole. Why is he beating the horse?"

"He has his reasons. Maybe it's not going well."

Later I understand that Jimena is a passionate animal lover. She doesn't even like the simple fact that people sit on horses and ride them. I am trying to persuade her that horses like to run, but Jimena won't hear of it.

"How would you know? Did you ask them?"

Then whenever we see a rider, Jimena pokes:

"Hey, another very happy horse!"

Vaquero passes the cows at a decent speed and his sharp call - *¡Vaca! ¡Vaca!* Cow! Cow! - gets the herd moving. He's now choking on the road from left to right. We are at the end of the woods. The cows and the cowboy move ahead of us in the light that will give way to night in a few dozen minutes. A glance at the GPS tells us that the destination is close. After a while, I see the blue expanse of the Caribbean from a hilltop and arrive at the village of Guardalavaca, whose name could be translated into English as "watch that cow." One of the versions of how this small village got its curious name has to do with pirates and the suspicious looks they were said to cast from their ships at the local herds. Today, the pirates no longer operate off the world-famous beach; they are all based in government offices in Havana.

Initially, Guardalavaca does not give the impression of being the second largest holiday resort on the island, which it is after Varadero, but the medieval huts are definitely behind us, and this is a visible change of scenery. From rustic we enter late modernism. We pass several unfinished brick houses, clearly planned to be rented out to foreigners. I stop at a light blue apartment block opposite the police station, built of rough concrete, a kind of poor relation's brutalism. The prefab is part of a small tenement. In Cuba they tend to be eerily run-down, but not here. The apartment blocks are in decent condition. The ground-floor apartments have well-kept front gardens full of colorful flowers and green shrubs.

On the recommendation of our Santiago landlord, we rent a small apartment on the second floor for $50 a night. We deal with a smiling elderly lady who takes care of the apartment. The price seems inflated. The lady asks if she would discount it, would we stay more than one day. At this point, however, we don't know if independent journalist Juan Miguel will confirm an appointment for tomorrow in nearby Holguín. I agree to fifty dollars and the lady looks like she has hit the jackpot. I'm told we're the first tourists in two years. The resort was closed during the pandemic and all foreigners are now staying in nearby hotels. We'll get a chance to check them out later. They're big buildings on the beach and probably half full. People from Banes, Holguín, and other cities work there, bussed in every morning.

I park in front of an apartment building under a gnarled tree and look anxiously towards the police station. Fidel's bearded face, in paint, stares back at me.

"You don't pay anything for parking here and it's safe. Police takes care of everything," the lady assures.

I couldn't be calmer. I look forward to sitting on the balcony overlooking the Revolutionary Guards' quarters at night, with geckos rustling on the bluish panel and me reading anti-revolutionary literature. But now it's time to check out the beach and see if there's a place to eat. From the police station, we walk across a large meadow of dead grass to where we suspect there is life. On the right is a closed CubaCAR/Havanautos car rental agency, which provides foreign currency for the army's budget. It's dark. After a while, the hotels built in the park on the coast appear before us.

The resort bears the name Brisas. It's not very lively and I soon find out why. Most of the guests are pensioners from Europe and Canada, who don't do much in half-empty hotels. The plan to eat at a hotel restaurant doesn't work out as the food is strictly for hotel guests and we don't have the required yellow wrist band. A reconnaissance of the terrain yields valuable information. There's a restaurant at the end of the beach where you can eat. It'll be a solid establishment, listed on Google Maps. But it's a long way away, and that worries us as it starts to rain.

"How far?"

"Far out, *amigo*. All the way to the end of the beach."

There's nothing to be done. Fortunately, the park between the roaring sea, which is close by, but I can't see it from here in the dark, and the hotel complex covers a path and part of the beach, so we are not exposed to direct rain, which, as it turns out, lasts only a few minutes. We walk past several half-empty outdoor bars and one large hotel pool. There's not a peep anywhere, but still the Hispanic pop roars into the space. The mood is like an apocalyptic movie. Big raindrops splash the surface of the illuminated pool in the shape of a giant kidney. On the steps of the restaurant, a cook in a dirty apron sits smoking. During a brief conversation with Jimena, he tries to flirt. He confirms that our restaurant at the end of the beach is *really far.* And indeed. After an endless walk of full fifteen minutes along the crescent-shaped beach, we reach the recommended restaurant, El Ancla, built on a cliff. It's closed! There's a waiter standing outside, and he's smoking too. He informs us that they will be closed today and tomorrow.

"They're moving us into a higher price category," he says proudly. "We're getting ready for an inspection."

"You've been preparing for it for two days? Isn't that too little?" I ask ironically.

"Three," he replies dryly.

Behind the cliff in the hillside, we can see two more restaurants. One of them is overpriced, a plate of food without a drink and an appetizer costs twenty dollars, American or Canadian, or euros, they don't count change here. The other, called Linda Luna, is much nicer, has a direct view of the bay and is reasonably priced. It's a small, bright orange wooden house with a patio on which four tables sit. They are all covered with clean white tablecloths that flutter in the breeze. The waitress is a girl with good English. She looks like a student, and a smile spreads across her face when she discovers that we are staying at the police station in Mrs Odelsa's guesthouse. Odelsa is her aunt.

We are hungry, as we hadn't eaten since the morning. Birán didn't prove to be a hospitable place. I order pork fajitas with rice and beans, sweet potato chips and Cristal beer. I down the green can with the distinctive palm tree logo and immediately order a second. Rice and black beans is a traditional Cuban dish, called *moros y cristianos,* or Moors (black beans) and Christians (white rice). Here, however, I somewhat disappointingly count only four Moors in the mound of rice. Otherwise, the dinner is very tasty. Afterwards we ask the waitress if she would call us a taxi. It's about half an hour walk home and we don't feel like getting wet again. She's going to the living room. I can see in through the open door. In the dark, a chef in a white apron lies on the couch, watching a flat screen TV. The wind is picking up, brushing the long white tablecloths of the neighbouring tables in vigorous gusts and shaking the perfectly polished wine glasses, stem upwards. I look north into the darkness towards the United States. It's pitch black. It must be a beautiful view of the bay from here in the daytime. The girl comes up and asks if ten dollars for the trip is okay.

"Are you kidding?" comes out of me faster than I meant to. It's the fatigue. She immediately bursts out laughing and says:

"That's right. Ten dollars is really too expensive."

The trip ends up costing us $5. We're in an American car from the late 1940s. It stinks of oil, gasoline and a better past. The interior has been completely gutted, no upholstery, just rusty sheet metal. It used to be red, but I can't tell you what color it is now. As the driver starts the engine and pulls out of the woods onto the main road that lines the coast from nearby Esmeralda Beach, the sound that comes from the car's innards has something hellish about it, and here on the surface of the earth, it most closely resembles a tank backing up. I look at the gearshift, which is probably of a tractor. Even the huge steering wheel won't be original. The Communists forced the Cubans to become world champions in circularity.

The driver apologizes for the smell. He said he was carrying some lobsters and didn't have time to air out the car.

'Lobster is the least of your problems, hermano,' I say to myself.

In the morning, I lie on the beach under a mossy tree. It's the seventh day of our trip and we haven't reached the sea yet. Now we have two hours to rest. Juan Miguel called. We're meeting him in Holguín this afternoon. I mentally prepare a few topics to discuss with him and observe a guy in a knotty, white, rather see-through swimsuit with a massive belly hanging over it. He's standing in the direct sun, a thick layer of sunscreen on his skin, watching the ocean. The wind is blowing hard, making big, foamy waves. It creates a dangerous illusion of the cooler weather, and so I stay under the tree.

The Brisas Resort is huge and surprisingly pretty. The hotels here, unlike in Varadero, look more in tune with the surrounding nature. The architecture is imaginative. Large buildings alternate with smaller villas in pastel colors. The outdoor restaurants are shaped like spacious halls, covered by huge pitched roofs in the traditional palm-leaf style. Everywhere there are paths, palm trees, landscaped shrubs and trees of all shapes. In one gazebo, a morning salsa lesson is held. A lithe lady with snow-white hair dances with a bronze-skinned instructor to music from a cassette twin. The singing sea behind the white gazebo provides a backdrop to their movements. I hear Russian, Hungarian, Polish, German and French. An older black man in uniform walks past me, a shovel in his hand, picking up trash on the beach. He smiles as he passes me.

Переход

Arenas describes Holguín, his almost hometown, as irredeemably boring. I was here for the first time more than a decade ago in the main square, and all I remember is a quick and nervous conspiratorial meeting with a human rights activist. He advised caution: the repression in the province is harsher than elsewhere. About three hundred thousand Holguinos live here, making it the third or fourth largest city in Cuba - numbers that are in flux due to emigration. I'm driving down a dirty boulevard that the *carretera* turns into inside the city. I keep an eye on the dilapidated brick houses and the smaller buildings of businesses and

Chapter 6

offices. The roadway is Caribbean-busy: you must ready yourself for anything. There are trucks, horse-drawn carts and rickshaws moving along the four-lane road, no one really keeping to the marked lanes, and there are plenty of pedestrians, too, in all sorts of places but the crosswalks. Typical provincial Cuban chaos. It seems to me that, unlike downtown Havana, people walk a little faster here, as if they have a clear destination in front of them. They're also more carefully and cleanly dressed. On my left hand I see a large Russian sign: Переход. Pedestrian crossing. It refers to an underpass under the road, once built here by a Soviet architect in the hope of teaching Cubans to cross the road in a safe way. Nice idea.

We go to the only remarkable place in this northeastern metropolis, the Hill of the Cross or Loma de la Cruz, towering over the city. The summit is reached by car via a serpentine road that rises steeply from the centre. Weaving between scooters and horse-drawn carriages, I soon find my way up. At the top I reach the car park in front of the huge cross that gave the hill its name. A group of young people sits by, singing Christian songs. It's a pilgrimage site visited by Pope John Paul II. He celebrated mass here and in Santiago, as he toured the Oriente.

Historically, Holguín was Catholic, but the belief in Jesus is mixed with Afro-Cuban, especially Yoruba, religious traditions. The indigenous Cuban population was nearly wiped out by the Spanish, who imported African slaves to work the plantations. The Indians retained some of their beliefs. Among the slaves, a specific tradition gradually emerged called Santería, a syncretic religion of Caribbean blacks that mixed elements of African and Indian spirituality with Christianity, a truly Catholic or universal religiosity. Yoruba gods and goddesses, known as orishas, play a central role in Santería. According to tradition, they are connected to the forces of nature and the elements and can intervene in human destinies. In Santería rituals, people interact with the orishas through sacrifices, dances, and other forms of worship. The connection between Yoruba and Santería reflects how the African diaspora has shaped the religious traditions of the Americas and how cultures have adapted and changed over time.

The top of the hill offers an impressive view of the city and its surroundings on this clear day with good visibility. Juan Miguel is standing by the souvenir stand, which is located across from a small outdoor bar near the cross. A young black man with a cheeky expression watches us from inside the open bar, and when he realizes we are not going to him, he exclaims that I can't park here. Before I can open the car door, the black man runs out of the bar with a box of cigars, which he offers me. He's wearing flip-flops.

"*Cohíbas,* my friend!"

Despite the initial feeling of anger, I can't help but appreciate his chutzpah. First he kicks me out of an empty parking lot where I'm not in the way, and now he wants to make a deal.

Juan Miguel Fernández Capote, a good-looking man in his thirties, is a journalist and gay rights activist. He is deputy director of Centro Esperanza (Centre of Hope), an organisation that supports sexual minorities and helps people infected with HIV. He runs the independent magazine *Palabras Abiertas* (*Open Words*). He earned a bachelor's degree in accounting in college and also studied communications. He worked as a voice actor in radio before the police forced the station management to fire him.

We sit far from the kitchen door, where two waiters in black and white outfits stand. The walls glow orange and contrast with the black solid wood furniture. The waiter, a young man with dark hair, a stubborn expression and a face mask, the top edge of which cuts into the wart at his nose, walks deliberately in our direction. Everything here is perfectly clean, they've just opened. The cut wart is already standing over us with his back to the sun, so we squint at him a little. The silhouette of his face is completed by his protruding ears. We order a beer.

"Beer is only for eating."

He makes me laugh - I haven't heard that sentence in a restaurant in thirty years! I should be angry, but a wave of warm nostalgia runs through my body.

"We're not eating."

"We have big platters," the cut wart beckons, poking a finger into his face mask.

We order coffee.

"There is no coffee."

"What do you have to drink?"

"We have beer, but you have to have a plate with it."

Just when it looks like our conversation is at a standstill, it turns out that the Loma de la Cruz Sightseeing Restaurant also offers fruit juices. I choose the guava juice.

Juan Miguel gives the impression that nothing can throw him off balance. He wears a black leather jacket, which he takes off after a moment and carefully places on a nearby chair, as well as stylish leather shoes and sunglasses with a large gold logo on the side. He places them methodically on the table. He has dark eyes, black, carefully trimmed hair, a sharp and friendly expression. He smiles slightly, occasionally, not very often, as he speaks. It's a remarkable smile that comes slowly, in stages. It is both familiar and somewhat resigned, especially when talking about opposition activities.

"Here in Cuba, everyone wants to be a leader. Everyone thinks they are leaders, even though they are not. There are many chiefs and few Indians. Even among the activists, you find some of the human misery, you find people who want to increase their own importance, to increase their own status. It will be difficult to unite the opposition. Some dissidents believe that the way forward is open confrontation, demonstrations in the streets, but so far these have led more to dispersal, brutal beatings and arrests. I don't think violent confrontation leads anywhere. Look at Santiago. The head of UNPACU, José Daniel Ferrer, is already back in jail.

Founded and led by Ferrer, UNPACU, or the Patriotic Union of Cuba, is one of the most visible civil rights organizations. Its stated tactic is nonviolent resistance. Ferrer himself spent the years 2003-2011 in prison for his activism and is considered a respected, if very hardline, activist.

Juan Miguel is the opposite of Ferrer. He's not a street fighter, he has inner strength. At the invitation of foreign NGOs, he has traveled to the United States, Trinidad and Tobago, Slovakia, Barbados and Peru for study visits.

"Weren't you tempted to stay abroad?"

He replies with a sigh, and despite the somewhat lofty content of his words, he says it civilly, "Too many people are leaving. I want to keep fighting. I want to strive for a better life through non-violent, peaceful means."

I'm asking about *Palabras Abiertas*, the magazine he founded five years ago. It used to be printed as a monthly magazine, but today, due to distribution and financial problems, it only exists online.

"We deal with topics that concern young people, such as the unequal status of sexual minorities. Although the government has been trumpeting information to the world about equal rights for the LGBT community and recently passed a law to that effect, this is just a theory. Like other Latin American societies, Cuba's is homophobic. Gays, lesbians and transsexuals are discriminated against and do not find much representation. In our society, for example, they find it hard to find space for intimacy."

If you are gay, it is dangerous to hold hands with your partner in public, let alone kiss them. Foreigners are not held to these standards with such rigour, after all, they have a reputation here as sex-starved creatures who have come to Cuba to enjoy themselves. Tourists tend to be under informal protection. And there are enclaves where looser rules apply, such as progressive locales like Vedado in Havana or central Cuba's Santa Clara, which has a vibrant LGBT scene and hosts many events, including a trans carnival. There, one can go to a gay club that is generally tolerated and allowed by the authorities.

Juan Miguel's personal life here in Holguín is complicated. His friend hides what he really does from his parents. He is unsure of how they will react. He doesn't want to get them into trouble and force them to make uncomfortable decisions. Their activism occasionally takes them out of the city, to other provinces.

"How do you travel?"

"As we can. By bus, train, and hitchhiking."

"Does the railroad really work here? I've hardly seen any trains."

"It works in a limited way. The train to Havana goes every four days. The trip takes about 16 hours. You get a small snack along the way. However, the official ticket to Havana is cheaper than the bus, costing 500 pesos, while the bus ride, which is more comfortable because the bus is air-conditioned, costs 1,200 pesos. The bus used to run four times a day, but now it only runs in the morning and evening. It is not easy to get a ticket for the train. A black market has developed."

These are not small sums. A person with a university degree in Cuba has a salary of around 5,000 pesos a month, most other salaries are between two and three thousand.

"I bet that guy over there doesn't make more than two grand," Juan Miguel points to the parking lot attendant. "In contrast, police officers and soldiers take between nine and 15 thousand a month and have other benefits, such as a steady supply of fuel at the Interior Ministry's gas stations.

Most people work in the state sector. Low salaries and inflation lead to people stealing what they can at work and then dealing with it."

Juan Miguel believes that the government's current priority is to bring social networks under control.

"They passed a law that toughens the penalties for criticism of the regime. People are no longer afraid and are expressing themselves critically on Facebook, YouTube and other platforms. I observe a real change around me. The people I talk to are not so much afraid of repression anymore, but of being fired from their jobs and losing the opportunity to steal. The state is also forcing private companies to fire civil activists, and it has the tools to do so."

We look around. Only a few other guests have come to the restaurant. I wonder who's going to eat all those plates today? I look at my watch. The unwritten rule is that public meetings with activists should not last long. Since it's a long way down, I offer to drive Juan Miguel, but he politely declines.

"It's better if we go separately," he says. "Anyway, I'm meeting a friend here."

I pay the bill and we go to the parking lot to help out the poorly paid security guard. He's also a government employee.

In Ocho Ríos

Juan Miguel's story in Holguín did not surprise me. I had already discussed the repression of sexual minorities in 2019 with several Cuban activists in Jamaica, where I had led workshops for them. At the top of

Loma de la Cruz, I suddenly recalled the raven hair of Leodán. We were talking in the dining room of a mountain resort high above the Jamaican port of Ocho Ríos. The large windows of the spacious room were wide open, and it was getting darker by the minute, bleeding the light out of the expanse of the Caribbean hundreds of feet below us. Soon it would be black and blend into the sky. There were lights on the patio to keep the mosquitoes from flying in. Cubans in fashionable ripped jeans and designer shorts walked past us, getting ready for dinner. At the picturesque, remote resort built on a mountaintop for ecotourism by a member of the famous Bacardí family, I gave several lectures to activists, independent journalists, and dissidents.

Leodán Suárez Quiñones is a transsexual woman from the Party for an Independent and Democratic Cuba. When I met her, she was 26 years old and had a life journey that no one could envy. Weeks before our interview, the media abroad had written about her. She had published a text message threatening to kill her. She received it via WhatsApp from a number made up of several zeros, but she knew very well who the real sender was: the State Security Service.

"This is a warning to leave the gay issue alone or you will regret it. You have no idea how much you'll regret it. Remember, you're alone and the sun can rise in any swamp, think about it."

She got other threatening texts. She replied to one, but knowing it was from an automated switchboard, she posted the reply just to be safe:

"You have done me so much, so much harm that I am no longer afraid of you. Long live free Cuba. Down with all Communists!"

Leodán comes from the small town of San Juan y Martínez, a famous tobacco region in the province of Pinar del Río. She was born a boy, but she tells me she felt like a woman from a young age.

"There were problems with that."

In the context of her life, the word 'problems' is a real euphemism. As a child she wanted to wear colorful dresses and soon ran into a barrier of misunderstanding. There were conflicts with children at school, in the family. Her parents are simple farmers working in the tobacco fields. They forced her to behave like a boy, to walk properly and make boyish movements, to dress appropriately. Her mother divorced her biological

Chapter 6

father when she was three months old and later remarried. Her stepfather forced Leodán to work in the fields, but she wanted to stay home with the women. When she resisted, he beat her, and her mother let him. He also tied her to the furniture so Leodán couldn't leave without permission.

"It was probably their way of trying to make me more resilient."

She sought support from children at school and on the street. Some of the girls took her in, played together, but the boys never did. They called her names, slandered her, rejected her. Sometimes they beat her.

"The attitude of some of the girls was nice, but I can't say it represented enough emotional support."

At eight, she attempted suicide.

"I was in a pretty bad place for a long time. Later on I managed to overcome the depressive feelings and since then I have never stopped hoping that everything will change for the better in the future. I still have it today."

Leodan speaks matter-of-factly, slowly and clearly. She reports her suicide attempt as if it were a minor inconvenience that every kid has to go through. Measles. Mumps. She blinks the flexible arches of her eyelashes toward the terrace over the bay. A group of workshop participants pass by, heading for a cigarette.

She didn't like it at home, so she wandered around. Often and sometimes far away. She went to the fields, hid in huts to dry tobacco leaves. Her mother and stepfather often got drunk. They fought.

"They were constantly yelling at each other. Sometimes I went to my grandmother's. When it got dark, my grandmother would convince me that I had to go home. She had a spare bed at home, but she wouldn't let me sleep over. I always had to go back home."

She tells me as if seeking reassurance that she was right. That Grandma should have let her stay the night. She pauses, looks at me, then to the end of the room where there's a large flatscreen. A few hours ago I showed a presentation on it and Leodán discussed it with ten other students. It was about politics. Now I'm trying to bring back memories that I'm sure she doesn't like.

"I went to school until I was 14. But then I didn't go anymore. My neighbor raped me.

He was a man close to her family, she knew him well. He brought them gifts, sometimes precious powdered milk. When her mother was in the hospital, Leodan would go to her grandmother's house and he would wait for her. He had a knife in his hand, there was no way she could defend herself. The police caught him and he was sentenced to ten years for rape. After five years he was released for good behavior.

During the trial, her stepfather and mother came to her defense, acting like normal parents. They helped her through the criminal process and she is sure that their support also led to his conviction. Still, she was looking for more.

"Maybe another father, if his daughter had been raped, would have tried to avenge her, would have wanted to kill the rapist, or something like that, but the stepfather didn't react that way. Nevertheless, they both supported me. They attended the trial, they went to the courtroom with me."

Or *something like that*. What does that half sentence mean? I don't have time to meditate on its meaning. Leodan's memories have taken on the energy of a waterfall.

"I applied to a university in the provincial capital. They didn't want me there either. They told me to dress like a man. I refused. That's why I lost the opportunity to study at the University of Pinar. I started taking independent courses in computer science and telecommunications. I got professional certificates."

She joined the work of opposition groups. She was not motivated by ideology. She saw a few demonstrations and thought she wanted to do that too, she wanted to work on human rights.

"It was clear to me that too many things were wrong here and needed to be fixed. At the beginning I was very scared. I was young and didn't know how to do it. I asked a friend how one gets into activism and he said, 'Just come to our meetings and join,' so I did. First I got involved in the Cuban Republican Party. Since then, I've worked in several different opposition groups. Today I am active in the Party for an Independent and Democratic Cuba. It was founded a long time ago by Huber Matos and now his children are also involved. At first, I was a normal local activist in my hometown of San Juan y Martínez, but gradually I became the party's national delegate."

"You didn't experience discrimination in dissident politics?"

"No. I finally started to feel normal among activists. I have not experienced any discrimination, my colleagues treat me with respect and as a woman. Men protect me, for example in moments when someone wants to attack me. As I told you, I first started going to meetings in my province of Pinar del Río. People would come to us from elsewhere, from Havana and other places, and I would ask them if they knew people like me, transsexual women with the same or similar problems. I didn't know any transsexual women who were involved in politics, and it seemed to me that it would be beneficial and interesting if we could incorporate them into a political party. I was able to meet a number of LGBT people in our province who were not activists but were interested in politics. I encouraged them to join us, to work in the party."

"The nice thing about my job is that I can see the change for the better around me. It's not perfect. But when you compare it to 15 years ago, I can't help but see progress. Let me give you an example. A few years ago, when a group of transsexual girls were walking down the street, people were shouting at them, calling them names, mocking them, some even throwing stones at them or hitting them. It doesn't happen anymore. Murder, violence and rape still happen, but they are mostly linked to prostitution, to this underworld of crime and sex. You more or less don't see them anywhere else. We have a park in Pinar where trans girls go and there's prostitution and that kind of thing. There are crimes, what they call 'crimes of passion,' but really they are based on prejudice."

In April 2015, six teenagers stoned a transsexual prostitute named Yosvani Muñoz Robaina, who went by the pseudonym La Eterna, a name that has a sadly paradoxical translation: Eternal. The murder was brought to the attention by 14YMedio, the web portal run by Yoani Sánchez. Authorities classified the crime as a crime of passion. Leodán has objected. Her name appeared in the foreign media.

"Everyone knows this was not a 'crime of passion' but a simple homophobic criminal act," the *Washington Blade*, a magazine that reports on issues affecting America's LGBT community, quoted her as saying.

I ask whether people's attitude towards sexual minorities is improving everywhere in Cuba.

"The situation varies from province to province. In Havana there is the least prejudice. In the capital, the cultural level of the people is much higher and characterized by respect. We are an agricultural province, the people are less sophisticated than in Havana, and the eastern provinces are similarly backward."

Our conversation is going in circles. We start on the perimeter. Leodán speaks like a politician, generalizing, using theoretical language and sophisticated formulas, but gradually, after my persistent query, we reach the center of the circle, her life.

"You come across as a strong person. Where do you get your strength?"

"But no, I have problems. I suffer from depression. Moods affect me a lot. Every little thing can bring out the sadness in me, bring me down. My grandmother once told me that my mother didn't want me. You grow up with those feelings and they become part of your personality. But at one point I promised myself that I would keep going, that I would keep fighting. For myself and for people who suffer like me, for trans people, for people who grew up in similar circumstances to me. I've had these thoughts since I was a child, thoughts that we need to change things for the better. But I didn't know how. It was just a vague feeling inside. Only today do I know that we need to achieve legal equality and a certain level of education and awareness so that parents of children belonging to sexual minorities know how to treat their offspring. So that these children do not suffer."

"I've always had trouble with the authorities. I couldn't find a job. I used to make money in prostitution. Back then, me and other transsexual girls were in big trouble with the police. And then, when I joined opposition groups at the age of 19, I was arrested and beaten in prison several times. Or they drove me somewhere far away to an unknown place, threw me out of the car and drove away."

"I know," I interject. "Many dissidents experienced this in the 1970s and 1980s in Czechoslovakia. Where did you find the strength to overcome all this?"

Chapter 6   171

"I have it because of my belief that my struggle is meaningful, that it will lead to changes in our society. Cuba is a sexist country, but that's why we need activists and organizations that fight for our rights. Mariela Castro boasts that she is fighting for gay rights, but I don't believe her or people like her. I don't think they will really change anything for the better. In fact, they do nothing. I have contacted their organization many times because I have sought a sex change surgery. But no one helped me. Only those who do and say what Mariela wants will eventually get the sex change."

Leodán's opinion of the work of official institutions, especially the one called Cenesex, which oversees sexual minority equality under the leadership of Raúl's daughter, is not unique among dissidents and independent journalists. Nevertheless, the fact that even the Communist establishment feels it must move with the times has had a positive, if limited, effect on Cuban society. Fidel Castro eventually reversed himself and admitted his mistake in his autobiography. In it he criticised Cuba's macho culture and called for a tolerant acceptance of homosexuality. In an interview with the Mexican newspaper *La Jornada* in 2010, he described his regime's persecution of homosexuals as a 'great injustice' and said he took responsibility for it. How? Only in rhetorical terms, of course. And that claim of responsibility was not without various excuses. It wouldn't be Fidel if he didn't blame others.

In that interview, he noted that in the 1960s he had been focused on dealing with vital issues such as the missile crisis and was therefore, in his words, unable to devote himself fully to gay issues. He also could not resist offering another excuse - the negative attitude toward homosexuality before the revolution, which Castro said led to the mistreatment of gays in Cuba. Who knew that Fulgencio Batista was ultimately responsible for the labor camps where Che and Fidel imprisoned homosexuals? After all, nothing is known about Batista's regime, disgusting as it was, torturing, beating, raping and working homosexuals to death in the name of the revolution, as comrades Che, Fidel and Raúl did.

But even a half-hearted apology has its value, and it is not fundamentally important whether Castro came to it sincerely or whether it was another calculation on his part: he saw that the progressive left, which was his ally in the free world, cared about gays, and so he made a mea culpa.

Night fell outside the open windows of the Jamaican mountain resort. The light in the room is dim. Tired Cubans sit on chairs inside and on the patio. Their faces are illuminated by cell phone screens. Some are Skyping with their wives and children, others are reading uncensored news reports and watching videos, taking advantage of fast and free internet, an unexpected luxury.

I ask Leodan to give me an idea of how she lives today. What's an ordinary day like for her?

"I live in a wooden house that I built myself. It's just one room, which is also a bedroom, kitchen and living room. I have a small toilet and a bathroom. The house is in a neighbourhood with other similar houses that are a bit bigger than mine. It's a cozy neighborhood. I have a pretty good relationship with all the neighbors. I've had a friend since I was 15 who has helped me tremendously. When I was down, she comforted me. When I had to go to the hospital, she visited me there. When I didn't have a place to stay, I could stay at her's. When I had nothing to eat, she gave me food. We still keep in touch even though we each live in a different district."

"Have you had a chance to travel outside of Cuba? Other than this stay in Jamaica?"

"I have also been on various political trips abroad - Argentina, Brazil and Guyana. The situation in those countries is different from ours. The level of human rights and freedoms there is incomparable to Cuba, and the majority society accepts sexual minorities with more tolerance."

"Yet you say things are moving in the right direction in Cuba. If you compare the situation ten years ago and now, is it better?

"Incomparably better. People treat us transsexuals better. Contact with the authorities is a bit more civilised."

"The police aren't beating you anymore?"

"Oh, yes. Especially in other provinces, the State Security sometimes disperses our events and beats us. They do what they can to stop our political activities."

"How's it going? Are they treating you the same as other dissidents?"

"Probably not. Maybe they detain me and tell me they have cells for men and cells for women. And they start being funny. 'Where to, girl? To the men's cell or the women's cell? Maybe we'd better leave you in the corridor, because you don't belong anywhere.' Our State Security, as you can see, has a great sense of humor."

Yes, all Communist State Security was always full of big joksters.

"What's your goal?"

"My goal is a Cuba that is completely free and democratic, with a legal system that protects human rights and civil liberties, that also protects our community and allows us to live freely. That's what I want, because if we don't have laws to protect us, we're screwed. People are gradually losing their fear. They're joining us because we're protecting them. I know a gay couple. One of them was imprisoned and the other couldn't visit him in prison. Or I know people who lost their homes because of the authorities. We were the only organization that stood up for them and went to the authorities to defend them."

"Do you have any international support from LGBT organizations?"

"We don't."

Her answer surprises me. Isn't the proud rainbow banner you so often see flying in the suave gentrified neighborhoods like Washington's DuPont Circle, London's Soho, and Madrid's Chueca supposed to be a banner of solidarity?

"Really?"

"We have help from our political party from the national level. But nothing from international organisations."

"Nothing from the Czech Republic?"

"We have support from the Czech Republic for one micro-project. But it is not related to the LGBT community, and it is not funded by an organization that deals specifically with sexual minority issues. It would be great if we had some support for communication or for organizing our events."

Defibrillator

At the time of his birth in 1969, Oscar Martínez Ayala was already an uncle. He was born in the small town of Ciego de Ávila, the eighth and last child of a family of a teacher and a journalist. He had a happy childhood. He was a quiet, sensitive child, not into sports, not into boyish mischief, and instead lay in books all day. His parents and much older siblings protected him from his more pugnacious peers. Oscar also told me his story in Jamaica at the same table as Leodán. A great-looking 50-year-old, he would have fit right in with his peers in San Francisco, thanks to designer glasses and trendy clothes.

He had his first date with the world in the army, where he was kissed by a lieutenant colonel in an unguarded moment, and the shocked Oscar only discovered at the age of 19 that he was erotically attracted to men.

"Not before? No teenage crushes?"

"Not really. I was the youngest, most pampered child. I was probably a little late."

His father died in a car accident when he was 13. After a military kiss, he confided his sexual orientation to his mother, who accepted it generously and embraced Oscar. As was the custom in their home when important matters were at stake, his mother gathered the entire extended family around the table and broke the news to them. All the siblings, their partners and their adult children supported Oscar. No matter what anyone really thought, they offered to help him. Oscar was happy. After the military service, he went to Camagüey to study child psychology and special education.

"I studied honestly and conscientiously at the university for five years and decided to overcome my social handicap by becoming a professional. When you become a professional in Cuba, no one dares to pick on you and you are respected."

He returned from his studies and got a job at a center for deaf children. It was at this time that his mother was diagnosed with cancer and Oscar asked for more flexible hours to care for her. But they wouldn't give it to him. So, he quit his job and found another one with an organisation that helps people living with AIDS.

"At my mother's we took turns with my brothers and sisters. She died in February 2003."

He then devoted himself fully to working for people infected with HIV. He found a partner, Francisco Gerardo, who was a nurse there. They moved in together and figuratively speaking, took their work home. Over dinner, they discussed care settings and ways of treating patients. Some things they didn't like. For example, infected patients were interned, unable to leave the clinic and integrate into normal life, as was common abroad. Cuba was criticised at the UN for this. Oscar and Francisco spoke up and proposed a change. Not only did this not come, but colleagues and superiors began to view them with suspicion. In 2012, the government ordered them both to apply for an international mission. Oscar was not selected, but Francisco was. The following year, the regime sent him to work in Venezuela without a whimper. Since then, they have seen each other only a few times a year, when Francisco was given a "leave of absence."

"One day he came and explained to me that there had been an accident at work and that he had contracted the HIV virus. But he didn't know about it, they told him only after a delay. From then on we both lived with the virus, he and I."

Oscar decided to set up a new, independent organization, Centro Esperanza, with the aim of helping sexual minorities. Gradually, its activities have expanded beyond Ciego to other provinces and - as we know from the previous pages - its coordinator in Holguín is Juan Miguel. The organisation helps gays, lesbians and transsexuals with official and legal matters, organizes courses to increase their self-esteem, teaches them to act assertively and advises on how to protect themselves from violence.

"In 2015, we participated in the Hope campaign, which we funded ourselves. We tried to raise awareness among people in the 15-35 age group about the risks associated with HIV. This was the only campaign where we received funding. But we never received any funding from LGBT organizations despite my trying to get it. It could also be because our organization is peaceful and calm, not interested in any excitement. I believe that an intelligent approach can influence people better than violence. For example, I was in contact with an exile organization in Miami. They suggested that we make some noise on the streets, but I refused. I was afraid of being arrested. Since then, the most they've helped us with is buying data for our phones."

"Do you have lesbian women involved?"

"It's interesting, but hardly at all. They are reserved, they don't care about others. They live in their own world and don't pay attention to our questions. Most of the women I work with are heterosexual. When lesbian women come up, I try to welcome them and include them in the group."

He tells how he came to be recognized and how his views slowly made their way into the media. Marriage for all began to be publicly discussed and TV journalists from a provincial station made a documentary about same-sex couples. They wanted people to see how such couples lived, so they arranged a panel discussion with a psychologist. He and Francisco were featured in the documentary as positive examples for others.

"We were a well-known, long-established couple, so we were invited as an exemplary, reference couple."

Because of criticism of HIV care practices, Oscar and Francisco found themselves in increasingly uncomfortable situations at work. In 2014, Oscar quit his job and began to devote himself full-time to working for the sexual minority community.

A year before our conversation in Jamaica, Francisco's condition had worsened. The hospital lacked basic equipment. When he couldn't breathe, it turned out they didn't have any working oxygen masks. Through his contacts, Oscar obtained one and delivered it to the hospital. Still, Francisco's condition worsened. He complained that the doctors did not respond to his complaints. He was having trouble urinating. Oscar confronted the doctors. They insultingly told him what the limits were. Soon after, Francisco went into cardiac arrest. The defibrillator, which had not been used in a long time, was not working, according to Oscar, and was not properly charged. The hospital didn't even have adrenaline for an intracardiac injection. Francisco died at the age of 51. Oscar pauses for a moment and takes a deep breath.

"We lived together for 18 years."

"When did this happen?"

"Last year. In 2018."

"How did you get out of it?"

"I'm not completely out yet, but I'm not crying anymore. That used to happen to me a few months ago."

Oscar complained about the doctors in the ministry and, after considerable effort, succeeded in getting them partially disciplined.

"Several of them have taken pay cuts and been reassigned to lesser jobs," he says.

Then he did nothing for weeks. His siblings helped him. His nephew had just had a newborn, and Oscar helped take care of him, went for walks with him; slowly, week by week, he came to other ideas. At the Esperanza Center, he offered his colleagues that he would no longer lead them.

"I felt that after so many years it would be better if a younger generation, people with new ideas, took over the work. But they didn't want to. They chose me again," he explains.

Before Francisco died, Oscar started a small business. In the late 1970s, Ciego de Ávila became the capital of an independent province, and the authorities established a university there. In 2014, Oscar opened a small cafe called La Casa del Iyawo near the campus. Hundreds of students come to him every week. He is doing so well that he can afford to hire two employees to work on the premises while he takes care of supplies. They are closed during the holidays and Christmas, but in high season he reports sales of about three thousand pesos a week. He pays 750 pesos a month in taxes and fees.

I'm interested in the unusual name. Iyawo is a term used in the Yoruba religion of West Africa and in derivative diasporic traditions such as Santería and Candomblé. It refers to a person undergoing initiation to become a priest or priestess of a particular orisha. During this process, the iyawo undergoes a series of rituals designed to strengthen his or her connection to the orisha and prepare him or her to serve as that orisha's representative in the community.

Oscar's business is official, he has obtained a business license.

"After I left public health, I was out of work. We were living on one salary. My family helped me, but I felt I had to do something. My boyfriend wasn't completely happy with the idea of starting a café, he wasn't thrilled that there would be college kids around, but he respected me. I told him I needed something to keep me busy. I started frying food for the students and over time I registered a business. Francisco was a practitioner of Santería, he told me about the orisha gods, so the name of the café is also in his honor."

"Given your experience, tell me, what is the situation of sexual minorities in Cuba today?"

"In Cuba, it is mainly trans people who have problems. Gay people like me don't have it easy, but today they no longer face open discrimination. A big handicap is the limited access to education for trans people, not only because of the system, but also because of the classmates and teachers themselves, who are very macho. I was able to study. Trans women are rejected by teachers from the moment they start dressing how they feel and are forced to leave school. Sometimes they don't even get a basic education. Because they have no other choice, they often must prostitute themselves. There is violence in trans prostitution. Trans women look for a man to protect them, but he often abuses, exploits, beats and steals from them. Compared to them, I went through my life stages quite easily. When I was studying at university, I didn't feel discriminated against. Even though I lived in a room with six boys and everyone knew I was gay, I never perceived any negative reactions."

"What would move your situation forward the most?"

"If I had a magic wand and could choose what I wanted for our organization, I would ask for educational and methodological materials from abroad. I think that would help us the most. In Latin America, people are often busy with all kinds of things and don't pay much attention to organizations like ours. That is why I would choose materials from Europe, because there similar organisations are bigger and stronger. In Europe people are more willing to help institutionally, whereas in Latin America people think more about themselves. If someone helps you, it is often because they want to increase their own importance. I talk about this because I was recently at a peace forum in Brazil and I met several people who were there just for fun."

"What do you mean?"

"It seemed to me that they weren't so much interested in social movements and changes, but whether they had the right wig, cool shoes or dress like in the last movie."

"Anything else?"

"First of all, we need change on the political level. People from the LGBT community cannot be members of political and youth organizations. For example, when the new constitution was being debated, there was no one who was strongly in favor of this change, except for Mariela Castro. And even her support was weak. Mariela is not the kind of person that her mother, the revolutionary Vilma Espín, was, who was a real defender of trans people and the gay community, and she did it at a much worse time."

"Cenesex, led by Mariela, was a center that educated society about sexual issues, taught people about these issues, and distributed different materials. It had a social mission. But then money came in from the world and Cenesex became a bit of a business and a bit of a travel agency for the members of the leadership. Before you could contact them, describe your situation, for example if you were abused, and they would give you support. I saw more sexual and reproductive awareness events from them, more documents and materials. They used to prepare people for life, they used to run hairdressing, cooking and make-up courses, but these courses have disappeared. Now you see on social media that the national coordinator is traveling around the country and that the deputy director has been to this international conference and that international conference."

34 Dead

One of my Jamaican workshops was attended by Caridad Santí Núñez, whom Jimena and I visited in her hometown of San Antonio de los Baños in the province of Artemisa, about a half hour's drive west of Havana. The airbase there was home to part of the 32nd Guards Fighter Aviation Regiment of the Soviet Air Force, with its modern MiG-21 fighters, during the 1962 missile crisis. You can tell that San Antonio is a military town by the access to the Autopista Este-Oeste highway, which for several kilometers is just a wide strip of asphalt that can be turned into a runway if necessary.

A few months ago, a series of riots began here over the government's incompetence in dealing with the new coronavirus pandemic. Cuba has seen its largest anti-regime demonstrations in many years.

Caridad lives in a small one-storey house in a nondescript neighborhood near downtown. We hope we won't have to wait long after knocking, but it doesn't occur to me that there could be several apartments in one entrance. As a neighbor opens the door, a young girl in shorts and a t-shirt comes out of the bowels of the building. She has a sporty haircut, a brisk walk, and is holding a dog leash. A hunting dog runs obediently behind her. Their step is well synchronized, they've practiced it. The girl passed us and silently indicated that we should go further into the yard and knock on the last door on the left.

Caridad welcomes us into a dark apartment consisting of a bedroom and a kitchen that doubles as a living room, a study, and her nine-year-old daughter's room. She's home alone, sitting in a chair with her back to the desk. A wooden bunk bed for her daughter is draped over her head. She offers coffee, which she makes from bottled water.

"It's not running again," she says matter-of-factly.

She has large dark eyes and is introverted. In Jamaica, she mostly listened, but when I gave her the floor, she spoke confidently and surprisingly loudly. Her wavy auburn hair flows down to her delicate shoulders, she wears denim shorts, and her left leg is adorned with tattoos of Indian patterns. She casually drapes it over her right and holds a cup of coffee in her hand. She has studied acting and also paints, and it is clear from the subject matter of her work that this is a form of protest for her. In one of her paintings I see an elongated female head with an antique nose, inspired by Modigliani. A crown of thorns sits on her forehead, and her mouth is bandaged with red tape. The second painting also has a feminist theme. The owl-eyed face, reminiscent of the style of 1970s Czech singer Nadia Urbánková, is set against a background of a target with red arrows pointing at it from all sides. Caridad works with strong colors and their contrasts.

"Women are still judged and criticized," she says, pointing to Urbánková. "Society has made them a target. But it doesn't apply the same standards to men."

For a moment, I wonder if I am passing judgment when I write that Caridad is an attractive little brunette.

Chapter 6 181

In addition to painting, Caridad is narrating a film about a black woman named Gladys. She moved here with her family from the Oriente to escape the worst poverty. But she did it without permission, so she's not registered. She does odd jobs in the fields, has no electricity, and gets her water from holding tanks. To make matters worse, Gladys is a polio survivor.

"Without immunization. She couldn't get the vaccine because she doesn't exist officially. I'm proud to be working on this film. Gladys fights like a gladiator, a strong personality who has had to overcome many obstacles. It's terrible that even though they're Cuban, they live here illegally. The movie is about how you can become a stranger in your own country."

Caridad's feminist fervor is not the ideological feminism of a university department fueled by pseudo-themes. She doesn't want to make a career and make herself visible at international conferences through eccentric theories. She wants to make things easier for herself and other Cuban women. She talks about domestic violence.

"No one is dealing with it. It is not a topic for politicians. And this year alone 34 women have been murdered in our country, most of them apparently after incidents of domestic violence. In the last few days, it's been three. I'm trying to find out as much as I can about these murders. But it's not easy. The police refuse to talk to us, or indeed any type of citizen oversight. Sometimes these attempts are dangerous."

"How do you find out what happened and if the police are investigating?"

"We have a network of collaborators in different places in Cuba. We are pressing the authorities to investigate all the murders properly. When it's not too far away, I travel to the site and talk to people. But I can't go to Camagüey, for example, it's too long a journey and I must look after my daughter. A lot of women are afraid to talk about their experiences of violence."

There is no doubt that Cuban society is dominated by men with a power-dominance complex. Very few women have risen to prominence, and only by the grace of men. Before the Moncada coup, they sewed uniforms, ran up and down the Sierra Maestra as couriers and carried guns in pugettes, or later became mistresses and wives of leaders and secretaries of the Central Committee of the Communist Party.

I'm asking about the recent riots.

"Sometimes the electricity didn't go for 14 hours straight," says Caridad. "People took to the streets to protest, mostly at night. They were banging on everything they could get their hands on, especially pots and pans. At night it was completely dark everywhere, and people were a little less afraid, believing that they couldn't be seen much, that if the police wanted to film them, they wouldn't be recognizable. At first nothing happened, the police left us alone. But then the riot police stepped up, their 'black caps,' and they started to come after us. Soldiers surrounded the town, just in case. They restored the peace by force. They handed out huge fines for rioting, even 5,000 pesos. They arrested a lot of people here in San Antonio. After the riots, many police officers stayed on the streets as a warning. Undercover cops abound. They're everywhere, even in the parks."

The black caps, *boinas negras,* are the units used by the regime against the demonstrators. Caridad lowers her voice, as if she is afraid of being heard from outside, from the small courtyard.

"Not far from here lives the former president of the provincial assembly in Artemisa. An elderly gentleman, but still a staunch Communist. I keep an eye on him. I have a polite, superficial relationship with him, but I prefer not to say anything to him."

We're asking about her daughter, who's visiting a friend. Caridad takes her to school every morning before starting her work day herself. She shows us her drawing of the human body. She has inherited her mother's talent.

"She captured the body proportions, head and limbs well. It's not common for children her age," she says proudly.

It's getting late and we have another journey ahead of us. Caridad assures us that the friends of freedom always have an open door.

7.

Seminar with Fidel.

Ciego de Ávila

After a few hours of continuous driving, the indicator light shows that my tank is half full, so I look for a gas station. To my amazement, I quickly find it between the motorway lanes. A chaser picks me up at the stand. He offers to fill up and pay for me. I must have switched off my brain at that moment, with the result that I get ripped off like some damn sucker. The guy gives me a full one, I give him a twenty-dollar bill, and he promptly disappears into the clutter outside the entrance. After a while, I realize he's not going to come back with change. When I find him after some effort in a crowd of similar hucksters, he pretends that twenty dollars for half a tank is a good price, even though it's four times the stipulated amount. The haggling begins. First he gives me back 400 pesos. After a while, he ups it to 600.

"That's all right, I deserve something for my work, my friend!"

I end up knocking eight hundred out of him. I still left him about twice as much as he deserved, but I'm comforted by the thought that today, in inflationary Prague, *twenty dollars isn't that much*! There's nothing like the power of self-deception in such situations. My mood is lifted by the great coffee that Jimena and I have at a small stand by the highway.

"How much do I owe?" I ask the stallholder.

"Ten," says the man, who has been standing there all day, without blinking. Dumbfounded by my previous experience, I ask:

"Ten dollars?"

The man rolls his eyes at me.

"Ten pesos. *Peso cubano. Moneda nacional.*"

In other words, basically free. I'll have another one right away.

Around the highway they are now showing a continuous documentary on both sides about the beauty of the island. Here in the province of Sancti Spíritus, the countryside is hilly. Green trees and shrubs with colorful flowers grow near picturesque restaurants with thatched roofs. We stop at one, but it's fully booked. In front of the restaurant, Soviet trucks are parked on a muddy patch and there are also three tethered horses. Two *vaqueros* with sombreros pass by and two dogs run close behind them at the hind hooves. A yellow cab pulls up, maybe straight from New York. The endless fascination with America in countries with anti-American regimes...

Change. There are more fruit and vegetable stalls along the roads. They're filled with bags of onions and bunches of tomatoes. Garlic necklaces hang from spikes, which also adorn the chests of the vendors. The relaxation of small business is palpable. There used to be almost nothing around the roads, just a few vendors selling Cuban cheese cubes. I tell Jimena and we agree we could buy *queso* for breakfast. I stop at a vendor, only he is unwilling to cut us a third of a huge cube. He's forcing a whole loaf that we could eat for a week.

"Ten! Only ten," he calls to me from two metres away, as if I were hard of hearing.

"Ten pesos?"

"No, ten dollars," he replies.

None of this is gonna happen. The disappointment on his face. Stubble, black hair, dark, sad eyes, a crumpled hat on his head. But he has no business acumen. Most Cubans don't, unless you count the art of conning someone. Where would they get it after 60 years of socialism? It's similar to the habits of dependency that a totalitarian dictatorship breeds in you.

Suddenly I think of the few activists I used to meet here, but in the meantime they decided to emigrate.

Those Who Left...

Many of them went to the States and Spain. The tall, black poet Jorge Oliveira Castillo lives in Pittburgh. A war veteran from Angola and a prisoner of conscience from Guantánamo, where he was in solitary

Chapter 7

confinement only in the company of "wasps, bees and ants," it is only in his upper middle age that he is able to pursue another passion, jazz music. It wasn't possible at home. The famous student leader Eliezer Ávila even became a farmer in Florida. His YouTube reality show, Ávila's Farm, is popular in Cuba.

And then there's Robertico, full name Roberto de Jesús Guerra Pérez. He was born in 1978 in the province of Granma into unimaginable poverty.

"I didn't even have shoes. And I couldn't study."

He soon became an enemy of the regime. I mean really soon. As a schoolboy, he criticized the food rationing system. He was sentenced to forced labour for that when he was 14.

"The police slapped me with the Idleness Act and I was off. For a year and three months I chopped wood, then I harvested sugar cane with a machete, worked in a quarry. When I got out, I was herding cows near Havana."

In 2003, he moved to the capital and began to work in the dissident community. He saw his first *acto del repudio*. He first went to prison in 2004 for participating in a protest in Revolution Square. Together with him, 60 other people were arrested. He got two years. And then again - nine months "for assault."

"At my sister's house, two strangers beat my brother-in-law. He got into some kind of argument. He just wanted to give the kids toys for Three Wise Men Day. I went to defend him and a fight broke out. I was in solitary for six months and eight days. I went on hunger strike several times. Eight times in all."

While in prison, Robertico had the idea of starting a news agency. That was in 2007.

"I read about an agency that started out as a journalism agency and then started helping people on the street. I was interested in newspapers before that. I was featured on Radio Martí a few times. But in Havana this station is not heard. It used to be possible to listen to Radio Prague in Spanish, but not anymore."

So in 2009 he founded Hablemos Press, an agency focused on human rights violations and the dire social situation that the official media was silent about.

186 Cuba: A Brief History of the End

"There were six of us and we didn't know anything. Today there are 36 of us," Robertico told me ten years ago. "We have people in Santa Clara, Sanctí Spiritus, Santiago de Cuba and Las Tunas. We had help from Radio Martí editors. We downloaded manuals from the Internet, and I went through a course organized by the American Embassy. Our first report was about farmers in the Sierra Maestra. I took pictures of the dire poverty there, how they don't even have drinking water..."

We chatted in his small apartment in Centro Habana, where he lived in a nondescript corner house on Calle Santa Marta. He was thirty-five and slightly overweight. His short black hair was combed up. A group of young reporters hovered around him, all of them squeezed into the top of the built-in floor of the dark apartment. Very quickly it was impossible to breathe, the house had no air conditioning, and there were about eight of us crowded around several donated computers under the ceiling. I conducted a seated workshop there; I couldn't stand up properly in the space with the lowered ceiling. With a height of about 165 cm Robertico didn't have that problem. He wore a dirty white tank top and, in contrast to other dissident leaders, led his people in a gentle, consensual manner. He complained of poor access to information sources.

"They don't want to talk to us. They're hiding everything. That goes for the official Granma journalists too, they don't get to see anything unless they have special permission. How many buses does the city of Havana run? We don't know. How was lunch today at which restaurant? Impossible to find out. I once managed to find out what hospital Hugo Chávez was in. I was awarded the Ortega y Gasset Prize for that information."

He was also nabbed because of cholera.

"Cholera is taboo. The hospital in Bayamo province where the outbreak is said to have occurred has been surrounded by police officers to prevent doctors from speaking to the media. I found out that cholera has emerged in neighbouring Matanzas. I was arrested for that. It was forbidden to use the word cholera. So we tried it with the official scientific name."

One day he was suddenly beaten in the street so badly that he had to go to the hospital. Warning. The authorities didn't like the *Hablemos Press* for covering issues they wanted to cover up. Like when they wrote about corruption in the police force, about some police officers pimping out their prostitutes. Some were underage.

"We're doing a video report on it. About child prostitution. We're editing it now. They're underage girls, thirteen, fourteen years old. We have testimony that the cops are pimping these girls. They take them from the Oriente and then they send them around here on the Malecón or Calle Obispo, where the tourists are."

"How do you get to these topics?"

"I listen a lot to what people are saying on the street. Then we follow it. I went to a concert in Miramar and we were filming with a girl there. We had a drink and she got talking. Suddenly she's like, 'I know you, I know *Hablemos Press*, my uncle reads your newsletter. And my aunt is the Lady in White.' She's from Guantánamo, she's twenty-one and has two kids. She gave us contact information for younger girls, 16, 17 years old. There's a street near here that's known for prostitution. I know a whole family that goes there. The mother and her daughters, too. The police used to go there, plainclothes cops used to go there for marijana and cocaine."

Because I look surprised, he explains the sexual customs in Cuba, which are different from those in Central Europe.

"Girls here usually have sex from the age of eleven. Theoretically, they're under the law until they're 18. My daughter is twelve now. She doesn't live with me, she lives with her mother. She was raped when she was seven.

"Who?"

"The man my wife was living with at the time."

Robertico has four sons and two daughters. His sister is involved in child rearing and educational programs. She gets money from foreign non-profits.

He recently discovered an abandoned prison on the coast, where many families with nowhere to live have moved illegally out of desperation.

"It's not safe there. The house is on shaky ground, on sand. In fact, it's sinking. It's a terrible story. There are a lot of mosquitoes. The police threatened me not to write about it. They told the families that if their names appeared in the media, they'd be evicted. There are about 60 people there. So I preferred to stop and not write about it.

I imagine an abandoned prison on the coast, the wind blowing in the rusty bars of the windows, small children and stray dogs running around. Laundry flutters on the lines. But Robertico is not a poet. He has no time for that; he's been locked up again recently. They stopped the bus he was on and dragged him out. This time they didn't beat him, they just took his camera and never gave it back. When he asked for it back, they said someone must have stolen it. They're after his people, too. At the time of our interview, two Hablemos couriers were in jail for distributing the magazine without permission.

As I prepare for my current trip to Cuba, I check my contact information and find that Robertico isn't in Cuba anymore, either. As of 2018, he lives in Atlanta, where he's trying to establish himself as a freelance reporter, editor, and photographer. Years of hardship have caught up with even an energetic machine like him. When we talked years ago at his home on Santa Marta Street about where he finds collaborators, he told me that he suspects some of his people are dissidents just so they can emigrate.

"Some have told me so openly. That's why I nominated my brother and some others I trust for your workshop, so as not to waste resources.

I should point out that I was doing the workshop for free, so by "resources" Robertico meant mainly my time. He was in a good mood, he was gregarious. He hoped that he had become so well known that the regime could not fundamentally harm him. He and his wife were planning a major renovation of their apartment. I remembered this exact conversation when I learned that Robertico had emigrated to the United States. But what I remember most about what he told me is this:

When he went on hunger strike in prison, the guards denied him liquids. So he wet his lips with a cloth soaked in his own urine. His chapped lips burned. He mentioned this in passing.

The Inverted Tree

And again a large number of hitchhikers. Waving bills over their heads, signalling they will chip in for gas expenses. Then the *punto de control*, a peculiar "border crossing" between provinces with a police box and unpleasant-looking gunmen menacingly wielding small semiautomatic guns. I slow down to 40 km/h. We are not eager to have a talk with the guardians of the revolution, it's enough that there are still plenty of signs with Fidel's likeness around the roads. Forever, comrade. Some of the slogans sound bitterly ironic, especially the one about how we go from victory to victory.

In the car, we listen to Radio Reloj, a "news" and talk channel, where you can hear the ticking of the clock in the background. A beep every full minute gives the idea that the station, founded in 1947, still has its finger on the pulse, and the inexorable passage of time will not stop it. This hour is spent discussing the genius of Fidel, six years since his death. Driving through Ciego de Ávila, I recall my two previous visits to the local poet, Francis Sánchez.

It's so hot I'd like to hide under a cold shower, but that's not an option here in this arid province. I don't plan to stay overnight or for long. Ciego de Ávila is a typical small town that doesn't offer much to tourists, so there aren't any. That means, among other things, that I'm conspicuous. I park off the main street, which is lined with arcades of low houses painted in bright colors. It's neatly swept, only the small center is busy. I leave the main street and find myself in a neighborhood of houses with front and back yards. Some streets are paved with a thin layer of asphalt, others have a surface of crushed dirt. I clutch my camera and feel the sweat under my hat. Afternoon, siesta, the unmarked streets empty. I am looking for the house of Francis Sánchez Rodríguez, whose visual poetry, short stories and essays are famous in independent circles.

The story of the arrest of two of my friends from Prague, Ivan Pilip and Jan Bubeník, which led them to the State Security prison Villa Marista, began here in the winter of 2001. They found themselves in the crosshairs of an ambitious country cop who saw a spy behind every telegraph pole. Learning from Ivan and Honza's experience, I decided not to stay overnight. My goal, meeting Francis, will be a precision landing. Quickly in and out.

Finally I'm in the right place. I climb the exposed outside stairs to the first floor, look around discreetly, and knock on the door. A middle-aged woman with close-cropped black hair answers. She is the poet and essayist Ileana Álvarez González, Francis's wife.

"He's not home."

"When is he coming back?"

"He and his son are at a baseball game. You can wait here for him."

Convenient offer. I don't want to stay, but in this case it's better to wait inside than to hang around in the city. I sit down on the small couch in the hall. In the corner there's a Christmas tree. The sight of trees with ornaments and candles in a climate where it's thirty in the shade still strikes me as unusual, which is surely an expression of residual Eurocentrism on my part. The walls of Ileana and Francis' home are bold and freshly painted, the turquoise in the living room contrasting with the brown-red frame and tropical wood doors. It's relaxed and inviting. Unlike Francis, Ileana had no dissident status when we met in Ciego, but she was in a gray cultural zone. On my next trip to Cuba, I will see her poetry collection in a Havana bookstore. When she finds out that I'm from Prague, she tells me that some Czechs before me had taken Francis's photographs to Germany for an exhibition. He also exhibited his work at the Langhans Gallery in Prague.

I ask why Francis no longer writes his blog, Man of the Clouds, which he started a few years ago and then suddenly stopped. Ileana explains that it's mostly due to discrimination. Their pressure was unbearable. They blackmailed him over his children, among other things. There was also a problem with access to the internet. Connecting to the web is expensive and slow. In Ciego de Ávila they have an ETECSA shop where eight computers are available for rent, but they are under surveillance. When Francis needed to publish something, he could use the services of the Swedish Embassy, but it was impractical. After all, it's more than four hundred kilometres to Havana.

At that time, Francis and Ileana were already editing a famous cultural and political magazine called *Árbol Invertido* (The *Inverted Tree*), published three times a year with a circulation of about one hundred copies. According to Ileana, it is difficult to raise money for such work. They have some from foreign NGOs, but that is potentially dangerous. Francis has been falsely accused of taking money from the CIA. He needs to be careful.

Ileana talks about her own work. She founded the feminist magazine *Alas tensas* (*Tight Wings*), which writes about sensitive issues such as violence against women. She shows us a short poetic video she directed and produced called *And Seeing Everything Differently*. It's a dreamy, black and white clip.

"We shot it in the city. That was also a problem. In a small province everything is more complicated than in a big city."

"For example, our son is a talented football player. At school, he was told, 'Daddy's against the government. We don't know if we're going to let you play...' They put similar pressure on our friend's son. It got to the point where the child started having mental problems and they had to get him a therapist."

Her eyes glisten with impending tears.

"We have no one to share our dreams and opinions with. Everyone is afraid."

She wipes away a tear, clicks into her laptop and closes the video. To watch it, we went to the study, a smaller room with no windows. Bookshelves surround it all the way around. A stream of cold air from a fan ruffles the Cuban flag on the sturdy, wooden desk.

Here comes Francis. He has a bald head, straight eyes and broad shoulders. He moves deliberately and slowly. We return to the living room and exchange a few casual sentences about baseball. Then we get to his journal, *The Inverted Tree*. The name is inspired by the kapok, a tree sacred in Cuba, shrouded in myth. Francis shows some more recent typographic poems. One features the Spanish word *libertad* (freedom), with the "d" at the end drawn like a broom about to sweep the trembling letters before it onto a scoop made from the first letter "l." It's as beautiful and simple as a fleeting goodnight kiss.

I wonder how much it matters for Francis' artistic expression that he lives in Ciego and not in a major cultural center. He explains that he wants to preserve a regional identity for the magazine, but he is aiming for a universal readership drawn to authentic culture.

"The magazine's regional cultural identity builds on the strong regional identities of the republican era. This promising trend was violently ended by the Communist revolution, which homogenized everything. But not only that. Even dissent has these tendencies, everything is guided by the optics of Miami."

The chandelier's dim light illuminates the orb of Francis's bare head. His face is sombre, he speaks quietly. He looks older, he is just over forty at the time. He presents me with a work-in-progress issue of the magazine he is dedicating to the imprisoned writer and journalist Ángel Santiesteban-Prats. In well-considered sentences, he paints the oppressive reality of the place before my eyes.

"Independent-minded people are under constant pressure in our province. They are in danger of persecution. In the centre of Ciego de Ávila, the blind dissident Juan Carlos González Leiva was recently subjected to an act of repudiation for several days. At first the police wanted his neighbours to organise this, but they refused. They support him and are disgusted by the regime's treatment of him. So the police herded people from elsewhere onto a bus and took them to his house. Only these hired miscreants threw eggs, stones, poured paint on his house, shouted all day, played loud music and also broke his water meter," Francis says in disgust.

Juan Carlos González Leiva is a well-known dissident. He was born almost blind and, according to the Czech organisation Post Bellum, working on a plantation at the age of twenty-one deprived him of his sight completely. Nevertheless, he studied law and in 1998 founded the Brotherhood of the Independent Blind and also the Cuban Organisation for Human Rights. In March 2002, he was arrested, interrogated and imprisoned for two years. He was tortured in prison. He was repeatedly on hunger strike. In April 2004, he was sentenced to four years and, with his health seriously damaged, served the remaining two years under house arrest.

"Recently the police picked him up again," Ileana says. "They took him to the train. They were plainclothes cops. Then they took him out of the train in the hills and led him somewhere in the forest. They left him there. A blind man. All alone."

Francis shifts to optimism. He says more and more people are refusing to join in acts of repudiation. Even officially sanctioned artists are beginning to speak out.

"People in culture - not dissidents! - express their views publicly. The jazzman Robertico Carcassés, son of the famous Bobby Carcassés, recently let his mouth go and shouted 'Freedom to all Cubans!' Then he said on television that he would like to elect his own president. He said it live on the air! His concert was subsequently cancelled, but the legend of the Trova genre, another official musician and singer Silvio Rodríguez, supported Robertico on state television and then invited him to play at his concert. Fear leaves the artist."

Ileana nods. At the Writers' Union convention, some members let it be heard publicly that citizens should have the right to vote for their president. But despite the slight relaxation, the mood of the society weighs heavily on Ileana and Francis.

"I feel intellectually and spiritually isolated here," says Francis.

He knew life off the island. He visited Mexico and was going to Prague. Even here in Ciego, sometimes things happen. Occasionally, they both attend public events.

"We went to a public poetry reading followed by a discussion. It was in the official Writers' House. We talked about Nelson Mandela, who had recently died. Some people were praising Mandela and also Gandhi, and indirectly contrasting them with Fidel, whom the official media tried to compare to Mandela and keep him on a pedestal. The result of the contrast in these discussions was devastating. People commented on Mandela's life and work to highlight his ability to forgive former enemies and lead the nation in generosity. They explained why Mandela is considered such a personality. He did not act out of revenge. It was stressed that Mandela had been imprisoned for a long time but had not led the nation in resentment. He was president for four years, managed to unite the nation and then left office. Nobody mentioned Fidel's name even once, but of course everybody knew what was going on. Mandela's legacy is forgiveness, Gandhi's is passive, peaceful resistance. But Cuba is full of violence: against dissidents, against the Ladies in White..."

The totalitarian state perfects in people the ability to speak indirectly. To praise Madiba, as Mandela was called, is to criticize Fidel. At the same time, you cover yourself. But everyone knows that. The problem is that after a while we become proud of these detours. It becomes part of our identity. We broadcast ourselves indirectly.

Ileana lights candles on the Christmas tree. Meanwhile, Francis has brought his next drawing, his latest typographic poem:

Saying I'm afraid illuminates the darkness.

I wish for a moment of silence and contemplation. But that's nonsense, of course. I'm here on business, so I listen and make quick notes that I'll have trouble deciphering.

"Great harm has been done to intellectuals and thinkers. They have cut off the head of the nation. There is no democratic culture, they destroyed the economy. The only industry that worked was sugar cane, but many sugar mills had to close! The state used to pay people who lost their jobs to go to university, but that has stopped."

After we met, Francis started traveling more. He also attended the opening of his exhibition at the prestigious Dox Gallery in Prague, where he presented his typographic poems along with the work of several other Cuban artists. And then one day, he, Ileana and the children decided that they couldn't go on, that the overwhelming meanness of totalitarianism (as Francis would later put it) was too much for them. They said goodbye to the province for the last time and moved to Madrid in 2018. From there they edit *Árbol Invertido*, which is now available electronically.

I walk out into the street, which has filled up after siesta. I've lingered longer than I expected. I look around. I am the focus of curious glances. I'm some ten minutes away from the car, walking faster. Ivan Pilip and Honza Bubeník stayed here at the Hotel Ciego de Ávila in January 2001. They moved around the city in the presence of dissident Antonio Femenías. These were two mistakes I tried to avoid. I meet with dissidents at their homes or at agreed third places. I don't walk the streets with them if I can, but the situation doesn't always allow it. I certainly don't spend

Chapter 7

the night with them, as a friend once did who was later expelled. I avoid if I can state-owned hotels, which are under more scrutiny than private accommodation.

Ivan and Honza were picked up by the local plainclothes police after breakfast. Ivan told me a funny story, from today's point of view, about a Ciego officer who saw him as a trained 007 agent and treated him with a mixture of disgust and admiration. Ivan's Palm Pilot, a sort of precursor to smartphones, was considered by the State Security agent to be sophisticated spy equipment. After their capture, they were transported to Havana in a transfer that looked like something out of a Jiri Menzel movie. Scene:

Ivan and Honza take turns driving their own car. In the back seat two plainclothes agents sit. Occasionally they all stop for coffee. Honza and Ivan pay. While driving, they have a bottle of rum by the gear lever, which they sip from to make the journey go better. The two Cubans in the back don't make a sound.

First they were locked up in a light regime immigration prison, then transferred to the infamous Villa Marista prison. Things got tough.

"I remember the transfer," Ivan recalls. "During the arrest we were kept in the dark. They didn't tell us what was going to happen to us, and when we were taken away from the immigration prison I thought we were going to the airport. That we were going to be deported. But as we drove, I noticed that the road was not widening, quite the opposite. There's a four-lane road with palm trees leading to the Martí airport. However, we drove through smaller and smaller streets until we stopped at the gate of the prison and I saw the black insignia of the State Security on the guard's uniform. I knew it was bad."

Czech diplomacy has begun negotiations with the Cuban authorities, which culminated in a meeting between Senate President Petr Pithart and President Fidel Castro. Foreign mediators who had good relations with Havana, such as Juan Pablo Letelier, were involved in the case. Valtr Komárek, who spent several years in Havana in the 1960s as an advisor to Che Guevara at the Ministry of Economy, also sent a personal letter to Castro. His and Pithart's communications with Castro will one day be studied in diplomatic schools. In Pithart's case, it was a top act, a kind of masterclass; in Komárek's case, I'm not so sure. In a dispatch to Castro, Komárek recalls his dispute with Che Guevara over whether it was possible to produce ten million tons of sugar a year, a megalomaniacal plan of Castro's to which *the comandante* had totally subordinated the entire system in the 1960s. This policy of Castro and Guevara caused considerable economic damage. At the time, Komárek, according to his own account in the letter to Fidel, contradicted Guevara and argued that the optimal economic target was eight million tonnes. In the end, ten million proved to be unrealistic. In the letter, however, Komárek quotes Guevara's response:

"Professor, we were shot at the moment we landed from Granma, and when the few survivors managed to reach the Sierra Maestra, Fidel counted us and said, 'Twelve, gentlemen, congratulations. The Cuban Revolution has won!' And today, Professor, you want to tell this brilliant triumphant that his directive lacks a sense of reality? Then you don't stand a chance."

In the spirit of the "historical lesson" he had received from Guevara in the sugar dispute, Komárek then asked Castro for Ivan and Honza's release. He wrote that he did not want "to argue vehemently about the legitimacy of his request, much less to elaborate on the detailed reasoning. It would be unwise to stir up the human rights controversy. After all, even with different political approaches, some understanding can be reached. I therefore ask you very much to make a generous gesture..."

Pithart took a roundabout way to Castro. He had a lively discussion with him about modern Czech and Cuban history. They clashed on several points, such as the Cuban reaction to the Soviet invasion of Czechoslovakia in 1968 or Czech diplomatic activity that led to the UN resolution condemning Cuba for human rights violations.

"In a way, I invited myself to the meeting," Pithart told me in his apartment in Prague's Petřiny district in the spring of 2023. We sat in his study, surrounded by bookshelves. The political legend, signatory of Charter 77, and former prime minister of the Czech government seated me in a leather guest chair and let me generously discuss the events of twenty-two years ago, which were one of his political high points.

"I met Honza Ruml, who was a senator at the time, and he said to me, 'You should also write something,' and I said, 'Why, everyone has already written to them anyway, so what else could I add?' But, he maintained, after all, as Senate President, you are number two in the state hierarchy. So I decided to write a letter to Fidel Castro. At the very end of the letter, actually after we had already finalized the text, I added a sentence, which I had not consulted with anyone, that I would offer him, if I had the opportunity, to add a personal handshake to my arguments. That I vouch for them."

"Then we were in the inspection room at Sumava national forest, borrowed from the Forestry Administration, and just a few hours after the letter was sent, the foresters were standing at our door, completely terrified: 'President, we have a fax from Castro for you!' 'Yes, I'm going,' I said immediately."

"When you were strategizing for your interviews, what was most important to you?"

"I knew I was not there to lecture them and convince them of my truth. I kept asking questions. I had meetings with the Attorney General, the Secretary of State and other officials. I asked them how things worked in their country, I took note of it, and I didn't argue with them. I did not say a single sentence that indicated that I thought the worst of their regime. That was the mistake of all those who wrote letters to them trying to prove what democrats they were. I told myself beforehand that if I was going to do it, it would be to let these two go, not to triumph in argument. So I had it all figured out. Not a word about their 'democracy'."

"During the preparation and then on site, I was greatly helped by our Foreign Ministry, especially by Jakub Karfík, the son of a literary critic and historian, my former editorial colleague in the 1960s. I intended to keep my trip as secret as possible, so as not to create an atmosphere of pressure beforehand. It was only when I was changing planes in London for my flight to Havana that I had an appointment with a BBC reporter to whom I told where I was going and why. Our preparation was very thorough. One thing, however, did not work out as we thought it would, and that was an estimate of when Castro would receive me. I was told that it would definitely be around two o'clock at night, that I had to allow for that. That's how Castro worked. That's what dictators do. They have a different sleeping rhythm. Stalin did it, Hitler did it. Late at night, their partner wasn't at his best, whereas they were on top."

Castro really was an owl. He stayed up late into the night and usually got up around 11 a.m., so he started his workday around noon. Hitler behaved similarly. So Pithart adapted his preparation to this assumption. He could not have known at the time that the exercise would have lasting effects on his body.

"I prepared myself by going to bed late after midnight every day in Cuba despite the time difference and jetlag. I broke my sleep rhythm, which hasn't been fixed since. I had no trouble sleeping before, but I've been on sleeping pills ever since. Well, you see, and Castro received me in the early afternoon."

"Where did the meeting take place?"

"In the hotel. As soon as the Latin American summit on globalization at the Havana Congress Palace ended. We were led through a long corridor to the back. I didn't recognize that I was suddenly in a hotel."

"Our conversation was really great in its own way. I was watching my balance. He talked for five minutes, I took five minutes. We teased each other. He was prickly, I was prickly. I didn't want Castro to dominate, to have the upper hand. When he was aggressive, I was aggressive. When he was questioning, I was questioning. I caught him in a good mood. And he was terribly vain. He told me how dozens of assassination attempts were made on him. He also boasted of his modesty. 'Look at my watch,' he showed me. He had a pretty ordinary, cheap watch. He was trying to tell me that he didn't go for luxury."

"I have prepared for our meeting very honestly. I played on his vanity. I told him my wife would be delighted with an autographed photo of him with his personal dedication. I made that up, my wife didn't care. But it worked."

"'Of course!' he says. And immediately to his adjutant: 'Bring it!' During our conversation, at Castro's command, he runs off several more times and always brings something. I thought it was an aide-de-camp, and he was the Speaker of Parliament!"

"What did he bring you?"

"In particular, the timing of the arrests. Exactly when the two boys were picked up. Castro was very insulted that he learned about everything from the world media, that they didn't tell him in time. The world was already beginning to see the pressure. I could see how he couldn't accept not knowing something a minute after it happened. Ivan and Honza took the fall for the fact that there was some miscommunication and his people just didn't tell him. That infuriated him."

Castro and Pithart then spoke for several hours. The President of the Senate even had to gently remind the Commander-in-Chief that he was invited to lunch, because Castro was so engrossed in his topics that he forgot about the meal. Somewhat surprisingly, the first few hours were in the spirit of a historical seminar. The topics were raised by Castro.

"I say that our relations were going surprisingly well, but everything went wrong after the Soviet invasion in August 1968, which you, Mr President, unfortunately approved. We used to go on holiday to Cuba, but August spoiled everything. I said that even many Communists at the time thought that he would be the one to stand up for us."

"How did he react to that?"

"He came right out. 'No way! Bring me the materials, he says to the Speaker of Parliament. 'Look, here, I waited one, two, three' - he counts - 'I waited for days, Castro says, 'if you Czechs defend yourself!' That was terribly unpleasant for me.

'Mr. President,' he says to me, 'every Cuban will protect every inch of his land. And we expected you to defend it. But you didn't. It was only when we saw this that we began to weigh all the pros and cons' - well he lied to me. Their statement was kind of two-faced. Like the invasion was illegal in terms of international law, but politically it was okay. I didn't know what to say. I remembered my feelings at the time in August 1968. I knew that we would not defend ourselves with arms, but I did not expect such a rapid slide into submission to the Russians. This submission, this "normalization" of the occupation, as you write (in my book of essays *Perhaps Even a Dictator Will Show UP.* T.K.), is constantly influencing us."

"I would say much more than the Communist terror of the 1950s."

"Exactly. I didn't think that the army would defend us, but that maybe some guerilla or resistance groups would form and operate in our country. In August 1968, I was in Israel on a trip organized by the writer Ladislav Mňačko. There were writers, intellectuals, student leaders, and we worked in the kibbutz and explained to them that in reality the sympathies of the Czechs and Slovaks were on their side. The official Communist policy supported the Arabs. People in Israel followed the occupation of Czechoslovakia closely and quite emotionally. Just a year before, they had experienced the Six-Day War. Immediately after the invasion, Eda Kriseová and I wanted to go to the Minister of Defense, Moshe Dayan, and ask him if he would supply us with some weapons. In those weeks, we thought that there might be some kind of resistance hotspot in our country. That's how it appeared to us from Israel at the time. Well, it was totally nuts, wasn't it. We only got to the Dayan's son in the end. He was a grown man, and he tactfully indicated to us that that was not an option. We sat in his garden for about two hours."

"It was at Castro's that I remembered our trip to Israel. I'm sure he was serious about every Cuban defending every inch of his territory. Latinos are just different than us."

"What else did you discuss?"

"He was very interested in our history. He knew a lot and had very good questions. There was not and is not a politician on the American continent who knows as much about European history as he did. He would say, for example, 'Oh, so in the Austro-Hungarian period you had the Landtag. What about the Moravians?' I said, 'The Moravians too.' 'Oh. What about the Slovaks, they didn't have one? And why not?' We discussed it like that, he enjoyed it and I enjoyed it too. He had excellent, informed questions. He was interested, he had a spotty but surprisingly deep knowledge of history. I said to him, 'Yeah, you know even that, too, you're good...' And he said, 'Well, you know, I'm not an idiot!' He was very vain and boasted of his modesty. It was such a paradox."

"Yet he lived in luxury. He had about two dozen houses. In Havana he lived on a large, inaccessible plot of land where everything was grown separately for him. He had a private island, a yacht..."

"He played coy with me. He sat there in his green uniform without any distinctions, showing me the watch. 'Look, look at my watch...' He said he lived modestly, but I didn't know if that was true. They might not even know properly that they live in a complete bubble."

"I looked at him and was surprised at how much older he looks than in the photos. I wondered to myself if maybe he had forgotten why I was there in the first place. We had been talking for about three hours, and he hadn't mentioned Ivan and Honza at all. We discussed the cooling of our relationship. I told him it was after August 68, and he said no, that it came after Havel, that Havel was responsible."

"He had no use for Havel, did he?"

"Exactly. He didn't like him one bit."

"Because of his past as a dissident? And his criticism of the Cuban regime?"

"And he was also terribly jealous of him. Havel's worldwide popularity. It was very personal, bad chemistry, all wrong. He probably felt that people like Havel were beginning to eclipse him in the world."

"Have these two met together?"

"I don't think so."

"What was next?"

"We discussed our Communist presidents. Gottwald, Zápotocký and others, and he always had a good question. I realized he was still intellectually sharp, but I wasn't sure if he had forgotten the reason I had been there for three hours. I wanted to talk about the arrangement, how to do it with the guys, but before I could get to it, he suddenly says:

Hey, you don't think I'm going to put your guys on the plane now, do you?

Suddenly he was familiar, using the informal 'you'.

'You don't think so, do you? That would be too spectacular!'

I said I certainly don't think so, and in my mind I thought, well, just let them go.

And he says the boys have had enough of their fame and glory, so let them go!"

"Is that what he said?"

"Well, yeah. It was funny and generous, actually."

"When you think of your meetings in Havana, and especially of Castro, what is the first thing that comes to mind after all these years?"

"I always wonder why he let them go after talking to me. I think he was waiting for me to save him. He was just waiting for someone to talk to him with recognition so that he could let them go without losing face. Unfortunately, those who protested with him did not give him that opportunity because they did not understand. I did. I didn't come to teach him a lesson. I was on a diplomatic mission. He was pleased and grateful. I think it was my game. He was happy to let them go. But he had a sense of a certain theatricality, so I told him I wasn't going to put them on the plane indeed.

"I didn't have it easy at home. Here, Václav Klaus [the speaker of parliament] and Miloš Zeman [the prime minister] were all over me in the media."

"And especially Klaus' Civic Democrat MP Jan Zahradil, right?"

"What Zahradil said was disgusting."

At the time when Ivan and Honza were in Villa Marista and it was not at all clear when or if they would get out, Zahradil gave an interview to the daily Právo. In it he said:

"I know Ivan Pilip well. He is a very focused and, to put it politely, very pragmatic person. Knowing him as I do, I can hardly imagine that he would go to Cuba with the sole intention of helping development or human rights there. It just doesn't fit with his personal characteristics."

Zahradil later apologized for his comments. Immediately following Pithart's mission, Klaus said:

"The real result of Senate President Petr Pithart's mission to Cuba is zero. However, it does not seem to have worsened the prospects of the imprisoned Czechs."

Politically, Pithart was in a difficult situation at the time: he could not realistically defend himself. He had to keep quiet.

"When I flew from Havana to London, I got a little drunk. Well, to celebrate. For the first time in my life I drank this Guinness. I had about three. I didn't expect there to be so much media. Even in the tunnel coming off the plane, I could see it was full of cameras and journalists. I knew I couldn't say anything or hint that Castro would let them out because I would have canceled the game."

"Then he wouldn't let them go out of spite, would he?"

"I couldn't say. And then all of a sudden Klaus calls me and says he's sorry."

"For what Zahradil said?"

"Yes."

"That's interesting. I wouldn't have expected that from him. I have never heard him apologize for anything."

"Neither have I. I heard it from him once in my life. I always admit that it must have happened once in my life that he apologized for something. I stood there sleepy and a little drunk at first, but I couldn't tell them that he was going to let them go. I said it would take time and it would work out. I couldn't have known that in less than a day I would get a positive report and that the responsible officials would come to my apartment near the Charles Bridge at two o'clock at night with it. I had not yet recovered from the time delay. At half past one in the morning, I went out on the square in my nightgown, and there was the charge d'affaires, and that was the end of it. Castro had a sense of drama and timing."

Seventy-two hours later, the guys were out. They spent about a month in jail. The drama ended happily, but it didn't have to. The case of American Alan Gross is proof. He was arrested by the Cubans in 2009 while delivering satellite phones to religious activists and imprisoned for espionage. Heavyweights like former President Jimmy Carter and former New Mexico Governor Bill Richardson lobbied Fidel for his release, but to no avail. Gross spent five years in Villa Marista until 2014, when he was exchanged for three Cuban spies imprisoned in the United States.

Never, Never, Never!

None of us were as unlucky as Gross, but several of my friends got into trouble in Cuba. Former Foreign Minister Karel Schwarzenberg, who came to help the dissent, was even pulled out of a hotel shower by the police. He was a senator at the time, but they didn't care. Karel had barely put on his dressing gown and as he was, he was whisked into a car, to the airport, and poof, he was deported.

There are cases of travelers who make mistakes and those who get into trouble by accident. Cuban dictators are unpredictable and pride themselves on their unpredictability. You don't know what you might get arrested for. And then there are those who want to make a name for themselves. One Czech senator behaved in such a way during his mission that, according to a friend of mine who accompanied him on the trip, he explicitly sought to be arrested by the Cubans. He went to local government offices and hospitals and provoked them. He traveled after Ivan and Honza's arrest and probably thought that this was the way to improve his reputation. Fortunately, they didn't give him the satisfaction and left him alone.

The Czech film director Jan Gebert went through some Cuban travails. When I traveled with him on one of my missions, not much happened. On his next trip a few months later, which he dedicated to teaching filmmaking and working with video, Honza had an unwanted adventure. He told me about it later in Prague.

"I went to Cuba with my friend, filmmaker Ondřej Provazník, to conduct a series of workshops for independent video journalists across the country. The basic idea was to show them how to easily tell a story using three types of footage, so that their reports could be broadcast on foreign television and report on the real situation on the island. As soon as we arrived, we were the only ones on the tour who were singled out and interviewed by a man in civilian clothes who wanted to know who we were going to see and what we were going to do in Cuba. He kept asking me why I was in Cuba for the third time and if we had *amistades* in the country."

An unusual word, like from a Spielberg film, but very important for Honza's narrative.

"Somehow that term stuck in my mind. It's a hybrid between 'acquaintance' and 'friend,' a word from a handbook, because I'm not used to hearing it in everyday conversation. It popped up again less than a fortnight later in a similar context as a red warning light."

Despite the initial interrogation at the airport, which may not be unusual, Honza and Ondřej made it to Havana without any problems and checked in downtown.

"The first workshop took place in Havana. Immediately after it was over, we got into a rented car and headed towards the provincial town of Santa Clara, because one of the basic rules of this work is to leave the province within three hours after the end of the lesson and not to return to it during the same journey, if possible. This is done to make coordination between the different branches of the Cuban police and State Security more difficult. The following workshop was scheduled to a wooden shack near a tall housing project on the outskirts of Santa Clara at the home of dissident Yoel Espinosa Medrano. On the way, I told Ondřej about my previous visit to Yoel a few months earlier, which you and I had attended together."

At Yoel's hut we were with Honza at a coordination meeting, where Honza arranged a video workshop. I did a workshop with Yoel and some of his colleagues at the same place, focusing on written journalism and the role of journalism in a free society. Yoel is an oddball, to say the least. He lives in a colony of shacks in the shadow of a huge apartment building. Several of his relatives live in the block of flats. We initially met in their apartment, but later I only saw him in his shack.

"I remember you mentioning to me that Yoel was rumored to be working with the Cuban secret police," Honza tells me.

Such talk is made about various dissidents. Mutual slander is not uncommon among activists. Since such accusations cannot be proven, I proceeded on the basis of the presumption of innocence. At the same time, I realized that, statistically speaking, it is almost certain that some of the many activists I have met in Cuba and elsewhere in the world have productive contacts with State Security.

"I didn't give much weight to these reports at first either. However, Ondřej was clearly impressed. I guess that's why he followed our action with slightly different eyes than I did during the following hours."

They got to Santa Clara and found the green apartment tower.

"Immediately upon arriving at the parking lot near Yoel's cottage colony, we saw two unsympathetic apparitions sweating in the forty-degree heat in a black boxy Lada. They watched us through dewy dark glasses. I think they were there to supervise the main access to the colony. So we parked elsewhere and entered the colony in a roundabout way.

Several dissidents from the region were already sitting in Yoel's shack. I met all of them on our previous trip with you. Actually, it was a positive experience. They were interested, hungry to learn."

"Only Yoel himself was out of his mind somehow. His cell phone kept ringing. Having your own cell phone wasn't exactly common in Cuba back then, it was a bit of a rarity. Yoel only answered it affirmatively every time:

'Sí... sí... claro.'

I found it somewhat disrespectful to our work, but I paid no more attention to it during my lesson. Ondřej told me later that he saw it differently, and he certainly read the situation much more accurately than I did. Yoel, in my opinion, was reporting live, maybe directly to the two slimeballs in the Lada."

Honza took a break and Yoel showed them through the cottage colony.

"He showed us his kingdom with a kind of pride, but perhaps also with some apology, where, he said, he could lead a surprisingly happier life than in the apartment block above us. In the shack he had found his freedom. He had luxurious acquisitions by Cuban standards, a pig and chickens. At the same time, he seemed to be revealing his weakness. It was as if he was telling us what he had to lose, what he could be blackmailed with if he didn't go to the police."

After the workshop, Honza and Ondřej got into the car and drove further east. Santa Clara is relatively close to Havana. They basically followed our previous route through the provinces to the very eastern end of the island in Guantánamo.

"We moved further east on the island and held workshops. Some were attended by just two people, others were well attended. We went to Camagüey, to Guantánamo. There, about twenty people from the video agency Palenquevisión were at our event, organized by the coordinator of Eastern independent journalism, Rolando Lobaina. He was in total control. He was surrounded by young people who listened to him on the word, to the point where I was a little uncomfortable. But in terms of participation, Guantánamo was the highlight of our trip."

I recalled several of my meetings with the organizationally savvy Lobaina in Baracoa and Guantánamo. He was one of the first to understand the importance of video for the dissemination of independent internet news. His outputs were not as high quality as those produced by Claudio Fuentes in Havana, but that's what Honza and Ondřej were there to help his team from Palenquevisión. Rolando rode to our first meeting near the Malecón in Baracoa on a brand-new mountain bike that must have cost around a thousand dollars. This both intrigued and a bit puzzled me. I had never seen anything like this luxury in an independent Cuban activist. Honza continues his story.

"Then we decided to take a few days off. We drove along the coast to the Sierra Maestra, the highest mountain range in Cuba, from where *the barbudos* started their revolution. We disappeared from the signal for two days. We climbed the tallest mountain, Pico Turquino, and then descended again to the coast. Then we got back in the car and drove in one go back to Havana, back to the province where we had already had one workshop, which we suspected was a risk."

Honza foresaw that after the Santa Clara experience there might be troubles. However, the rest of the tour was without them, so the gloom was not the main thing on his mind after returning to the metropolis.

"That evening, we decided to visit what was probably the only free-spirited hipster club in Havana at the time. It was in a former theater in Vedado, not far from the guesthouse where we were staying. We wanted to have a few drinks and get a taste of the independent cultural scene. From our previous experience, we knew that the only women who started conversations with us were prostitutes. We definitely didn't want to talk to them. There probably wouldn't have been anything to talk about. That's why I was surprised when I was approached by an intelligent-looking girl at the bar around one in the morning. She invited us both to her table where two of her 'cousins' were sitting with her. How to describe them? They were two hardened, extremely serious looking guys. They were a handful in the club. They looked really out of place with their very conservative clothes. The girl got straight to the point: what are we doing here and why am I in Cuba for the third time?"

"How could she know? You told her? You did not!"

"Exactly. Of course I didn't. I ask her how she knows I'm here for the third time. I had a couple of drinks in me at the time, and we were pretty tired after the trip, but her question had the same effect on me as if she'd punched me out of the blue. It was like she slapped me. She totally woke me up. She was like, 'Well, your friend here told me.' I guess she was under the impression that Ondřej couldn't hear the conversation and didn't understand Spanish. But Ondřej heard and understood and kicked me under the table saying, 'Honza, I didn't really say anything like that to her!'"

I try to imagine the scene and put myself in his shoes. I say to Honza: "Maybe she said it on purpose. Undercover cops are no idiots. Maybe she wanted to intimidate you, put you on the defensive?"

"Suddenly it was obvious that she was not a prostitute, but neither was she an ordinary girl who came to talk to tourists. She keeps asking us questions, and the red-light bulb goes off in my head. 'And what kind of *amistades* do you have here in Cuba, she says? Where have you been everywhere?'"

"Hm, not exactly normal conversation for being in a club and it was after one in the morning."

"Then she switched to politics. 'What do you think of the Cuban revolution?' I answer very carefully. I said something like, 'Every major event has its positives and negatives. And she said, 'And in the case of the Cuban Revolution, do the positives or the negatives prevail?' I simply said something evasive and vague. And she kept pushing: 'So you think the Cuban Revolution brought about more bad things, then?'"

I remembered a university classmate in the second half of the 1980s, whom everyone thought was a snitch for the Czechoslovak State Security (StB). I just didn't believe it because his methods were naive. At that time, a rumour spread around Prague that the Communist journalist Julius Fučík had not died in World War Two but was living in South America. One day I am on a tram and this classmate enters on the Smetana Embankment, sees me, immediately comes up, and without saying hello, goes to the point: 'What about this Fučík? Do you think he's really there?' In my head I think to myself that he's definitely not an StB snitch. If he did, he wouldn't do it so idiotically. The StB has to train its spies well! After 1989, we got acquainted with our files and lists of StB collaborators. And he was on the lists! He was an informer for the State Security.

Honza continues his story from Havana Vedado:

"When she didn't get a clear answer, she pulled her last trump card. She began to stretch herself, saying that 'there's nothing more beautiful than a sunrise on the beach and we can do whatever we want with her there'."

"Wow. How about that?"

"We got up and disappeared."

Of course. The last thing Honza and Ondřej needed was a false rape accusation.

"We were not far from the guesthouse. We got there and I had this suffocating feeling. I thought to myself, are we worth the secret police putting this sleazy operation on us in the middle of the night that could have been aimed at discrediting us? In the room, we immediately started deleting all photos and videos of the workshops. Then we looked out the window. On an otherwise quiet side street in the middle of the night, there were two men standing by a tree, another sitting in a parked car, and another crossing the street back and forth."

"Not exactly an ideal situation. It's like a B-movie thriller."

"We were expecting a knock on our door any minute," says Honza. "It didn't happen. So in the morning we went downtown and called our coordinator in Prague from a pay phone. She told us that we should end the mission immediately and cancel the next workshops. We agreed and promised that we would indeed end the tour."

"Really?"

"At the time we thought so. We thought we would spend the rest of our stay on the beach. But on the way back to the *casa* we changed our minds. We decided to stick to the plan we came for."

"What else was waiting for you?"

"A workshop in Pinar del Río, and then another one in Havana. So we went west to the dissident Dagoberto Valdés and organized two more. We left the most problematic one, with the Havana dissident Robertico, for the very end. We visited his apartment in Habana Centro at 1:30 a.m. and left in the morning. Although we had only a flight to catch, we also knew that if there was to be a moment of reckoning, all they had to do was wait for us there."

I imagine their night workshop in Robertico's dark apartment in an inhospitable part of Havana's downtown, and picture Honza and Ondřej huddled on the small elevated ground floor, where they have to keep bending down to avoid hitting their heads on the ceiling, while at the same time expecting at any moment a pounding on the door and shouts of "Security! Open up!" It must have been a quality experience. But surprisingly, nothing happened. Then it was time to leave.

"During check-in at the airport, we noticed that the man who interviewed us on arrival was standing nearby. He was soon joined by two other civilians, one older, one younger, both definitely undercover cops. As we walked past them to customs after checking our luggage, they stopped us and asked for our passports without explanation. We walked through the departure hall among the tanned German tourists, turned into a sort of corridor and found ourselves in a deserted arrivals hall. Two undercover cops led me into a miniature room and sat me down at a table. The older of the pair introduced himself as Major Ivan. I've forgotten his last name. At first he spoke calmly and asked questions again according to the standard muster. Why are we in Cuba for the third time? What are the *amistades* here? When he didn't get the answers he wanted, he banged his fist on the table:

'Since you entered Cuban territory, we know what you've been doing here! You are supporting subversive elements, and that is a crime against the Cuban revolution. The plane waiting for you will leave and you will return with us to Havana. And you may never see home again. So think carefully about what you say to me. Do you have any *amistades* here in Cuba?"

While the police apparently did not know much about some of the workshops, they had absolutely detailed information about others. He knew about the workshop at Yoel's in Santa Clara, who attended the workshop, when it took place, and even what was said during the workshop."

"So Yoel was really reporting?"

"It is possible. Someone must have. They were also quite accurate about the progress of the last workshop at Robertico's. Moreover, they obviously monitored our conversation with the coordinator in Prague, because they knew that we wanted to interrupt the mission, but in the end we didn't. Their anger was probably all the greater.

For half an hour I used our somewhat funny cover story about contacts from the Prague bar La Casa Blú in the Old Town and denied everything over and over again. Then I was escorted out, followed by an interrogation of Ondřej. Major Ivan's roar could be heard even through the closed door. After an hour they gave us back our passports and told us that we would never see Cuba again - nunca, nunca, nunca - the younger policeman repeated with gleeful hatred.

Honza got a kind of entry in his papers, something like persona non grata, and he hasn't been back to Cuba since.

"The story does not end there. A few minutes before I left, an announcement was made all over the airport with my name on it, telling me to go back to customs.

This has happened to us before. The last time Honza flew with me from Cuba, we were waiting in the airport lounge. Suddenly, the announcer asked him to come to security. Honza went. He went through a relatively harmless interrogation. His luggage was searched. They found a comic book about Fidel's revolution in the Sierra Maestra. I remember teasing him about buying it. The policeman asked him what the book was, why he bought it, what he needed it for - I was surprised he didn't confiscate it. And it was pure regime propaganda in pictures! After he came back and told me about his experience, I told him with friendly irony:

"See, that's what you get for your revolutionary fervor. Good for you."

But Honza did not make the same mistake the second time. He ignored the announcements in the airport lounge.

"It was clear that if I went to the checkpoint, my plane would indeed fly away. On Onřej's advice, I decided to ignore the invitation and not go. We stood in line for the plane and were in it within a few minutes. And flew back home."

Honza and Ondřej were lucky. They could have easily ended up like Ivan Pilip and Honza Bubeník. Or even worse. The case of the American Alan Gross still wakes up those of us who travel to Cuba from time to time. The Cuban State Security prides itself on doing whatever it wants. You can console yourself a hundred times: They can arrest you, they have

212 Cuba: A Brief History of the End

to let you go, but that's the Prague pub wisdom. When you are sitting in a small room facing Major Ivan, who is pounding his fist on the hideous metal table and yelling at you that you too may never see home again, you are not in the best of circumstances.

Something similar happened to a friend of mine later. She got arrested, too. Like Honza, she was surprised how much they knew. They went into great detail. They laid out the photos on her table - with icy calm, as if they were cards, and the comrade decided to take a long moment to lay out the solitaire. *"This one was here a month ago, doing this and this.* They knew everything," she told me. "They knew how to encrypt documents on the phone. They're no amateurs. They interrogated me for two days and then deported me."

Honza Gebert seems to be a magnet to Cuban drama. We had one together. It took place, of course, before his airport interrogation, which marked a stop for his further Cuban plans.

The Raid at Martha's

Honza and I walk down Havana's Belascoáin Avenue, which slopes down to the bay. We walk slowly, looking around at the tired facades. I was here a few days ago, just before December tenth, Human Rights Day. In front of the entrance, where the famous dissident Martha Beatriz Roque Cabello lives, were several athletic undercover agents and two uniformed policewomen. We were signaled not to enter, and then Martha was indeed taken away and interrogated for several hours.

It was far from the first time I had heard her name in connection with the jail cell. At a bar in Miami Beach, Martin Palouš, the former Czech ambassador to the United States, introduced me to some Cuban exile activists. The conversation turned to Martha Roque. Those present instinctively lowered their voices and expressed their concerns.

"She's been imprisoned again."

"They took her."

"Martha is on hunger strike."

"How is her health?"

On the sidelines of a conference in Florida, former U.S. Secretary of State Madeleine Albright expressed similar concerns.

"Martha has been locked up again," said Madeleine in Czech. "Terrible."

But now I have information that Martha is home.

As we approach entrance 409, we keep a close eye on the sidewalk near it. It looks normal. Honza calls the agreed number and a few minutes later Martha unlocks the door. A slim little woman in her seventies, her gray hair pulled back in a ponytail. The building is neat and clean. We walk up the stone stairs. Martha walks in front of us, one foot slightly forward. She points in front of her.

"This is where I was beaten. Two uniformed women dragged me by my hair up these stairs," she says. "I couldn't move for three days. I'm diabetic, and they didn't give me a drink. Not even water, juice, nothing. That was on November 19. And then the same thing happened on November 27. They surrounded our house and legitimized everyone."

Upstairs, we sit in the kitchenette. Martha suggests that her apartment may be bugged. Sensitive information and organizational matters are to be written on paper. She says that the State Security are inciting the neighbors against her.

"They cooperate with them."

She's got a hard look on her face. I've never seen her smile.

"I had a serious incident with a neighbor. I was repairing the electrical wiring in the kitchen and apparently I was making noise. And he physically attacked me. He hurt my arm."

She doesn't look like she's just gonna let anyone terrorize her. Must have been a regular fight. She wore her hand on the belt she's showing me now. The police were called on her.

"They took my camera. Later the police returned it to me damaged, without the photos they had deleted."

She's bringing in a police confiscation document. In addition, she has a long-standing dispute with the authorities over the apartment and is afraid they will try to evict her. But now it looks like the dispute will be settled and Martha will be able to stay here in downtown Havana.

"I met people from the Interior Ministry in a park not far from here. A general assured me that everything would be sorted out. He said he had issued an order to proceed in my favour in the matter of the flat."

Martha is under frequent police surveillance. The regime tries to get rid of her through persistent persecution and offers of emigration. In vain. The hammer and sickle hit the boulder. Sparks fly. But it fails to roll it off the property. They always wait for Wednesdays when Marta meets with her colleagues.

"The police keep disrupting our meetings. On top of that, I was recently detained on my way to Santa Clara. They pulled me out of the car and sent me back to Havana."

She tells how, with the help of mobile phones, she created an ingenious network of postmodern tamtams. She sends news via viral text messages. The system has three levels of distribution. She was forced to suspend it a few months ago due to lack of funding but managed to raise more money and get the system back up and running. She calls it *red de redes,* or network of networks. Work is also continuing on new issues of the two journals she manages. The news bulletin *Redecilla* has a circulation of 475 copies and the revue *Comunidad* is published once every three months with a circulation of 200 copies. It is always monothematic.

From the balcony she shows us the half-decayed buildings around.

"The next issue of *Comunidad* will be about the culture of destruction."

"Destruction?"

"Yes, destruction. Look around you, what Havana looks like. In 1959, there were 176 theatres and cinemas. Today there are less than 50."

Martha is an economist by training. In the 1990s she became a member of the famous Group of Four together with Vladimiro Roca, Felix Bonne and René Gómez Manzano. She was co-author of the manifesto *"Fatherland Belongs to All,"* seeking civil liberties and the international isolation of the regime. They called on foreign companies not to invest in Cuba as long as the regime violates human rights. She went to prison for her efforts. From there, she managed to smuggle out a treatise, written on toilet paper, about the harsh conditions and political indoctrination in the prison. In 2003, she was one of 75 dissidents imprisoned during the Black Spring. She was given 20 years hard labour. Her sister, Isabel, met with President George W. Bush in Washington about it.

In prison, Martha became very ill. She lost 14 pounds. Remarkably, advanced socialist health care somehow doesn't apply to political prisoners. Concerned about international embarrassment, she was released in early 2004, and the following year she founded and led the Assembly for Civil Society. She organized a public meeting that President Bush supported from afar. The authorities did not intervene, but they did prevent some of the foreign visitors Martha had invited from attending. Senator Karel Schwarzenberg came to Havana at that time and, as we know, the police picked him up at the hotel.

Some observers feel that Marta bangs her head against the wall too much. Her uncompromising nature has brought her into conflict with other dissidents. Oswaldo Payá Sardiñas, founder of the Christian Liberation Movement and author of the national petition Project Varela, criticized her for creating the Assembly, saying it only further divided the forces of opposition. He did not like the fact that she was working with the exiles in Miami, the so-called hardliners. In his view, this gave the regime a pretext for harsh repression. Disputes between Roque and Payá are not uncommon in Cuban dissent. Their different views on how to proceed against the regime may have stemmed from their different natures, as in the case of the disputes between Dagoberto Valdés and Antonio Rodiles. Martha is very stubborn, Oswaldo was a deliberate tactician and Catholic activist who always tried first to find consensus on the lowest common denominator. I met him in Prague at the beginning of the millennium when he was visiting and President Havel gave a dinner in his honor in an old restaurant near Prague Castle. An emotional Oswaldo spoke softly, almost as if to apologize for bothering us with his problems.

By the time we visited Martha, Oswaldo was already dead. He died under mysterious circumstances in a car accident in Bayamo in the summer of 2012. No one I spoke to in the dissent doubted that his car was forced off the road by the police, deliberately causing his death and that of his dissident colleague Harold Cepero. Eleven years later, in the summer of 2023, the Inter-American Commission on Human Rights concluded that the Cuban government was responsible for the deaths of Payá and Cepero. A month before their deaths, I visited Cuba for the first time. I drove around the island in a blue Hyundai Accent and also visited Bayamo, where foxes would say goodnight if there were any. The day of Oswaldo's accident, I was back in Prague. When I saw the photo of Oswaldo's wrecked blue Hyundai in the news agencies, I was breathless. Could it be that he had died in the same car in which I had driven through Cuba only a short time earlier? The same type of car, the same color, the same brown tourist license plate, beginning with the letter T. I search frantically among the photos I have taken to see if they show "my" car. It wasn't the same car. It was just from the same rental company and the same series that the company had purchased.

The animosity between Oswaldo and Martha spilled over into the relationship between Martha and Oswaldo's daughter. Rosa María Payá Acevedo went into exile in the United States, where she speaks for the organization founded by her father. Martha Roque accused Rosa María of using her father's memory for her own enrichment, practicing resistance to the regime from a safe distance, protected by the laws and institutions of a democratic society.

Cuban dissidents deserve admiration for their courage in the face of brutal repression, but to portray them as pure souls would be naive. They are only human. Some accuse others of wasting resources intended for activism. Lilia Castañer is no longer a member of the Ladies in White because of disputes with the organization's leader, Berta Soler. Along with six other Damas de blanco founders, she accused Soler of embezzling funds and behaving in a dictatorial manner. Lilia also accused Cuesta Morúa of embezzling funds. Some dissidents play a double game and collaborate with the police. I have heard so many times about a very well-known dissident who collaborates with the regime that it is probably not just a fabrication.

In Jamaica, I spoke with a Cuban woman who worked with a prominent dissident. She described to me his dictatorial behavior toward his collaborators, how he misused the money he received from abroad to fight the regime, how he bought houses and kept mistresses in them. According to her, she had a good working relationship with him until she refused to sleep with him. Then the harassment began. She claimed that this was the main reason why she left his organization and joined a feminist association. She made similar comments about another internationally known dissident who also allegedly embezzled funds intended for civic activities. Two things occurred to me as she spoke. If this is true and the current regime is replaced by one of these people, there will be no real freedom in Cuba. In that case, one kind of corrupt government would replace another.

But such allegations cannot be verified now. Are they true? Or is "my Jamaican activist" a regime provocateur spreading rumors? Or is she not working for the regime, but falsely denigrating her former associates for some other reason? Perhaps she is a repentant former girlfriend, or is she just doing it out of simple jealousy? As the independent journalist Juan Miguel Capote told us in Holguín, there is plenty of human misery to be found even among dissidents. Of course, none of this excuses the criminal government that has decimated Cuba for more than sixty years. But perhaps it explains why dissent has been so ineffective for so long.

Martha tells us about another project she has taken on that keeps her busy. It's the case of the people of the Havana suburb of Guanabacoa, whose houses the authorities want to demolish. A recurring story in this country. Out of desperation, people build houses in the open because they have nowhere to live and the authorities do not issue building permits. Then they are blackmailed, at their mercy. Martha tries to help.

"They want to intimidate us. They keep disrupting our meetings. They want to shut down our magazine *Redecilla*. They don't like our text news network. They know it works. People come to us with information to spread it, and we have collaborators everywhere, even in the East. We have 20 people in Manzanillo in Granma province. We are in touch through Twitter and texting."

She takes a pencil and writes on a piece of paper on the kitchen table how we should contact her in the future. Again, she suggests an indirect way - we should call a friend's phone number. We look through some back issues of *Comunidad*. A middle-aged woman enters the apartment. She has a wrinkled forehead and gestures towards us from the door. Martha introduces her as a co-worker from Palma Soriano.

"The police are surrounding the house," the woman whispers.

For a few seconds, I can feel my pulse quicken in my temples. Honza and I look at each other and then at Martha. She registers our frightened glances with calm and a little amusement.

"It's better if you go," she finally says. She points to her colleague.

"She'll unlock the main entrance for you. Downstairs, do as if nothing."

We run down the stairs to the lobby. Do I have anything compromising on me? Did I forget to encrypt sensitive information on my phone? The woman in front of us is unlocking the entrance. Chaos is brewing outside. There's a lot of people here. I take a decisive step out onto the sidewalk, Honza follows me. The woman locks the door behind us; I hear the click of the lock. Behind the cluster of civilians in front of me, I see two sparse cordons. The first consists of plainclothes police, or so I guess. Behind them, uniformed men stand at intervals. There are several women among them. I head towards the black female officer, avoiding eye contact, looking over and behind the cops, helped by the fact that they are all a head shorter. I pass between the black woman and her colleague. Every moment I expect her to stop and speak to me. Somehow, miraculously, that doesn't happen. Not bothered by anyone, we continue walking down the sidewalk, turning right around the building and speeding up. It's only after a while that we realise that it's not smart to go to the overpriced basement apartment on the Malecón now, where we're staying with a Swede, an over-aged hippie who invests here. We turn to the Prado and disappear into the alleys of Old Havana. We've escaped trouble for now.

Several years have passed since the hot days of the visit to Martha Roque. Fidel died, Raúl withdrew. Obama restored diplomatic relations. Díaz-Canel took over. Before my last trip, I tried to persuade Honza to try and fly with me. It's been a long time! They may have a mess in their records. I could see him thinking about it, how tempted he was. In the end, he didn't take up the offer and didn't test the validity of the ban, that *nunca, nunca, nunca*. Instead, I traveled with Jimena.

8.

Bay of Pigs.

Playa Girón

Twilight quickly dissolves the shadows of Camagüey. The historic centre lies opposite the baseball stadium across the St Peter's River, which skirts the rest of the city walls. One summer I saw children splashing around in it. The boys were jumping off boulders into the water, and I shuddered at the thought of the sewage and industrial waste that flavors the Río San Pedro.

Camagüey was originally an Indian village. The town that grew into its splendour was founded by the Spanish in the early sixteenth century further north, closer to the sea, as Puerto Príncipe. They soon moved inland here because of corsair raids. The city has a distinctive character unlike any other historic settlement on the island. The center is made up of buildings from the 17th and 18th centuries. The most famous, unofficial logo of the metropolis is the Iglesia de Nuestra Señora de la Soledad, the Church of Our Lady of Solitude. The simple white building is easily recognisable by its distinctive window trim and corners. Ten years ago, the trim was brownish red, but during the renovation it was painted over with ochre, giving the church and the small square in front of it a fresher look. Here they baptised their most famous native, General Ignacio Agramonte, leader of the uprising against colonial rule and co-author of the 1869 constitution. The square tower in the corner of the church, with three unequal floors, has become a symbol of the town.

Several other churches, classic Hispanic villas, inhabited colonial buildings and a labyrinth of ancient streets paved with polished cobble stones add to the character of the historic center. Proud, low Spanish houses smile at the streets from both sides. Through the open barred windows, one can see lit apartments, neat, with quiet, contented-looking people watching television. The city is relatively well-preserved, at least compared to Havana, but that's true of all Cuban provincial towns and cities.

This is the second time Jimena and I have been here in a few days. The first time we drove towards Santiago, where we visited Castro's grave and then his birthplace in Birán. We drove through the resort town of Guardalavaca to Holguín, where we sat with Juan Miguel on the top of Loma de la Cruz, and from there we headed back to Camagüey. I parked in the bowels of the old town in a paid parking lot a few steps from the Soledad church and found accommodation in one of those one-storey colonial houses with high ceilings. Our *apartmento* La Isabella is names after the lady of the house.

Mrs. Isabella is upper middle-aged, has long black hair that has not yet been dyed, an intelligent smile and does not worry unnecessarily about anything. She only asks for twenty dollars for accommodation. After she opens the large white front grill, we find that, like many other houses in this style, hers has a large hall just inside the entrance that also serves as a living room. The hall, as usual, flows seamlessly into the dining room. On the walls hang framed photographs of Mrs. Isabella from some thirty years ago, as well as a photograph of her daughter in an orange wedding dress. The two women resemble each other in such a way that the photo of daughter looks like a more technically perfect copy of her mother. The photos are set in ornamental copper frames, inspired by vegetation, consisting of a tangle of twigs and leaves that mischievously distract from the framed work.

"Frío!" complains Mrs. Isabella. She is cold. The temperature outside has dropped to a frigid eighteen above zero.

Shortly before we checked in, as soon as we found the parking lot under the church, we walked around town. We went looking for a restaurant. To my amazement, I found only two open, both obviously state-owned. Not the Camagüey I remembered from past stays, where there was no shortage of private *paladares.* I have noticed bored waiters in the state-run restaurants. On the tables were menus bound in leather folders. It reminded me of our former Communist establishments - a strange feeling, the subtle smell of *something* and a *Book of Wishes and Complaints* displayed on the table. This strange institution has been forgotten in our country, but here it brazenly prolonged its unwanted existence.

I give up trying to eat here. Instead, I get a Mahou Madrid lager from a nearby stand. Across the little square, I watch the illuminated back of the church, which is unfortunately closed, and listen to the incredibly loud reggaeton provided by the bartender from his phone via Spotify. Over a second beer, I take this genre in my stride. It can be listened to at these exact moments. Hundreds of kilometres echo in the back of your neck, you have two cans of beer on an empty stomach and stare into the void. Literally. It may be Saturday night, but the historic centre is unusually devoid of people. Tourists are few, locals don't want to go out.

"Frío!"

We don't find a paladar the next day either. Years ago I stayed just outside Parque Ignacio Agramonte, where it was alive. The excess noise from the dance clubs that no longer fit inside spilled out into the alleys, and the square pulsated late into the night with the activity of local and foreign youth. I arrived late that night from the east. I was followed by a relentless hustler on a bicycle who tried to force a casa on me. Around the bars and discos, you could take pictures right out of a sci-fi series. Outside one club was a bouncer with a red star badge on his jacket. There were soldiers and policemen with automatic weapons, dogs running around, prostitutes and homosexual prostitutes on display. The Cambio Bar, named after the currency exchange, was as crowded as the Blue Light Bar on Prague's Mala Strana. From my casa, looked after by an old lady, I remember the crosses on the walls and the smell of stone mustiness. There was a condom in the drawer of the bedside table next to the Bible. The lady was realistic. She knew what tourists came here for and she tried to help.

The image of the Bible with the condom, this postmodern still life, comes to mind as I finish my can of Madrid beer and walk slowly home. I ask Mrs. Isabella for a plate and cutlery so that I don't eat the canned tuna, pea chips, and protein bar like a barbarian. Without asking, she makes us coffee, even with real milk, and asks for nothing in return. Her hospitality culminates in a remark to Jimena:

"Leave the dirty dishes on the table in the atrium, I'll clean them up later."

Jimena relaxes in the rocking chair, looking contented. Unlike the other Cuban ladies, Isabella doesn't seem to look at her strangely. Maybe she senses that our bizarre landing party is not a romantic couple, maybe she doesn't care, or maybe she's just putting on a good front. In any case, her attitude is different from the experience we had with Yosvany on Ánimas Street and his platoon of stove-lined guards.

The morning heat returns, twenty-eight in the shade. A brisk breeze blows in from the distant coast, cooling the stone streets and houses. We walk past half-empty bakeries and grocery stores, or more accurately, no-grocery stores. Jimena still hasn't gotten used to the poorly stocked shops and every now and then she points out to me that they don't have this here and that there. We walk through a small square, on one side wall of which I see nice graffiti; portraits of historical figures in shades of black and white stare back at us. There is Martí and Agramonte, Maceo and Bolívar. Seeing the wall free of Bolsheviks puts me in a better mood, and I immediately find Camagüey a little more sympathetic, despite the lack of *paladares*. In Agramonte Square, the Cuban flag flies cheerfully by the equestrian statue of the general to whose legacy the space is dedicated. He died in battle at the age of thirty-one, like Martí and other great figures of the wars of independence. Their young lives are the opposite of the fidelist gerontocracy, whose fate only Che Guevara escaped.

A tree and Christmas decorations are prepared at the Nuestra Señora de la Candelaria Cathedral. In the Latin American world, Catholic churches, cathedrals and basilicas have dynamic names, as if one hears a bell being vigorously rung, and Candelaria (or Groundhog Day) is no exception. This name is one of the many synonyms for the Virgin Mary, for whom it is a common epithet in the region. Advent cleaning is in full swing here, with two younger women, both in tight yoga pants, in charge. Leaning against the last bench is a young black man with a meticulous haircut that I file away in my memory as a curly pineapple. He is wearing smart grey trousers, a white shirt with a blue collar, and two silver bracelets dangle from the wrist of his right hand. In his left palm, he carefully clutches a smart phone, his attention so fully focused on it that he doesn't notice anything around him, not even that he's in the Lord's Tabernacle during Advent, or that he might be helping the women clean up, let alone that I'm taking a close-up picture of him.

A few hundred metres further on, we lose ourselves for a while in a more conventional twentieth-century development and turn around at the birthplace of the poet Nicolás Guillén. It's a single-storey stone building with pale yellow plaster and a chamfered corner entrance with an ornamental grille. A black plaque with the artist's bust hangs next to the door. A banner with Guillén's photo and a quote from a political event we see a few minutes later on the local library building in the pedestrian zone between Agramonte Square and the Soledad Church. Guillén is the author of the famous fidelist slogan Homeland or Death! (*¡Patria o muerte!*), which the regime adopted into its thesaurus in the 1960s. He published the poem of the same name in the second year after the 1959 coup. At the end of the poem we read:

Homeland is humanity, we cry out all the time,
we all shout together, old and young,
and the air, the sea, the earth and the sky answer the call,
and men's faces will be filled with light.

Homeland is humanity, let's shout in unison,
and raise a fist and shout loudly:
Homeland or death! Homeland or death! Homeland or death!

Guillén was a journalist, political activist, and writer. From the 1920s, his poetry dealt with racial and social inequality and the rights of black Cubans, and he became an important figure in the Afro-Cuban literary movement. He joined the Communist Party in the 1930s and remained a member until his death. It came for him in the symbolic year of 1989. For his loyalty, the regime gave him privileges, attention and medals, including the Cuban National Prize for Literature and the International Lenin Peace Prize. Progressives celebrate him as a fighter for black identity, but for me, a child of communism, it is hard to take seriously slogans like "the homeland is humanity" from the servants of a dictatorship that enslaved and sent the wrong kind of humanity to concentration camps. When Guillén writes of the faces of men filled with light, I think of the ragged features of political prisoners in uranium mines, for whom the only "light" was the radioactivity that slowly but surely killed them. After the collapse of the Communist bloc, Castro and his regime were in a quandary, and Guillén's slogan was modified to reflect the new conditions: Socialism or Death! Between the two, I would have recommended the latter.

At Café Ciudad in Parque Agramonte, Jimena and I order coffee and juice. It's a large room with a high black wooden ceiling and two large French doors. It's elegantly and simply decorated. The decor consists of historical photographs of Agramonte's plaza, showing that a hundred years ago this was a drugstore and a pharmacy. I ask a young waiter in a well-fitting white shirt and pointed soft leather shoes if he would change our dollars. He lowers his voice and leads me to the back, where his colleague is standing at the counter.

"How much?"

I ask about the exchange rate, and he asks me, somewhat suspiciously, what do I suggest. I try 165 pesos to the dollar. The waiter nods and goes to the backyard to get change. I change a hundred. Back in the café, the morning is quiet. An older woman in a flowered dress keeps checking her smartphone. A girl with red hair keeps watching me. Black lacquered wood furniture, white walls and vintage photographs create a welcoming atmosphere. It's a government-run but pleasant place, with helpful staff, good coffee and honest fruit juice. The only place you know where you are is in the bathroom. There's no toilet paper, the stench is unbelievable and the water doesn't run.

Half an hour later we say goodbye to Isabella in the apartment and take her recommendations for accommodation in Santiago and Trinidad. When we arrive at the car, we find it washed and polished. For a reward of a hundred pesos and a compliment, a tall black man in overalls comes and asks if I need gas. You betchya! He gets on an old rusty bicycle and tells me to follow him. It's just a short ride, he says. It turns out to be a trip through half the city with relatively heavy traffic. The man in front of me is pedaling for his life, inhaling leaded gasoline fumes from cars without catalytic converters. He's sweating profusely in the late morning heat, the bike creaking and groaning, the chain straining. On a crumbling wreck without a derailleur, he stomps the pedals with a frequency I wouldn't expect.

On the outskirts of the metropolis we come to a gas station. A white Hyundai Tucson is parked there, and a guy in designer jeans is pumping gas. But when I want to buy 25 liters of gas, the attendant dryly tells us that there is no gas! I point at the Hyundai driving away, but the attendant ignores my questions. The black man on the bicycle smiles apologetically. This reminds me of another night trip to Camagüey from the east. Someone told me that in Jímbambay, a smaller town in the province, they were guaranteed to have gas. And they did. When I arrived there at night, two young men in thick sweatshirts and woolly hats were sitting on the curb nodding. There's gas, but not for me, just for the government officials. My attempts to bribe them were in vain, the guys were obviously under the cameras and didn't want any trouble. I had to find another station, just like now. The black cyclist asks me to follow him. He says it's only a short distance.

Who was that man in Tucson? High-ranking Communist? Prominent athlete? Or just a guy who knows his stuff?

Black Pogačar in overalls finally finds a working pump and collects his reward. We're on our way to Trinidad. In Ciego de Ávila I spot an ATM on a busy street. It occurred to me to see if it would give me a peso from my Prague account. I stop behind a mobile kiosk from which a small man is selling suspicious-looking sandwiches to schoolchildren. I get in line, enter my PIN and select the amount I need. The tired screen displays a barely legible message in English: "Your transaction has been declined." Aha, so it didn't work, I think, and I'm about to turn around and walk away, but then a familiar growl comes from the ATM and the amount I entered comes out! I ponder the existential significance of this evasive banking maneuver for a long time.

Back to the main road. *¡Bienvenido de nuevo a Carretera Central!* Terrible smell. Bicycles, motorbikes, chariots, dogs, all dusty, moskviches and zhigulis, and trucks half-hidden in clouds of greasy smoke. People in the middle of a four-lane road. A mother crosses it unperturbed in full traffic, holding the hand of a five-year-old boy in short pants, with big brown eyes and a blue pacifier in his mouth. This is where Oriente begins and ends. After leaving the city, we are surrounded by a landscape of tropical winter, royal palm trees and dried grass. Along the way it showers occasionally, but only lightly, no summer downpour.

I'm turning on the car radio, this time the Radio Rebelde station, but the content must be done in one newsroom, because Fidel's incredible pieces are on for a change. An expert on hurricanes and rebuilding devastated areas is gushing. "We were taught rescue work by Fidel himself! He's the one who gave us advice on how to handle natural disasters." Jimena doesn't know whether to laugh or cry. She notes that it was definitely Fidel who invented gasoline, he just forgot to figure out the supply. Then Radio Reloj again. Ticking as a soundtrack really isn't a good idea. The news is dominated by President Díaz-Canel and his video meeting with Russian official Ushakov. I wonder if he got anything out of it? Then I'm delighted to learn that Democrat Raphael Warnock won the runoff election for the Senate in the state of Georgia over the extremely obtuse Trumpist Herschel Walker, and Democrats will have a narrow majority in the U.S. Senate for the next two years. We're talking about Díaz-Canel, and he's here, or rather on the billboard we pass, whose hilariously ridiculous slogan he proclaims:

They wanted to kill us, but we're still alive!

The president's smile belongs to the artificial and slimy category, which Jimena noticed a few days ago:

"I wouldn't want to be alone in an elevator with him."

Nearby, more revolutionary slogans for the 61st Congress of Campesinos en Armas, which promises vigilance and militancy to passing motorists. We take the road to Sancti Spíritus and Trinidad. Further south the vegetation changes. The artesian wells, which give the impression of the Wild West in the arid landscape, disappear and the greenery increases. The landscape slowly undulates into the Escambray Mountains, famous for being the retreat of resistance fighters after Castro's coup. Independent journalist Robeisy Zapata Blanco, whom I visited in Santa Clara, showed me a video report on Idalberto González Gómez, a former rebel who fought against Fidel in the mountains.

Chapter 8

"He goes around Escambray looking for the graves of his fallen comrades. He's discovered several mass graves of anti-Castro guerrillas. As a young man, Idalberto acted as a liaison between the guerrillas and the villages in the area. He brought them food and intelligence. He was never captured. Now, decades later, he spoke for the first time in my report," Robeisy boasted, his eyes glistening with emotion and pride. I sat with him in an empty concrete house and organized workshops in Yoel's wooden hut.

In Prague, I looked up Idalberto's profile on the Memory of the Nation website. It says, somewhat contradicting what Robeisy told me, that he was captured in 1960 while working as a liaison in Escambray.

"After his release, he tried to join the Bay of Pigs invasion. But he did not. Shortly thereafter, he was interned in the forced labor camps known by the acronym UMAP. For the rest of his life, he struggled to find work. As a man whose views were known everywhere, he finally decided to dedicate his life to the peaceful struggle for freedom and democracy in Cuba. He participated in many dissident organizations, contributed to the spread of democratic awareness and, together with Tomás González-Coya, led the Operación Rescate project, which sought to identify the bodies of soldiers killed in the fight against Fidel Castro's government and buried in unmarked graves," reads Idalberto's profile on the Memory of the Nation website.

As in the Sierra Maestra, you will see many shades of green in the Sierra del Escambray. At the foot of the mountains, palm trees of all sizes and tropical deciduous trees of fabulous shapes grow, gleaming in the dazzling sunlight. I step on the gas. Emerald and golden blurs pass around the valley's winding road. Poor villages huddle on the edges. The road is empty now, with a few exceptions, and I occasionally pass old cars with sometimes ten people crammed into them. Rickshaw drivers, wearing Lionel Messi and Cristiano Ronaldo jerseys, drive through the villages, pedalling uphill, huffing and puffing, pulling yellow cages recently imported from China. I also spot a few Polish Fiats that look like matchboxes, and it occurs to me that I haven't seen a single Škoda, the proud Czech car, here this year.

Maura the Witch

Accommodation in the centre of Trinidad. We find the recommended corner house a few streets from the Plaza Mayor, the main square with the neo-classical facade of the Holy Trinity Church, after which the city takes its name. Driving slowly up the large cobble stones, you can tell there are a few more visitors here than in Camagüey. Trinidad is one of the most important destinations for the local tourist industry. The inner city has an intact historic character and is not far from beaches that, while not as famous as those up north, are certainly nicer than Santiago's Siboney.

Trinidad's pastel-colored colonial houses wave their red terracotta roofs in welcome. Inside, they're supported by wooden beams. Their main gates are oversized and have smaller entryways cut into them. As in Camagüey, you enter a spacious hall that doubles as a living room. The large windows, starting at pavement level, are not glazed, but are usually fitted with a wrought-iron grille to let in fresh air but not burglars. I'm dragging a suitcase behind me. I carefully avoid the well-maintained motorcycle that the man of the house has parked on the living room pavement. There are several brown antique rocking chairs around, the kind you'd pay a fortune for in the centre of Prague. Like most Cuban colonial houses, this one is built around a small courtyard, with rooms facing it. Our room boasts a high ceiling, finished with white-painted beams, and a large window facing the street with a white lattice. In a small fridge in the corner I find a few PET bottles of water, a couple of cans of beer and a cucumber.

Finding vegetables is an unexpected thing. Despite the fact that Cuba theoretically grows just about anything you can think of, in practice there is nothing easily available and I haven't seen cucumbers for some time. I assume - correctly, as it will later turn out - that while the drinks are for guests to buy, the cucumber has been kept by the lady of the house and is therefore not for us. Leaving the cucumber to enjoy the cold, I open a can of beer, sit down in a chair and observe the goings-on in the street. Most of the pedestrians are locals who don't bat an eyelid at me. But the tourists stare in. Occasionally someone says hello. The sidewalk in front of me is massive, concrete, raised above the level of the uneven historic pavement. Traffic is virtually non-existent, except for cyclists and rickshaws. A

Chapter 8 229

perfectly blue-sky looms over the house opposite, and in the corner of this realistic frameless image I can see the front of my car. The owner of the apartment, a middle-aged, sporty man with a bald head, assures me that I can park here without any problems, so I sip and enjoy the time saved by looking for parking. I pay nothing for parking and only twenty dollars for the room. Sometimes a little is all you need to be satisfied.

About an hour later, something happens to me that has never happened before. I return the food I ordered without touching it. I order bistec de cerdo, a pork chop, in a neat restaurant that turns out to be a state-run tourist trap. You can't go wrong with a grilled pork chop, can you? When I order it, I make sure that the meat is really grilled. The young black waiter assures us that it is. Then an unappetizing slab of fat lands on my table, moist and slimy, with a side of wilted vegetables and overcooked rice. I'm not picky, but I'm not going to eat that. I return the food immediately. The bewildered waiter asks what's wrong and offers to cook it again, but I've had enough. And I am determined not to pay for the returned food and get into a conflict. I have a second Cuba Libre. Jimena orders a suspiciously colorful cocktail, and we make a contingency plan. Option A is that I refuse to pay for the food, period. If that process leads us to an impasse, I offer Plan B: I won't pay for the meal, but we'll have an extra cuba libre or two. It will be a compromise that exceeds the cost of the meal. If that doesn't work, then we go to plan C - blackmail. I'll say I'm going to post about them on social media.

"You can tell them you're a famous journalist," Jimena says with a stony expression. The girl has a sense of humor.

I imagine a scene: I see an angry superintendent, his forehead sweating, yelling at us that he's going to call the police. But I am sitting firmly in my seat, my index finger in the receipt, leaning against the fence of principle. People gathered around and divided into two camps. One cheers for us, the other sides with the outcast in the black bow tie. When we've laid everything out in detail, I take a deep breath and head for the fight - waving to the waiter and asking for the check. A moment later he comes over and hands it to me with a smile. The food I ordered and did not eat is not on it at all! Because I don't want to believe it, I look at the

230   Cuba: A Brief History of the End

bill for a while and give it to Jimena to count. It really only contains coffee, water, Cuba Libre, another cocktail and Jimena's salad, which she did eat.

But I notice something else. The cost is miscalculated. The waiter was off by less than 300 pesos, and it's to his own detriment! I have noticed several times that average Cubans are not exactly world champions in counting. I often see three or four numbers, quickly add them up in my head, tell the salesman, and he looks at me with great admiration when, after a moment of clumsily working his calculator, the same amount comes out. I'm not a financial type, there are times when I struggle with calculating percentages and trinomials, but I could start here tomorrow as the head of the statistics office. I toy for a moment with the idea of punishing the establishment and not telling them the mistake, but our better selves win out. We point out the waiter's mistake and leave him the correct amount. We leave the patio as winners, just as some Canadians enter. It occurs to me that I should warn them about this venture. But to each his own, maybe they're just out for a drink.

A little further down the street, at the corner Paladar Santander, which can be reached via a small staircase, we have a delicious meal. Tasting aguardiente, a sugarcane brandy, I order fried malanga, a potato-like root vegetable, and chicken fajitas, vowing never to set foot in a Cuban state restaurant again. From the aguardiente - the best brand is called Black Tears - they mix a local specialty, the canchánchara, Cuba's oldest cocktail, dating back to the War of Independence. It contains ice, aquardiente or rum, honey and citrus juice and is served in small ceramic cups with a colored rim. These cups can be purchased at the market in Trinidad. They make very nice gifts. As we wait for meal, the houses around the paladar plunge into pitch black darkness and the smell of a diesel generator wafts from the kitchen, a sign that the power is out again. Paladar Santander is owned by an elderly man who runs a ceramics workshop in another part of Trinidad. Photographs of his work and utilitarian dishes adorn the walls of the restaurant.

After dinner we walk through the winding streets of the historic centre. Trinidad is a regular city, but it feels like a village. I get pulled into a tobacco shop and get a small fat Partagás cigar, which I immediately light up. In complete darkness, we tread carefully on the uneven pavement. To our left, a gallery is lit up and the bulky owner stands on the steps at its entrance. We exchange a few cordial words. He invites us in and offers to give me a haircut. It turns out that he is not only a painter and gallery owner, but also a barber. We promise to stop by tomorrow morning, but we have something to do now.

We're looking for a bar whose name Jimena's friends in her town wrote on a small scrap of paper. Salty air blows in from the sea, it's crisp and cool. Despite the thick darkness, we manage to find the bar after a while. When the bartender sees my lit cigar, he sends me hurriedly to the smoking room in the back wing, as if under the watchful eye of a stern superior. There's no one inside but him and a colleague. We walk through the empty establishment to the back and look around suspiciously. If Raúl wanted to get even with us, this would be the perfect place. In the emptiness and darkness, one usually thinks of many things, which I dispel with a mighty puff of a tasty cigar. After a while, the bartender's partner comes into the room and asks who we're looking for. As agreed, we answer that we are looking for Maura. At the sound of her name, the young man lowers his voice.

"Maura?"

"Yes. Do you know her? Do you know where she lives?"

The young man nods. He says she's on this street. But he doesn't know if she's home and asks what we want. We say our friends from Jimena's homeland sent us to her. No wonder he watches us with measured apprehension. Maura is a true Caribbean witch. When Jimena's friend was with her the other day, she predicted his girlfriend's pregnancy. He laughed at her and said, "No way! Then he came home and his girlfriend told him the good news. Jimena had been insisting for days that we visit Maura and have her lay out the cards. Maura's small house is located a few dozen yards south on the same street as the bar that now serves as our landmark in the dark. She opens the door after knocking a few times and invites us in after a brief introduction.

Maura Jiménez is a perky little octogenarian in a plaid dress. She has short silver hair, a rough voice after a lifelong friendship with cigarettes, very dark skin, and vivid brown eyes that at times look at us amusedly and at others dart around the small living room. She sits us down on a stool, sits across from us in a rocking chair, and when I apologize for still having a lit cigar, she just waves her hand. "Never mind, I smoke too," she says good-naturedly, laughing. She has a lively look on her face, constantly gesturing and changing facial expressions. Behind the rocking chair, a large stuffed tiger lies on a table, and above it hangs a picture of a young man, presumably son, in a military uniform. To my left, at the entrance to the kitchenette, is another table covered with a lace tablecloth and on it are neatly arranged pieces of fruit, a glass of red wine, a red and white candle: a small shrine. A red and white curtain hangs behind the shrine.

"Each of the candles cost me a hundred," Maura complains when she notices me inspecting her shrine. "One is for a Yoruba orisha, the white and red one is for St. Barbara, my protector. And the wine goblet is there for money, naturally."

"Naturally," I nod, not knowing what I'm talking about.

"I am a strong believer. I was seriously ill and my faith healed me. I have been a strong believer ever since," she stresses. "I go to church on Thursdays and Sundays. Not many people here believe anymore. There are a lot of Communists in Cuba and they don't have God."

Maura says it cheerfully, so you can't tell she's complaining. She notes.

"Where are you from?" I ask. "Are you local?"

"Nope. I was born in Santa Clara. City of Che!"

In her brief remark, I can see how deeply the regime's propaganda has penetrated. She refers to the fable of how Guevara, in a clever military maneuver, seized an armored train in Santa Clara. That at least is the regime legend. He actually bought the weapons from a corrupt Batista officer. I'd expect Maura to say, "I'm from the town of Saint Claire." But no. Che's town. Unless she told me with an irony so subtle that I missed it. It's possible. Maura continues.

"I have lived almost my entire life in Trinidad. I was brought up by my aunt and grew up with cousins. I have one son, the one in the picture here. He's still young there. He's 50 today."

Maura talks about her difficult life and mentions in passing, rather vaguely and in hints, the mistakes she has made.

Chapter 8

"Only love gives meaning to life," she says, looking at Jimena, who is devouring Maura's every word. "But I'm tough. I'm not sentimental. When love ends, it doesn't come back. I don't believe in second chances."

She lets her words reverberate, leaving their recipients in mild amazement as to their true meaning. I don't ask. A witch is supposed to be mysterious.

"Cuban women are complicated," she winks conspiratorially at me for a change. "They're hot-blooded and do stupid things. Mostly for money. They do all kinds of things for it."

She laughs out loud. She's a happy character with lots of energy. Also because, as she later reveals, she drinks thirteen cups of sweet coffee a day. With that, she smokes a pack of filterless cigarettes. She complains that she has trouble breathing. She has asthma, and there's no medication available.

"There is nothing to be had. I have no money. My pension is about a thousand pesos a month. Isn't that something? Besides, the economic situation is bad.

I'm trying:

"Why is the economy bad?"

She looks at me silently. I think she's wondering if I'm crazy. Or a provocateur. Instinctive caution prevails.

"You know...there was a pandemic. We have a new president."

The news is on the television in the next room, the sound turned down. Archival footage of Fidel Castro appears on the screen. Maura jerks to attention.

"Fidel. He's had it too."

We watch the screen in silence for a while.

"The media is always lying. They lie, even if they only talk about the weather. They said there was electricity, but we didn't have it. And Fidel is gone."

We come to the purpose of the visit. Jimena's friends sent us here to check on Maura and ask what she needs (medication!), but also to have her lay out her cards for us. I've never done anything like this, I don't believe in fortune tellers, but if I'm going to try it somewhere, the myth-ridden Caribbean is the perfect place.

"I've been dealing cards since I was five years old. My aunt used to get mad at me for it. But I couldn't help it."

We're moving on to the house. We walk past the TV into the simple kitchen. It's very poorly furnished. There are a few pots, a sink and a simple gas stove.

"I love this kitchen," she says. It's open to the darkened backyard. Maura reveals that she has an orange tree growing there. She says it as excitedly as if she were five. I thought oranges were a common thing in Cuba. I remember they were importing Cuban oranges into Czechoslovakia. They didn't have a good reputation because of their thick skin, tough flesh and lots of pits. They were mainly used for making orange juice.

Even though it's around nine o'clock, Maura makes strong coffee for us. I'm afraid I won't be able to sleep, but she just laughs at my fears.

"Coffee doesn't affect me like that. It makes me fall asleep without any problems."

She's lighting a cigarette. I look behind me, where through the open door I can see the bed in the small bedroom. Maura brings out a pack of cards, places it on the plastic tablecloth and crosses herself. Jimena is first up. She must double down on three stacks and pick out eight cards. Next to the pile is a glass of water with a few stones inside. Maura dips her fingers in it, picks up the cards and explains what is happening and what is about to happen. This ritual is repeated a total of three times, so it takes longer than I expected. Her explication takes the form of test questions. She always raises a half-question, which she directs to a topic she assumes Jimena is interested in and waits for a response. Jimena looks serious, almost timid.

"Someone is keeping a protective hand over you," Maura tells her slowly and quietly. "Someone up there. Someone you loved very much."

"Grandma," the girl gasps, tears appearing in her eyes.

"You were very close, weren't you?"

Jimena nods. In a similar way, Maura gets information out of her about her boyfriend. Their conversation reveals that Jimena is not yet sure she wants to marry him. Maura informs her that her boyfriend is going to attend a party where he doesn't really want to go and where she will be gossiped about. Jimena's pupils dilate in surprise. Most of the conversation is about the partnership and some of it is also about university studies. Maura assures her that everything will work out. The prediction of a party where she will be gossiped about becomes the subject of our conversations in the car over the next few days. Jimena will text her boyfriend and ask how the party went. According to his information, the prediction will not be confirmed.

Then I sit across from Maura. I also must take down a deck of cards three times and go through the same, somewhat lengthy ritual. Even the prognosis about my affairs is - how else - optimistic. Maura, however, is not concerned with my marriage or my children this time, which disappoints me somewhat. I'm wearing a wedding ring, so I expect her to try to guess something on the subject, but not a word is said about my wife and my two daughters, and I'm not helping her. Most of the séance is about my health, profession and money. Maura has people pigeonholed like this - a young girl is interested in boys and studies, a man in advanced middle age is more interested in business, money and health. At one point, however, she warns:

"Watch out for the women," she says. "Some of them are just after you for the money!"

Apparently, that's what she assumes about men my age. I don't react to her hints and smile inwardly. There are no gold diggers around me, and there would be nothing to dig for. Although from her point of view it seems that way. Still, during the séance, she makes some successful guesses, even disturbingly detailed and accurate in some aspects. They concern work matters, expectations and dilemmas, as well as my brother's personal life. Maura is a good psychologist. For a moment I wonder if she really is a witch. Jimena seems convinced. Later, on the street, she shakes her head in disbelief:

"She knew almost everything. I cried when Grandma died. She loved me very much.

We pay what we owe and leave Maura's modest but well-kept home.

The next morning we have breakfast at the casa. The food is good. For the first time there are two kinds of fresh bread and even butter! A rarity.

Admittedly, only two small travel containers, but who can complain! There's a sweet, spongy dessert and a Brazil-Croatia match as an encore. I promised the hairdresser that I'd stop by his place, so I reluctantly leave the apartment and walk alone to the gallery. There's also a TV on, showing soccer. I order a haircut à la Richarlison, but without the coloring. All the Cubans, including the burly barber, are passionate about Brazil. So I keep it to myself and wish the Croatians success. From the way the game was going, it was clear that for the first time in the championship, the Brazilians were up against a strong team that they couldn't use their usual tricks against. I ask my hairdresser if he is more of a hairdresser or a painter.

"Of course the barber. My father trained me when I was fourteen. The painting came later."

Normally I'm quite happy if the barbers don't have this professional conversation with me, but here I would welcome it. It's just that the painter is a bit taciturn. He only talks when he's trying to sell me his work. On the wall is a faded, framed photocopy of an article about him from a Madrid newspaper, and above it a large, colorful tourist kitsch, with black women with cigars and American cars. It's interesting how the imperialist roadsters from the height of the Cold War have become a symbol of Havana. Fidel would not have been happy.

"You pay two hundred dollars for that painting in Havana," he points to a glossy image of the Havana Capitol. "That's you, I'll give it to you for a hundred."

I have to pinch myself if I don't see through his transparent ruse. But no, I don't pinch myself. Instead, I'm itching like hell for the tiny hairs that have invaded my shirt. I beg him to rinse them off.

"Sorry, buddy. There's no water."

"No water? In the barbershop?"

"Well. For two days now. I'm sorry."

I choose a poetic naivist picture of the spires of Trinidadian churches, painted by a friend of his. It costs only six euros, because the gallery apparently prices its canvases according to their size. I say goodbye and flee back to my own casa. It's thirty in the shade, my hair itches behind my T-shirt. I wonder if the water will run and I'll be able to take a shower. Luckily, I do. I make it to the end of the football game. The master and

Chapter 8

mistress of the house are sitting in the kitchen, nervously watching the screen, looking devastated after Marquinhos's botched penalty that means the Croatians are through. And so is Jimena. All three are down, reeling from the Brazilian defeat. The wife of the man of the house, a sporty woman in her forties with the first strands of grey hair in a short haircut, who has been cooking soup during the match, asks if we are staying for lunch. We gratefully decline; we have a journey to Cienfuegos and on to the Bay of Pigs.

"You said you were from Czechoslovakia?" asks the man of the house, the owner of the motorcycle.

"Yes, from the Czech Republic."

"Actually, the Czech Republic. We have such a nice story here. Years ago, a boy from you visited Cienfuegos. He liked a Cuban girl on the street, a friend of ours. He didn't speak much Spanish, and of course she didn't speak any Czech, but he approached her anyway. They started dating. Today they're happily married and have two children. You reminded me of that. It's a beautiful story. Wait, I'll give you a recommendation for accommodation in Playa Girón. It's a very nice guesthouse."

These recommendations are worth listening to in Cuba. There is an informal network of acquaintances who vouch for each other.

The road from Trinidad to Cienfuegos is one of the most scenic routes on the island. It runs along the sea, which is on my left. Today it's calm, dark blue and the sunlight shines on its surface. The gently undulating landscape glows with emerald green. A well-maintained tarmac road winds through valleys and passes lagoons with a plethora of water birds.

In the centre of Cienfuegos, I park in Marti Square. A doorman runs out of the palace and calls out that this is the provincial parliament, and I am not allowed to park here. When I ask where I can park, he points about fifty metres away. In the expanse of Parque Martí, everything is as it was. The houses have been repaired, and among them the Tomás Terry Theatre, where Sarah Bernhardt played and Enrico Caruso sang, shines like a pearl. The elegant, eclectic building from the 1880s celebrates the entrepreneurial skills of Venezuelan industrialist Terry. The first performance held here was Verdi's *Aida*. Inside, the auditorium is decorated with marble and a hand-carved parquet floor. Standing inside, the empty theatre with its less than a thousand seats feels cosy and intimate. Years ago, I was here in the daytime. For one euro, I bought a ticket that entitled me to a thorough tour of the stunning interior. Through the half-open wooden shutters, ropes of sunlight streamed in, with animal dust flying about like in any proper art stall.

Now the theater is closed. Mothers sit on the benches in front of it, watching the nearby antics of their naughty children in pioneer uniforms. The yellow Cathedral of the Immaculate Conception (Catedral de la Purísima Concepción) has also closed its gates. On another December evening years ago, I mingled in the Advent procession here. At its head was a priest with a monstrance, followed by a gold-clad statue of Our Lady of Charity of Cobre (La Virgen de la Caridad del Cobre), the patroness of Cuba. The statuette had a puffy face with red cheeks and large black eyes. Her black hair peeked out from under a massive crown. It emerged from a lighted building with towers topped with a red roof. The procession went around the square and was imbued with a mood of resigned reconciliation. There were no policemen, at least no uniformed ones, in sight.

The Cuban cult of Our Lady of Mercy began in the 17th century, when a wooden statue of the Virgin and Child was allegedly found standing in the waters of a bay near Santiago by three men, all named Juan. Shortly before, they had survived a fierce storm at sea and the wooden statue, which they first thought was a dead bird in the water, amazed them by being supposedly dry. Thus begins the sacred tale of Cachita, who became a guardian against pirates, a symbol of the struggle for independence and a protector of the faithful against the Communists.

But no procession today, except perhaps a stream of people from bar to bar watching the climax of the thrilling match between Argentina and Holland. Jimena is very keen to see Argentina succeed, especially as her boyfriend is a Leo Messi fan, as are the other twenty billion or so Spanish and Catalan speaking boys. And, in fact, not only these languages. Messi has become a planetary phenomenon and everyone wishes him success at the World Cup. Everybody except the curmudgeon from Central Europe. But this time I'm out of luck. Messi and Argentina triumph and despite the early afternoon, the celebrations begin in Cuba.

"Why do you care about some Argentinians?" I ask Jimena.

Chapter 8

"Because they represent South America. It's time for someone from us to win."

"Don't Argentinians have a reputation for being arrogant nabobs?"

She looks at me and I think she pretends she's never heard of it. It doesn't change the fact that Argentines are unpopular in their own continent. Argentina was rich and developed for a long time before it was gradually destroyed by socialist populists, military juntas, and incompetent democrats who brought it to its current state of mediocrity. Those who want to understand Argentina and its mentality should read the brilliant essays of V. S. Naipaul from the seventies.

But I prefer not to tell Jimena, who is beaming with Messi-anic enthusiasm. From Parque Martí we walk towards the port and find a nice café, the Café Centro Mercantil, which we enter. It's crowded, although there's no TV, so no one has come to watch the soccer. It is, at first glance, a cave of artists and intellectuals. On the back wall I see various percussion instruments, other instruments and microphones, ready for musical production. We sit down at the bar. We are served by two nervous mulattos between fifteen and twenty years of age, watched from behind by an older man and woman, presumably their parents. The boys are on a roll and their hands are shaking. I order a coffee and a soda.

"Do you want coffee or lemonade first?" one of them, the younger one, asks me.

Faced with a dilemma, I choose coffee. I get it a good five minutes later, a little disheveled. I don't get my lemonade, the boy forgets about it in the rush.

The café has large windows and entrances open to the street. It's casually nice and there are lots of flies, especially around the bar. It has a Caribbean feel - except for the two painted Central European plates hanging above the bar, which have somehow mysteriously made their way here. Maybe they were found in a shipwreck. They've got a fox and a pheasant on them, and they don't fit in at all. There's a white man sitting at a table a few yards away wearing John-Lennon spectacles. He's got a sweaty complexion lined with sparse, unwashed hair. He's having an engaged conversation with a black man who looks like a slim version of Big Papi, former Boston Red Sox baseball star David Ortiz. The

240 Cuba: A Brief History of the End

bespectacled intellectual is wearing a tattered T-shirt with a picture of Curious George, the cartoon monkey. I'm sorry I can't hear their conversation. Are they discussing Foucault and Derrida? Maybe they're just complaining about inflation. It's an engaged, friendly conversation, with the black guy mostly nodding and listening. The intellectual may be absorbed in the topic, but he doesn't look unhappy. I guess he's not an intellectual then.

Originally, I wanted to show Jimena the old Spanish cemetery, but the time has imperceptibly dripped into late afternoon, and we have to go to the Bay of Pigs, where I have not been yet and I have no idea what condition the road will be in. The cemetery will have to do without us. It's a strange place with a macabre charm, but perhaps late millennial Jimena would not have been sympathetic to this type of poetics. Its official name is Cemeterio de la Reina, the Queen's Cemetery. It's away from the centre in a quiet part of town. Outside its entrance, horses graze and stray dogs roam. On the way there, under the scorching summer sun, I passed an old rusty moskvich without wheels, set on four logs, and something tells me that even today, years later, I would find it there. The cemetery is entered through a gate that is part of a low, long building, considerably dilapidated. The most striking impression from inside can be expressed in a word: cramped. There's tombstone upon tombstone, the aisles are uneven and narrow, baroque decoration everywhere, dingy marble and granite, angels and almost no vegetation. The cemetery was completely empty when I walked there.

Remembering the silence and the cracked marble, I think of a huge abandoned cement factory outside the city. That's where I met Alejandro. It was after the botched conference at Antonio's.

Fernandina de Jagua

"My parents taught me the basics of solidarity. They believed in socialist ideas until the Soviet invasion of Czechoslovakia. Then they lost their illusions," says Alejandro Tur Valladares, an independent journalist.

We met in a wooden hut in a small colony outside the city. As I drove through the moonscape of an empty cement factory not far from the cabin, scenes from the David Bowie film *The Man Who Fell to Earth* ran through my head. In my mind I ask why the cement factory isn't working on a weekday, but the same question could be asked of the Cuban economy: why the hell aren't you working?

Alejandro borrowed the cabin from a friend. This is where he receives foreign visitors. A slender, greying man with the face of a stoic checks to see if I'm being followed. He goes to the window, leans out, then returns to the wooden table. He limps as he walks. He is wearing frayed jeans and a black short-sleeved shirt.

His fate could have been very different. He studied electrical engineering and from the age of seventeen worked as a service technician, repairing televisions and VCRs. When he started writing and doing opposition work, Mefisto came with an offer of a well-paid job as an official writer. He would travel. But he would have to leave the opposition, and he didn't want to. Here in Cienfuegos, he publishes a community newsletter called Jagua Press, which takes its name from the black and blue ink used on temporary tattoos. It comes from genipa americana trees that grow in the rainforest. The Indians used it for decoration and medicine. The city itself, Cienfuegos, was originally named Fernandina de Jagua, after Jagua, the Indian chief and Spanish King Ferdinand VII.

"Jagua and the tree it comes from have symbolic and historical value for us," says Alejandro.

He recently began teaching journalism classes, each with about five students. They meet once a week for three months.

"I give them an assignment and then I correct it with them.

I get it right away: most of all, Alejandro reminds me of a favorite high school professor, the one who doesn't give out Fs, but gets students excited about his subject. Something that sparks in them for life. The students look forward to his classes, even though some of them have been harassed by the police, who have threatened them and their families. For example, they have threatened to shut down their illegal sources of income. The father of one of the students is a fisherman.

"Fishing for one's own needs is almost impossible here. Well, our journalism student was blackmailed through his father's black market income. But despite these threats, the parents allowed their children to attend my course."

I am silent for a while, as the information that it is not legal to fish for personal consumption in the land of Hemingway's Santiago sinks in. I think of Fidel's many fishing trophies displayed in his many Cuban mansions.

Although Alejandro was born into poor circumstances, he remembers his childhood fondly. Soon, however, he was struck by cancer at the age of ten. He commuted to Havana for treatment, which his father paid for with a monthly fundraiser he organized with his work colleagues. Alejandro didn't tell me this. I have found out later on his profile on the Memory of the Nation website. He spent several years at home in bed, reading classical literature, history, psychology and philosophy. He tells me he used to be a fierce rebel, but it went nowhere. So he turned to journalism instead.

"I was a member of the Central Cuban Coalition of Opposition Activists for the provinces of Villa Clara, Sancti Spíritus and Cienfuegos. But such activism brings open persecution and consequently discourages many people. They are afraid and have no real information to back it up. If we give it to them, a whole new space opens up before them. That's why I decided to pursue this."

The wet sound of a whirring engine comes in from outside. Alejandro jumps up nervously, the hard wooden chair he is sitting on falls to the floor, he limps to the window of the hut and looks around cautiously. Inside the almost empty room, I can hear my own breathing. After a moment, the car drifts away against the tide of uncertainty, but we both prick up our ears until the end of the meeting.

"I grew up listening to Spanish radio. When I was 16, I joined the Cuban Human Rights Committee and became a member of the opposition. I was with them for six months. The organization was led by brothers Gustavo and Sebastian Arcos."

Gustavo Arcos took part in the attack on Moncada's barracks alongside the Castros and was shot. After the coup, he became ambassador to Belgium, from where, among other things, he organised arms deliveries. However, he soon sobered up and joined the opposition. In the early 1980s, Castro had him arrested.

Chapter 8

"After that, I was out of the opposition for a while, but in 2004 I joined Oswaldo Payá's Christian Liberation Movement. I worked with Héctor Maceda Gutiérrez, Laura Pollán's husband. Today I belong more to the liberal opposition."

I'm gonna take a detour here. Alejandro mentioned names that are fundamental to modern Cuban history. Maseda Gutiérrez, a nuclear physicist by profession, was imprisoned for many years in 2003 during the Black Spring along with many other oppositionists and was only released in 2011. His wife founded the Ladies in White, originally an organisation of women and family members of imprisoned dissidents. While in prison, Maseda wrote a memoir, *Buried Alive* (*Enterrados vivos*). He managed to smuggle the manuscript out, allegedly page by page, and Laura then had the book sent to Fidel Castro. Maseda later claimed that he was released against his will, as he first demanded a release and rehabilitation for himself and all those imprisoned during the Black Spring.

There is a memorable photo from the time of Maseda's release in February 2011, in which he and his wife are hugging. Her head rests on his chest, looking into the camera lens and smiling happily. Maseda is smiling the same way. He looks relaxed, wearing a blue hoodie, glasses and a digital wristwatch with a leather strap on his right wrist. The image radiates the warmth of their embrace. Laura has waited eight long years for him. Eight months later, she was dead.

"The loss of Oswaldo Payá was terrible," Alejandro continues. "When I learned of his death, the first thought that crossed my mind was that there would be a vacuum in the opposition. He is irreplaceable. With the Varela project, he managed to win the support of the masses. He outlined what a transition to democracy could look like. He invited people to discuss in groups what they wanted to change, and then collected and combined it and deduced the next course of action from it. Today the opposition is not in good shape, it has no real leader. Without a unifying personality it is impossible to achieve anything."

"And there's another element. Raúl's reforms have forced the opposition to change course. We have criticised some of the partial things that have changed in the meantime. We can have mobile phones. The government has started issuing building permits. It's a little easier to get

244 Cuba: A Brief History of the End

on the internet. We can go to hotels. We can travel. But I think ultimately these changes will lead to the demise of the regime."

A year and a half later I meet Alejandro in Prague. He is there with other independent journalists at the invitation of several NGOs for a journalism course. We met at the editorial office of the Czech Press Agency (CTK) in Opletalova Street. On nearby Wenceslas Square, with the remnants of melted snow, in the fog between the car headlights, he looks smaller, uncertain. Catfish in the pool. Like Guillermo "Coco" Fariñas, who once flew to Prague one winter with his old mother. At the airport, he told the people from an NGO who were waiting for him there that he wanted to go immediately to Havel's grave and pay his respects. But Coco flew in lightly, forgetting that it's cold here in the winter. So their first journey did not lead to the cemetery, but to a shopping centre where it was necessary to provide them with winter clothes. When I picked them up to take them to Havel's tomb, they were both wearing coats about two sizes too big. I will never forget the scene of Coco standing in front of the grave, his head bowed, his arms crossed on his stomach, and his mother standing a few feet away. Or the two huge winter coats from C&A. The thought always creeps into my mind of a kind of Cuban dissident out of place, out of his element, in a different context.

I once came across Antonio Rodiles in the New York University center in Prague's Malé náměstí, quite surprisingly. He was there for a meeting. We exchanged a few words. The distinct impression I formed and stored in my memory from the brief conversation was about Antonio's defense of Donald Trump. I knew that Antonio supported Trump's harder line on Havana. I understood his position, even if I didn't share it. A man who is dangerous to the American Constitution is not a credible defender of freedom in the world. Back then in the NYU hallway, I found myself thinking that while I would have been receptive to such positions in Cuba, they sounded discordant in Prague. There is a time and place for everything. Context is part of content.

In the CTK editorial office, Alejandro Tur explained to me that the opposition is beginning to focus on practical projects at the expense of big, abstract proclamations and public protests.

"Rhetoric gets you nowhere. We have to work. Dissent is now more connected to NGOs in Europe than before, which makes a qualitative difference. Miami was dominated by an older generation of political exiles who wanted immediate change. Now we have a series of long-term projects. People in Miami wanted to control and manage everything. Now there is more diversity in our work. Journalists seem to be quite tolerated by the cops. I even had one tell me that they basically have no problem with what we do. But they're a little afraid of our foreign travel. When I came back from my first stay in Prague, they wanted to confiscate my computer and video camera at the airport. I told them I wouldn't give it to them, they'd better arrest me. In the end, they let me go and I could keep everything. Other people weren't so lucky, they had their equipment confiscated. I don't want to complain. If someone had told me five years ago that I would be able to travel, I wouldn't have believed them. But if they had told me that the Communists would still be in power, I wouldn't have been surprised."

"What do you think is most important for the regime to disappear?"
"Information. Dissemination of independent information."

December 2022. The road to Playa Girón winds through an agricultural landscape. Plátanos grow around the dirt road. The approach to the village through the sparse forest is surprising. A crucial chapter of the 20th century was written here, but it is just a quiet village of two thousand inhabitants. The bungalows along the main street are neat and well-kept. The village ends at the Bahía de Cochinos, the famous Bay of Pigs. They've built a resort with small cottages on the beach, which looks deserted. I look over the scratchy yellow wall that surrounds the campground and separates it from the village on the northeast side. A few maintenance workers and other staff cross the yellowish grass, but as far as I can tell from a cursory glance, there are no tourists.

We're staying at the Hostal Rachel, a casa particular and a great choice. We park on the grass by the road in front of a small turquoise house surrounded by flowers. Behind it is another smaller building with an apartment and two small guest rooms. Between the two houses is a few meters of covered paved area with an outdoor kitchen. This is where breakfast and dinner are served. Next to the door to the apartment are books in English, including a Bible, on a small shelf. The owner of the house, Lázaro, speaks English because he occasionally works in Miami. He has a cell phone with a Florida number. Parked outside his fence is a well-maintained Volga 24, the kind of car mid-level Communist apparatchiks drove in the 1970s and '80s. The wisecracking Czechs nicknamed it "piano in the front, piano in the back," and anyone who sees it has to admit it's an apt description. On a hanger next to the kitchen, Lázaro is drying a black sweatshirt with a yellow United States Army insignia. It looks rather ironic right there. The village is still littered with plaques commemorating the victory of Castro's forces over Cuban exile fighters in April 1961. There's also a museum dedicated to the multi-day battle.

There's a dog named Nina running around who doesn't like me at all. She just got scolded for going for a walk in the village without permission. She takes it on me, barking at me from two metres away. It sounds like a coughing fit. As it is getting towards evening, we immediately go to the beach, which they call Coconut Beach or even Pine Beach. It's adjacent to the tourist camp behind the wall. White sand, coconut palms, low trees and a few red wooden booths where you can get beer, cocktails and a solid dinner - grilled fish or octopus. You'll need to order in advance, though. I park right on the sand near the vegetation that separates the beach from where the fishing boats are moored.

There are a few local guys sitting at wooden stalls. For tourists, it's just me and Jimena. She sprays clouds of repellent on herself, but the mosquitoes don't seem to care. Their swarm surrounds the girl and doesn't leave her alone. The idea of having dinner here falls through. We take turns having a beer and a cocktail at each of the three booths and listen to the conversation of the guys sitting on the wooden benches near us. They are talking about the emigration wave and Venezuelan President Nicolás Maduro. As we walk past them to the booths for drinks, they lower their voices.

I'm going to have an interesting experience at the booths. When the cuba libre is ordered by Jimena, the cocktail is thin, as if the rum is losing a battle with the cola to see who can conquer the taste buds more. When I order the cocktail, it's suddenly a good old-fashioned cuba libre. The rum exhibits its signature immediately, tingling pleasantly on the tongue as its flavour rushes to the nose. The mystery is soon solved. Jimena orders the drink, but watches the sunset, which turns the sand of the beach pink and turns the coconut palms into big black brooms stuck in the ground. I, on the other hand, turn off the postcard from the tropics for a moment and watch the guy prepare the cuba libre and her mojito as if I wanted to learn how to do it too. So the amigo doesn't dare to cheat. When the fiery wheel in the west finally falls into the sea, the sky fills up with star-studded darkness and we move on to the last booth, manned by a burly guy and his wife, also in the flesh. He cooks, she takes care of the supplies. He speaks some English, *justeh leetle*, and offers fresh grilled octopus for dinner. If it weren't for the mosquitoes, I'm sure we couldn't resist. When he hears I'm from the Czech Republic, he lights up.

"Checo? Really? A bunch of Czechs were here yesterday. Young people. Drinking late into the night. *Amigo,* you all must have a good practice back at home. There were only a few of them and they drank a total of 40 mojitos, 34 cuba libre and beers I haven't counted yet!"

He says this with moved admiration. Some of the glory of my countrymen sticks to me. I can confirm. We Czechs are fond of educational field trips.

"What time are you open?"

"I close when people aren't here. I've been here till three. I open around nine in the morning. Come in for breakfast."

There are several stray but very friendly dogs running around the beach. A large black cat prowls around the booth. In a land of malnourished quasi-kittens, it's a phenomenon. The chef's wife says someone abandoned her, with a fresh litter of young ones, and brought her here. She's been distrustful of humans for a long time, and only now is she letting them pet her.

"But no one else, just us," she laughs.

It's nighttime on Coconut Beach. The tops of the palm trees rustle in the gentle breeze and the ocean murmurs behind them. The mosquitoes

248   Cuba: A Brief History of the End

drink Jimena's blood, literally and figuratively. They're giving me a break
for now. Sixty years ago, the blood stakes were different here.

Brigada Asalto 2506

Because of the intended element of surprise, the invasion of the Cuban
Expeditionary Force began at midnight on April 17, 1961. Four large ships
brought more than twelve hundred fighters, Cubans trained by the
Americans mainly in Guatemala, but also in Panama, Mexico, Puerto
Rico, and some American bases. But there was no surprise. The Castro
regime knew about the upcoming attack from its informants, since the
fighters were not exactly discreet in the bars around the bases where the
manoeuvres had been carried out for about three quarters of a year. Some
sources say that Soviet intelligence even knew the exact date of the main
attack. The English-language version of Radio Moscow broadcast a report
on April 13 that an invasion of Cuba would take place within a week,
plotted by the CIA with the participation of Cuban exile "criminals."

On April 15, eight B-26 bombers, falsely identified as Cuban military
aircraft, attacked the airports at San Antonio de los Baños, Ciudad
Libertad, and Santiago de Cuba in three directions. They succeeded in
destroying a few aircraft, but far from the majority. But the Expeditionary
Corps pilots exaggerated the damage they inflicted on Havana, and this
also contributed to the failure of Operation Zapata, the code name for the
invasion. Even before it, there were several false flag attacks in the east at
the port of Baracoa and in the west at Deep Bay (Bahía honda) in the then
province of Pinar del Río (now in the newly created province of Artemisa),
where the Americans had a base until 1912 but, unlike the one at
Guantánamo, abandoned it.

The April 1961 invasion was not the only attempt by the United States
to get rid of Castro. It was an attempt to correct the perceived mistakes
that led to the so-called "loss of Cuba. It was not the first time such
arguments had been made in Washington. When Mao proclaimed the
People's Republic of China in Tiananmen Square in the fall of 1949,
American pundits argued over "who lost China." Such optics, however,
tend to overestimate the ability of the United States to influence foreign
policy crises. America knows how to paint a picture with broad

brushstrokes, as it demonstrated in the missile crisis of October 1962, in the weeks surrounding the Suez crisis in the fall of 1956, and even more clearly in the invasion of Iraq in the spring of 2003. But with a few exceptions-such as the coups in Iran, Guatemala, and Chile-it is not capable of detailed work in complex situations. The latest visible evidence is the chaos in post-invasion Iraq.

Washington hastily recognised Fidel's government, but then relations only deteriorated. Castro denied being a Communist, but they played a vital role in his government. In Havana, Soviet advisers alternated with GRU agents, the regime received arms in large quantities from Czechoslovakia and the Soviet Union, cracked down on the independent press, unleashed retributive terror and launched Marxist-Leninist indoctrination in the schools. Many of the rebels who passed through Sierra Maestra felt taken aback by the radical turn. Matos ended up in prison and Cienfuegos mysteriously died. One of these young rebels was Dr. Manuel Artime, who took part in the fighting on Fidel's side in the Palma Soriano area in 1959. After January 1959, Artime, a Catholic, psychiatrist and professor at the military academy in Manzanillo, organized the rural corps, the so-called *comandos rurales.* They were made up of Catholic university activists from Havana and were under the umbrella of the Instiut for Agrarian Reform (INRA), where Artime was employed. Like the much more prominent Matos, who was the commander of the central region in Camagüey, Artime watched with concern the growing influence of the Communists. After Matos's arrest in October 1959, he went underground. He took refuge in Havana among the Jesuits and officially resigned from the INRA in November. His letter of resignation was published on the front page of *Avance*, one of the last freely operating media on the island. At this time, Artime founded the underground Movimiento de Recuperación Revolucionaria (MRR), the Movement to Restore the Revolution. In the middle of the following month, with the help of the US Central Intelligence Agency, he managed to board a Honduran cargo ship and flee Cuba.

President Dwight Eisenhower's government was taken aback by Cuba's rapid conversion to communism. The intelligence services therefore turned to the Chicago Mafia with the idea of getting rid of Castro by force. Organized crime was given an unofficial promise to control casino and prostitution revenues again after the change of government. According to some historians, the Mafiosi took money from the CIA, but behind the CIA's back they tried, understandably in vain, to negotiate an acceptable modus operandi with Castro. When the people in the CIA understood this, with the blessing of the government, they began to organize the Cuban Expeditionary Force. Work on it began in the spring of 1960. Gradually, the Movement to Restore the Revolution became the umbrella political organization of the landing. The 2506 Invasion Brigade was formed. In preparation, Dr. Artime worked with CIA operatives, especially Gerry Droller, going by the aliases Frank Bender and Mr. B, and also with E. Howard Hunt, who later became involved in the Watergate scandal, for which he served two and a half years in prison.

While troops were being formed in Florida and Central America to be sent to Cuba to overthrow the Communists, no precise plan existed. It was clear from the beginning that the Americans did not want to be drawn directly into the conflict. They intended to present the situation to the world as an internal Cuban dispute and they were more or less rooting for one side. Despite various myths, the Eisenhower administration did not approve any operational plan; there were only options that were discussed. The most viable of them at the time seemed to be a landing in the Trinidad area with the help of the US Air Force and Navy. For one thing, there were several military installations there that would be useful to the exiled troops once captured, and in an emergency it was close to the Escambray Mountains, where the troops could fortify themselves and launch guerrilla raids. The plan assumed – erroneously, as it became clear – the dissatisfaction of the majority of Cubans with the new regime and its eventual support for the invading army, as well as the international pressure on Havana that Washington would organize at the Organization of American States.

Meanwhile, Cuba was mightily reversing its foreign policy course. The Minister of Economy, Che Guevara, was still a supporter of the Soviet Union. He would only sober up about the Russians a little later. With Moscow's support, he wanted to make the island a base for the spread of Communist regimes to Latin America and Africa, exactly what the

Americans feared. The Soviets did not yet have an official diplomatic mission in Havana. The first ambassador from the Communist bloc was the Czech Vladimír Pavlíček, who had been there since June 1960. He oversaw economic assistance and arms supplies, although as he later stated in Matocha's book, the details were mainly handled by "the boys from Omnipol," a state-run weapons trader. Pavlíček coordinated with the Russians, and Czechoslovakia then represented Cuban interests in the United States after the two countries broke off direct diplomatic relations. The Communist Dr. Pavlíček would later serve as director of the Cuban department at the Czechoslovak Foreign Ministry. After 1989, he publicly boasted about his contacts with the Havana hierarchy, especially with Raúl, with whom he said he continued to meet after the Velvet Revolution.

During the spring of 1960, the government of Prime Minister Castro and President Dr. Osvaldo Dorticós began importing arms and military equipment from Communist countries under the pretext of the U.S. military embargo that had been in place since the Batista regime. The United States imposed this embargo in March 1958, effectively helping the fidelistas to take power. Ships with firearms as well as T-34 and IS-2 tanks were sent to Cuba, and these became fatal to the invading army the following year. In the spring and summer, the government began to confiscate Cuban assets from U.S. agrarian companies without compensation. In retaliation, Eisenhower reduced the quota on Cuban sugar imports. The Soviet Union responded by buying the rest of the sugar export quota itself. Eisenhower thus cancelled oil exports to Cuba. Castro ordered the US oil companies Texaco and Exxon to process Russian oil in their Cuban refineries. They refused, after pressure from Washington, and so Castro and Dorticós - really just a figurehead - decided to make a radical cut. They ordered the nationalisation of US oil refineries without compensation. In this way, the Cubans confiscated $1.7 billion in assets from US companies. In October, Eisenhower declared an embargo on all exports to Cuba except for medicine and some foodstuffs, and in early January 1961 he broke off diplomatic relations with Havana.

As late as April 1960, the State Department was recommending an effective but cautious course of action with respect to Cuba. A memorandum from Deputy Assistant Secretary of State Lester Mallory noted the majority support Cubans expressed for Castro's coup. Mallory describes the rapid spread of communism, the lack of effective political opposition, and suggests slowly but surely inflicting economic damage on the island that could turn people away from communism as a result of the lower standard of living. At the same time, according to Mallory, these policies must be "deft and as unobtrusive as possible" so as to deny Cuba finance, goods, and raw materials, which could eventually lead to the overthrow of the government. In the months from April 1960, however, the situation took a quick turn. There was no time for subtle and clever policies, and every move by both sides accelerated the fall into the abyss, so that by early January 1961 both countries were in a cold war.

The incoming Kennedy administration took over from Ike in a full-blown crisis. In late January, after his memorable inaugural address, Kennedy learned of the Cuban Expeditionary Force's invasion plan. In the presidential campaign, he had criticized Vice President Nixon for the administration's failure to prevent the spread of communism in the region, and now he was in a position to do something about it. However, it seems that JFK was more concerned with keeping the U.S. out of Cuba than with really effective policy. The landing in Trinidad, about 270 kilometers southeast of Havana, did strike him as too conspicuous, too revealing of the U.S. role. He ordered a less conspicuous location to be sought. The planners eventually settled on two beaches, Playa Girón and Playa Larga, at the mouth of the Bahía de Cochinos, across from what is now the Ciénaga de Zapata Nature Reserve. At a press conference, reporters questioned Kennedy about a possible Cuban invasion, and the president stressed that no U.S. troops would take part in the attack. Thus, direct U.S. Air Force and Navy support fell off the table. These political considerations proved fatal. Instead of dealing a crushing blow to the Communists, the expeditionary force was limited by politically crafted rules that undermined its strength. After the failure of the invasion, JFK privately complained that he had fallen for his advisers and Eisenhower and that he should have called off the action instead. But he had only himself to blame for the defeat with his half-hearted approach.

His other concern was that no figure of the Fulgencio Batista regime should be at the head of the invasion. Even before the election, JFK had criticized Batista as a murderer and dictator responsible for twenty thousand deaths. Some sources give this figure, but it is probably an exaggeration. There is no doubt that Batista's regime was disgusting and corrupt, but the real number of his victims is probably somewhere between three and four thousand. Kennedy, already ensconced in the White House, ruled out Batista's return from Madeira. The search was on for a political leader. The choice fell on Dr. Artime and his Movement.

Artime was a democrat, an intellectual, a soldier and an able organizer who hated the Communists. He had worked against Castro for more than a year, and he also had the advantage of being a member of the 26th of July Movement, which fought against Batista. On the seventeenth of April, Artime, as a member of Brigade 2506, landed in the early hours of the morning on Girón beach, code-named Blue Beach. Since the landing began, bad luck had dogged the Corps. Due to inconsistent terrain reconnaissance conducted from aircraft, one of the four ships bound for Playa Larga, code-named Red Beach, struck reefs and landed damaged. The reconnaissance troops thought the reefs were just colonies of seaweed. The soldiers thus lost, among other things, medicines and medical supplies that the wounded had to do without. Communications equipment also broke down, leaving the units with only sporadic connection with each other.

Castro's army reacted quickly and *El Comandante* himself took the lead in the operations. The fighting on the beaches, in the adjacent marshes, in the fields and in the forests was fierce and lasted less than three days. Brigade 2506 had several World War II-era M41 Walker Bulldog light tanks, equipped with a 76 mm cannon and two 0.30 caliber machine guns. These vehicles were not well suited for the terrain in the Bay of Pigs area. The Cuban army, well fortified and camouflaged, had the advantage of superior firepower, an unlimited supply of ammunition and air support from the outset. The first thing the Communists did was to cut off the invading army from supplies. The artillery and air force kept the exiles' ships farther from the coast, so the soldiers ran out of ammunition after a while.

Nevertheless, the exiles fought bravely and the short war was very bloody, unlike Castro's fight in December 1958 and January 1959. The world Communist bloc-equipped army in no way resembled Batista's lethargic corps of officers, many of whom were more concerned with the size of their bank accounts than with defending their homeland. Estimates of Communist casualties vary widely. Multiple sources give different statistics, ranging from 500 to 4,000 casualties, including those killed and seriously wounded. Of the nearly 1,300 men of the exiled army, 106 lost their lives during the fighting or as a result of execution. As many as 1 202 men were captured and taken prisoner. Nine of them suffocated to death in a cargo container while being transported to Havana, 160 kilometres away. Some were tried and executed for alleged torture in the service of the Batista regime, but more than 1,100 prisoners of war were returned to the United States in December 1962 in exchange for $53 million worth of medicine and food. These were not provided by the U.S. government, but by private sources. As part of the exchange, about 1,000 family members of prisoners of war left Cuba for the United States.

In its postmortem analysis, the CIA cited several reasons why the action failed. These include poor knowledge of the enemy's real strength, failure to organize internal resistance on the island, poor communications, and poor risk analysis. The invasion preparation team suffered from groupthink, during which they failed to deal adequately with potential critical issues, or rather did not vet them at all. They did not have the capacity for strong internal opposition that would have exposed the weaknesses of the plan in time. Hunt, who served as a CIA operative in Havana in the mid-1960s, said the Castro regime was still popular in Cuba at the time. Overthrowing it was beyond the power of airborne forces without support from the sea and air.

Castro used the defeat of the exiles to glorify the regime and launch a propaganda offensive. In August 1961, at an international conference in the Uruguayan resort of Punta del Este, Che Guevara met Kennedy speechwriter Richard Goodwin at a reception. They talked about all sorts of things, including the future of the US base at Guantánamo Bay. After the meeting, Goodwin reported that at the end Guevara ironically thanked him for the Bay of Pigs invasion, adding that "it was a great political victory for them - it allowed them to consolidate and turned them from a wronged little country into an equal." Guevara was thus figuratively trying to twist the knife in a fresh American wound and enjoy some gloating. Materially, let's not overstate the remark. Cuba never became an equal country after 1959; it always had to find someone to prop it up. Its anti-American campaign may have taken it out of Washington's political and economic influence, but it made it a vassal of Moscow, which held it until the fall of its empire. During the 1990s, Castro proved incapable of functioning independently. His country languished until another sugardaddy, Hugo Chávez, rescued it. Then, when he and his successor Maduro brought oil-rich Venezuela to its knees, Cuba fell even deeper under Díaz-Canel.

In traditionally anti-Yankee Latin America, Castro's victory in the Bay of Pigs quickly gained the status of a legend and Fidel became an international leader. Letting him grow up like that was Kennedy's biggest mistake of his very short presidency. Yet even before the fighting in the Bay of Pigs began, another conflict began to take shape. Khrushchev sent Kennedy a message warning him against invading Cuba and threatening that if it happened, the Soviet Union would attack with nuclear weapons in the American interior. The path to a Cuban missile crisis that would bring the world to the brink of nuclear apocalypse was open.

After the Bay of Pigs defeat, Kennedy authorized Operation Mongoose, the preparation for the assassination of Castro, which, as we know, was unsuccessful. Actually, not exactly. Information about Langley's intentions, to which the CIA had moved in late 1961, reached the right places in Havana and led to increased security for the leader. A monstrous system of personal protection began to take shape, with the First Department of the Ministry of the Interior in charge of Fidel, while Raúl was protected by the Second Department. The Third Department of Personal Protection is in charge of protecting all the other members of the Politburo. As Sánchez writes, the security detail will consist of three circuits. The third includes thousands of soldiers dedicated to organizational tasks, logistics, and providing for the first families. The second, operational circuit, consists of eighty to one hundred soldiers, and the third consists of two shifts of fifteen members of the elite bodyguard. One shift is on duty one day and off the next, and its duties are taken over

256 Cuba: A Brief History of the End

by the alternate shift. The leader is guarded 24 hours a day, seven days a week, anywhere on the planet.

Fidel and Raúl's family will move to Punto Cero in the Havana suburb of Siboney, a large, inaccessible and perfectly guarded complex that will ensure their comfort. The Castros lived in villas with swimming pools far from the poverty to which they had consigned 99 percent of their citizens. Here are pantries and refrigerators with delicacies most Cubans will never see even in a picture. A private farm raises chickens and geese for the first families, greenhouses grow organic vegetables, and there's even a private ice cream factory. The commander-in-chief's clothes and bedding are taken care of by a special platoon that tests them every morning for radiation and toxin levels. In fact, one of the ways the CIA contemplated getting to Fidel was by slipping him a neoprene diving suit infused with poison. Cuba is a dysfunctional state, but one thing works here, and it works according to the principles of first-class professionalism: protecting the leader and his loved ones. The CIA's most inventive action against them didn't stand a chance.

I see him aboard the Aquarama II, his private yacht. It's the early 1980s, Fidel is sitting in the armchair of a luxury cabin, reading *Newsweek*, which is banned in Cuba, and underlining an article. He has a small glass of whiskey on the rocks brought in. Lifting his head from the pages of the magazine, he squints his eyes and watches the spot where the dark blue ocean fades into the light blue sky. Life is good. Gabo sits in the cabin with Fidel, silently listening to Fidel's breakdown of the international situation. He knows well that he must be economical with words. Tension kills resonance and besides, the *Líder Máximo* tends to be prickly. After the withdrawal of the Soviet missiles, Castro realised that he was just a piece on the chessboard for the Russians. He decided to make the most of this status. He became one of the leaders of the Third World. He tried to play the role of regional power in Africa. He would help Ortega to power in Nicaragua. As he sits aboard a yacht sailing to his private island of Cayo Piedra, a pod of white dolphins circles by.

Sánchez reports that the vessel was always accompanied by two 18-metre jet-powered boats, the Pioniera I and Pioniera II. The ten men of

Castro's security detail were divided among the three vessels as they would board three cars on land. In one boat, the guards carried medical equipment, medicines and first aid supplies for every conceivable injury. The vessels are armed with heavy machine guns, grenades, Kalashnikov submachine guns, one of which is Fidel's personal, and ammunition for a minor battle. A short distance away, a Coast Guard vessel provides maritime and radar surveillance, with instructions to stop any ship that comes within three nautical miles of Aquarama II. A MiG-29 fighter pilot is on full combat alert at Santa Clara Airport, some 90 miles away. He could intervene in seconds.

"Few people in Cuba knew of the yacht's existence," Sánchez writes. Its mooring was well hidden on a private creek, invisible and inaccessible to ordinary mortals, located "on the east side of the famous Bay of Pigs, about ninety miles southeast of Havana. Since the 1960s, Fidel's private marina has been hidden here, in the middle of a military zone and under close surveillance. The site, named La Caleta del Rosario, also housed one of his many vacation homes and, in an annex, a small personal museum dedicated to Fidel's fishing trophies."

We have dinner with Jimena at El Butty restaurant near our Rachel bungalow. We're about twenty-five minutes down the coast from Fidel's former private marina, if a mere mortal could get there. My thoughts wander unbidden to the cozy beach a few hundred yards away. Sixty years ago, it was the center of the world. It was the scene of a decisive chapter in the conflict between the superpowers, where blood flowed on the white sands. Today, not a dog in the US barks about Cuba, except for the occasional snarl when there is a presidential election and the candidates need the votes of Florida's Cubans.

After the dispersal of Brigade 2506, Dr. Artime hid in the forests and swamps of Girón, not far from where we are now sitting sipping cold drinks. Communist troops caught and captured him on May 2 near the Covadonga sugar mill with two dozen other comrades. He was taken to Havana, tried and imprisoned. A year and a half later, he was exchanged with another thousand captives for medicine and food and sent to the United States. On December 29, 1962, he stood with President Kennedy on the lawn of Miami's football stadium for the traditional college football final, the Orange Bowl. He attended a ceremony honoring the victims of the Bay of Pigs battle. Then he organized another landing attempt. He raised the money and the manpower, began training an expeditionary force, but after Kennedy's death, President Johnson canceled the project. Artime befriended Hunt and became his son's godfather. That's why his name came up on the Watergate tangent. After the arrest of the "plumbers," he raised funds for their lawyers, for Hunt and for the Cuban-Americans accused of breaking into the Democratic Party headquarters. Some sources say that Artime was raising money to gag the defendants in the case. Then he got cancer. He died in 1977 at the age of the romantic poets. He was thirty-five.

The El Butty restaurant is a bright, spacious room lined with wood and stone, open to the garden at the back and sides. It is clean and well-appointed. National flags, including the Czech one, hang on the sides, and a flat-screen TV with Kremlin propaganda from RT hangs on the wall. Tired of being brainwashed, Cubans deserve real news, but they are not being indulged. After thirty years, they're getting back their Russian b.s. The sound is muted, and so is the "world news." Nothing about Ukraine. I choose grilled octopus from the menu; it would cost half as much in the beach shack. Then fresh vegetables, rice and beans. The owner of El Butty is a chef who made his money in the United States. The restaurant is expensive by Cuban standards. How does he make a living on the current tourist diet? Besides us, there's only a group of locals here to celebrate a birthday. The owner comes out of the kitchen to greet them. He's wearing a tattered T-shirt pulled tight over his bulging belly, with the words *Today we drink!* still visible.

Jimena talks about Latin hip hop. A track by Puerto Rican rapper Bad Bunny is playing right now, but it's not her taste. Instead of Rabbit, she recommends the hip hop formation Calle 13 and its frontman named Residente.

"Where are they from?" I ask.

She's hesitating. A common language and colonial history blurred the boundaries of Latin American cultures and created a shared space and sense of belonging. This was evidenced, among other things, by the Cuban

Chapter 8

tears today and the celebrations after the two soccer matches. Jimena eventually guesses Puerto Rico, which turns out to be correct after a look at Google.

"They sing about the whole of Latin America. They are critical of our culture and politics. Residente speaks for a whole generation of young *Latinos who are fed* up with corruption and all that stuff."

In Europe we do not have a similar sense of belonging and cultural affinity. What we do not lack, unlike in Latin America, are institutions set up for economic and political integration, and we Europeans do not experience these very emotionally. Well, it depends on the context. I once drove around Cuba for several hours in one go and listened to the radio, and *Ode to Joy came on.* I immediately thought of the flag of the European Union. Surrounded by a socialist dystopia, I felt, perhaps for the first time, a real gratitude for the Czech history of the last thirty years. We were lucky, thank God for the European Union, I thought to myself, without confiding the thought to anyone.

We're paying. Two waitresses are killing Jimena with their eyes. Lest I forget, I pick up a wooden block. I found it next to the beach shack for our landlady. She likes to carve and would like a piece of tropical wood as a souvenir. This one will have a special historical value.

9.

Hostage at Bella Vista.

Viñales

From the Bay of Pigs, I head west through Havana, where we make a brief stop to meet two independent artists, boyfriend and girlfriend in their early thrirties. It is a brief session in a dilapidated apartment they rent from a friend, who is in Madrid. Our final destination is Pinar del Río. Along the way we pick up a hitchhiker named Julio, a dark-haired man in his fifties who looks like the older brother of Brazilian soccer player Casemiro. I give Jimena the task of interviewing him, getting the most out of him and not forgetting anything. Julio Casemiro first wants to give me gas money.

"Is two hundred enough?"

I shake my head, wanting to add that I won't take any money from him, but he'll beat me to it.

"How about three hundred."

Jimena assures him that we really don't want the money.

"I thought you were Cuban," he tells me. "Cubans rent cars and then drive people around for money. Tourists don't stop hitchhikers, they're afraid of being mugged."

He asks Jimena where she is from, as her Spanish sounds foreign to him. When he learns the name of her Central American homeland, he surprises us with a question:

"Do you have black people living there?"

It turns out he's eager to disappear and is looking around for a place. He thinks of himself as "black," which he obviously isn't in the true sense, he just has very dark skin. Jimena, whose face shows the genes of Central

American indigenous people, assures him that there are plenty of blacks like him in her home. I ask why he wants to leave.

"Everyone wants to leave here. Everybody's running away. America, Mexico, even that stupid Jamaica, imagine that, anywhere is better than here. Our salaries are low, and inflation is eating them up, it's expensive. A pound of pork costs 450 pesos. Three lousy tomatoes at 80. Can you believe that? I have two daughters. I want to give them a better life. Then I have a daughter in Panama, but I've never seen her. My girlfriend left pregnant, she said she'd get everything ready for us and I'd come back later." He waves his hand in frustration. "She disappeared and I never heard from her again."

"I would like to leave. They offer language courses in Havana. They're expensive. I think I'm gonna die in this fucking country."

Jimena really got him talking.

"I work as a technician at the thermal power plant in Cienfuegos. It's not bad, I operate everything by computer. There hasn't been enough electricity for about six months. They had to ration it."

His phone rings. He quickly says something into it. He's babbling so much I can't understand a word he's saying. The call lasts a few seconds.

"Where are we? Yeah, my job. It doesn't pay much. I make rattan garden furniture to supplement my income. Two armchairs, a table and a double chair, would you like one? A set like that would set you back twelve grand."

I ask how many he sells in a month, and Julio Casemiro bursts out laughing.

"Sometimes I don't sell anything for months. It's just an occasional income. You have to be careful with the side job. When the government finds out you have a decent side income, they start auditing you, taxing you, fining you."

We're talking about Christmas. Christmas Eve is about two weeks away, and we've seen very few Christmas decorations in Cuban cities.

"Haven't you heard?" he asks, amused. "No Christmas this year. Christmas is cancelled. There's no money."

Julio Casemiro has a backpack and two large carry-on bags. He says he's taking food to relatives in Havana. He has to be back today. He's

Chapter 9

trying to hitchhike to save money on the trip. Sometimes he doesn't, and then he has to pay a lot of money for the bus. Then his phone rings again. Another urgent call I don't understand. On the outskirts of the capital, Julio Casemiro directs us to a motorway overpass where he gets off. Jimena is silent for a while. Then she breaks the silence. Her voice carries a trace of uncertainty.

"I think he was bullshitting. That he doesn't take food to relatives."

"Why?"

"His phone calls were suspicious. He looked like a drug dealer to me. He talked fast, in riddles, asking how the 'vuelta' was going, as if he was managing someone. Then he also asked how long and where exactly to wait under the bridge. I'd say he's a drug runner. He certainly didn't look like someone bringing his aunt a piece of pork from a farm near Cienfuegos."

"Do you think a drug dealer wouldn't have the money to rent a car?"

"It's hard to say. He may be low in the supply chain and wants to save money."

I'll shut up. We are, after all, in Jimena's hemisphere. In Havana, we quickly take care of what we need to do and continue west to Pinar del Río, where I want to meet an old friend.

Tripods and Weavers

Dagoberto Valdés Hernández is the future president of a free Cuba; at least that was my first impression when we met. An energetic man who looks like a theology teacher, he is one of the most important activists here. He was born in 1955. He soon had the desire to become a public intellectual. He applied to the university to study sociology, philosophy or other humanities, but Castro had a different plan for people of his faith: he kindly allowed him to become an agricultural engineer. Dagoberto worked and still works as a layman in the Catholic Church, which deprived him of a job in the tobacco industry and eventually earned him ten years of forced labor. In 2004, at the invitation of Cardinal Miloslav Vlk, he visited the Czech Republic, met Havel, and nine years later returned to Prague for the Forum 2000 conference, in which I had a bit of a hand.

Now, in December 2022, Jimena and I are walking around his little green house on Pedro Téllez Street in Pinar, trying to find out if he's home. A colleague in Washington tells me that Dagoberto may have been arrested by the police, but he's not sure. No one answered the knock; the low, one-storey house looked abandoned. I sent Dagoberto several text messages beforehand, but he did not respond. It's possible the police have taken his phone. We walk for a while through a neighborhood of small, stacked houses. We walk casually down narrow streets, avoiding the clutter. Then we come back down Pedro Téllez Street from another direction and slowly make our way to door number eight, Dagoberto's entrance. Jimena gets into conversation with some locals. We ask about him. No one responds. It's strange that they don't know him on his street, but so be it. The sun shines down on us through a filter of mushy haze, mixing a cocktail of harsh, pale light. I involuntarily clench the muscles around my eyes and squint at the opposite sidewalk, where a young girl is lounging. She's oblivious to us, focused on her Instagram. Still, we manage to draw her attention away from the screen for a moment.

"I know Dagoberto. But he's gone."

"Where off?"

"In Mexico."

We're looking at her uncomprehendingly.

"Dagoberto. You mean the boxer, don't you?"

We knock several more times that noon without success. We won't be able to contact him this time around. I'm getting a recommendation from Washington to give up. I'm giving Jimena a lecture on the old days, and I feel like a veteran. Long ago, when there were no smartphones in the world, a traveler was equipped with a sweaty piece of paper with an address and hoped to reach the person at home. It often didn't work out. Today, encrypted apps like WhatsApp, Signal and Threema aid the logistics of meetings, but as you can see, they haven't solved every problem.

When I met Dagoberto in the summer of 2012 in his small living room, entered directly from the alley, he was dignity itself. Standing before me was a short stocky man, a cross between a kindly wrestler and a vigorous priest. I was glad I had dressed decently in linen trousers and shirt - which was soaked through with sweat in the sweltering heat - and that I had put on a pair of polished black shoes. Dagoberto: a face with lively expressions, vigorous, well-considered arm gestures, the clear articulation of a Sunday school teacher. I never found him dejected. It's not that he has no opponents. His argument with Rodiles at the Stockholm conference is now legendary. But his name puts a smile on almost everyone's face. Dagoberto has a good reputation.

On a visit to Pinar, he introduced me to two young members of his team, Yoandy Izquierdo Toledo and Livia Gálvez Chiú. We met in the large house of his collaborator Karina Gálvez, who was on a trip abroad at the time. We walked through the corridor of the old stone building to the backyard in front of the wooden shed. There we sat down. The shorter dark-haired Yoandy was the editor of Dagoberto's magazine *Convivencia* (*Coexistence*), Livia a member of its editorial board. Dagoberto praised the cooperation with Czech diplomats, but when it came to the ambassador himself, he was, shall we say, "diplomatic." He was said to be walking down blind alleys and not open to advice.

"He's trying to fry snowballs."

I hand him a photocopy of the invitation letter to Forum 2000 in Prague.

"There are invitations that are not easily refused, and this is one of them," he says. "I was invited to Forum 2000 once before, but the government wouldn't let me go. How are my friends Archbishop Miloslav Vlk and Bishop Václav Malý? I met the Cardinal in Prague when I was staying at the Archbishop's Palace on Hradčany Square. Bishop Malý was here in Pinar on a visit, just like you."

Dagoberto then gets to the point.

"The European Union should demand a report on the state of Cuban civil society, prepared by its representatives, in order to avoid the regime's objections to foreign interference, but to allow independent voices to be heard in Cuba."

He calls this tactic a three-legged stool plan - each corner of which represents one side of a possible trialogue: the Cuban government - the European Union - Cuban civil society. He brings out the new issue of

Convivencia and shows a page where he has published a plan to create a kind of civil society consultants.

"Once every three months, the group issues a report on the state of Cuban society. This is also a way to build consensus. We have to leave politics out of it because the group is made up of people with different views: Christian democrats, social democrats, liberals. The core of the work is outside politics. We are all about the non-violent struggle for freedom and democracy. We have decided not to criticize each other in public. We know that the solution to our situation is here in Cuba. Exile can help, but the solution is here on the island. We believe in the principle of unity in diversity."

He calls the consultants *tejedores de la convivencia,* translated as weavers of coexistence. It is an initiative of his eponymous magazine, which he has gradually transformed into a movement and a kind of broader think tank.

"We want to put a big roof over diverse civic activism. We're going to be like a quilt maker who puts together one quilt of many colors. Each of us, each of our organizations, will keep our color and contribute to a unified effort. When we reach a free parliament, only there will we engage in concrete political arguments."

The Tejedores initiative was launched in March 2013. Our meeting at that time took place just before the aborted conference at Antonio Rodiles's villa. I asked Dagoberto if he would attend.

"I was informed about the Estado de SATS conference via text message, but I was not invited to it," he states dryly.

That answer says more about the state of dissent than all the tripods and weavers. Dagoberto, and a number of other dissidents, dislike Antonio's affection for the United States. Some activists spread the rumor about him that he would like to see Cuba annexed as the 51st state to the US. I have spoken to Antonio several times, but I have never heard anything like that from him. Later, Dagoberto complains about some statement by Rodiles that the Cuban people are incapable of governing themselves and that the United States should therefore take care of the island. The disagreement between Dagoberto and Antonio also stems from

Chapter 9

their different ages and life experiences. Dagoberto is a Catholic, a man of consensus. He doesn't like radicalism.

"People who look up to the United States are actually helping the Cuban government."

Leaving aside the disputes, which Dagoberto clearly doesn't want to talk about much, I turn my attention to how the regime is currently treating them. Dagoberto provides an illustrative story.

"Karina Gálvez went somewhere abroad. She was detained and questioned at the airport. They read our magazine, where we published a report about a meeting with a foreign ambassador. They didn't like it and wanted to confiscate it. So Karina decided to confront them. She asks them, 'Can't we meet and discuss with ambassadors? Then please put this ban in writing,' 'No, no, they said immediately,' 'of course you can. But you don't have to be so visible...'"

"This is a huge change from 2003. We would have been arrested for a lot less back then. But they're being forced by circumstances to ease up. The fact that people abroad know about us is a huge help. Yoani Sánchez, Coco Fariñas, Félix Navarro, José Daniel Ferrer and other well-known activists are irreplaceable. The Czech ambassador has officially visited us here in Pinar del Río. He met with the people of Convivencia. That's great!"

On the way from Pinar to Viñales, I explain to Jimena who Dagoberto is and what she missed when we did not contact him. I give her a more concise version of my memories of the weavers and the tripods. Darkness falls over the tobacco region. We reach Viñales at night. On the recommendation of the Hostal Rachel in Playa Girón, we easily find our accommodation. It's a glass villa on a hill above the village. The owner is waiting for us. Besides us, several students from France and Germany are staying here and sharing their travel experiences at a table on the terrace. I can tell from their conversation that they are serious young people, not a drunken bunch, and as we drag our luggage past them into the room, they measure us curiously. The lady of the house watches Jimena with a quizzical expression. She does not answer her greeting.

Cyclone

I'm sitting on the terrace of our villa, and below me is the Viñales Valley, a national park, a popular tourist destination. Foreign visitors come to this karst country to hike, trek up mountains, visit a cave with a small lake, ride rafts down the river, rent horses, or just stroll through the dreamscape, the land of Cuban vultures and tobacco. Viñales lies in the province of Pinar del Río, the terroir of the celebrated *puros,* cohíbas, whose name derives from the old Indian term for cigars. The whole of Cuba is a visual feast. It stuns with its tropical forests, palm trees, green valleys full of colorful flowers, cacti, beaches with white sand and a sea where dark shades of blue turn to turquoise and light green. Yet even in this context, Viñales is unique at first sight.

It is morning, and the clear blue sky promises a glorious day. Somewhere up there, the moon has forgotten itself. It occurs to me that it is practicing a policy of convivencia, cohabitation with the sun. Dagoberto would be happy. The moon over Viñales is a favorite subject of photographers, landscape painters and poets. Of course, they were looking for a nocturnal version of the moon, saturated with a dark yellow that gives the vast valley a fairy-tale quality. One night, Honza Gebert and I were sitting in the village square of Viñales when the power went out again. The area full of local youth was plunged into darkness, the disco club fell silent, and the moon shone above us, bathing the town in its silvery glow. The blackout lasted about half an hour. After that, everything came alive with the usual reggaeton rhythm, but the brief pause gave us a taste of something ephemeral from the old days, when one had to whisper by candlelight not to wake up the orishas.

I finish my cold coffee, set my cup down on the damp pavement of the terrace, and watch the strange shapes of the mogotes looming in the distance, narrow conical hills covered with jungle. Between them are patches of red earth, a tapestry of tobacco fields. Small tobacco curing huts are nestled against a backdrop of palm groves. Below me is a small town with terracotta roofs lined up in a pattern and large water tanks attached to them, painted an aggressive blue.

A few minutes later, we head for the coast, about fifteen kilometers away. I remember my first visit here. In the coastal village of Puerto

Esperanza, I stayed in a small house with a garden in a neighborhood. The elderly owner looked quizzically at my Korean car.

"Everything is coming from China and Korea now. This junk won't last. They break in a few years, and you can't fix them, it's all electronics. I used to have a Soviet washing machine. It was metal and it lasted me more than 30 years. When something broke, a neighbor came and fixed it."

I slept in my room under a mosquito net, with ominous gnats circling around me. I jumped into the blue bay from a long wooden pier with the local children, for whom I was a welcome attraction.

Years later, Jimena and I head to Puerto Esperanza again to see what has changed in the village. The road from Viñales passes by the mogotes, liana groves, sandstone cliffs, a newly built and apparently empty hotel resort with a swimming pool, and a small river with abandoned rafts moored beside it. Horses stand in corrals by the roadside. Occasionally I overtake a rider. They are sitting upright in the saddle, with hats slid down their backs, scarves around their necks and lassoes in their hands. They don't notice the passing cars, which are few, and anyway, they don't belong to their world. They look contemptuous. Normally it would take a few minutes to reach the coast, but the road, full of huge holes, allows only a careful pace. I zigzag between potholes from one side to the other and back again. It had rained during the night, and large muddy puddles, who knows how deep, had settled in the holes. It's Sunday, December, the countryside between Viñales and the coast is deserted, so when after a while I come across a work crew filling in the holes with hot asphalt, I can't help but be amazed.

A sad arrival in Puerto Esperanza. There is no one on the wide main street that slopes down to the sea. It used to be very busy. The village was devastated by the cyclone that swept through the region last summer. I look for the palm grove at the end of the village by the sea, where the road ends with a roundabout, but I can't find it. We get to the sea - and the grove is nowhere to be found. Am I misremembering? There was a grove with a volleyball court, a grassy patch where the boys played football, and a long pier next to it. I get out of the car. A continuous carpet of dead palm leaves crunches under my feet. The grove itself has been flattened by the cyclone, giving the expanse by the sea a bleak look. The elements have damaged several houses on the coast and many roofs throughout the village. Even my wooden pier is kaput. I won't be jumping in the water here today. Someone dropped an empty box in front of it, a black carton for *aguardiente*. It's proudly marked Black Tears on the side. On an empty basketball court at the seashore, a tattered net hangs from a basket. The former volleyball court is an unkempt patch with two netless stakes. A pensioner sits on a concrete bench while another shuffles in on a cane.

A middle-aged black woman comes in wearing a faded T-shirt and tight pants. She asks if we want to stop for lunch or dinner. She's insistent, offering fresh lobster. She explains how the cyclone hit.

"It's a disaster. And now there are hardly any tourists."

A sharp wind scratches the pale blue ocean, creating foamy ripples on the grating surface. To the right of the roundabout, a group of men are repairing a restaurant on the shore. The sound of hammers can be heard. They've already got a whole new roof made of layered palm fronds. They're doing a good job. They ignore us, even when we take pictures. I'm trying to remember exactly where I used to live here, but I can't find that little house off the main street in the vast village. So we go back, up from the sea, past the closed judo gym. It's a small, yellow, scruffy building with two stone columns in front of the entrance, a black sign that reads *gimnasio de judo,* a carefully brush-painted operating hours and a charming picture of two wrestling judokas. We continue at a snail's pace back to Viñales. Again we pass steep hills, a small river and tobacco fields until we reach the village. The drive from the sea takes about an hour.

The serpentine road climbs up a hill to a natural gate to the valley. There is a fantastic view of the whole region. We see again the upright royal palms, tobacco fields, herds of horses, water buffalo patiently pulling rickety wooden wagons through the red mud, mogotes of unlikely shapes and behind them the green mountains of the Cordillera de Guaniguanico, which follows the coast. Cuban vultures circle above the valley. On the hill, the large pink structure of the Los Jazmines Hotel, built in the early 1960s, stands guard. This mountain hotel has dozens of rooms, a restaurant, two bars and a nightclub. Next to the main building is a beautiful swimming pool overlooking the valley and distant mountain

Chapter 9

peaks. I park in the nearly empty parking lot. My idea of having a coffee here will probably come to nothing. The hotel is closed. A cyclone has battered it, taking off its roof and demolishing at least one room on the second floor. Outside the hotel, a few workers are resting in the parking lot by the mosaic wall. They sit on the concrete sidewalk, drinking water from PET bottles. Another group is restoring an abstract mosaic inspired by the elegant New York style of the 1960s. On closer inspection, it's not abstract. It features the stylized mountains and jasmine blossoms that gave the hotel its name.

At the top of the pink building we see new wooden beams, the foundation of the future roof. A large black dog lies by the pool, and a chicken is precariously perched nearby. One of several large pots of palmetto has been knocked over. We walk over to the upper parking lot above the pool, where there is an open bar with a television. A baseball game is on. They've placed a life-size silver and gold statue of clowns sitting at two tables. As we approach them, both statues suddenly move at the same time, look at us and light up - they are not statues, but street performers dressed as statues! Jimena almost has a heart attack. She screams, gasps, and when she recovers a bit, she starts to curse the actors in a friendly way.

We can have coffee at the bar, but no coke or beer, although I can see both behind the glass of the cooler. We can also use the toilets, but the barmaid warns us that the water doesn't run and of course there is no toilet paper, which is no surprise in Cuba. The silver and gold clowns reminded me of an old clown parade on the main street in Viñales that I stumbled upon on one of my previous trips. There were only a few clowns, but they created much welcome excitement. Young men and women on high stilts, dressed in brightly colored costumes, made up with white paint, red lipstick, and aggressive eyebrow pencils, walked through the streets in full traffic. Cars honked and stopped, clowns on stilts carefully perched on bonnets, children in pioneer uniforms and civilian clothes ran around. In all the colorful cheering and jumping of little boys and girls, you would almost forget that there were a few plainclothes policemen hanging around. Just in case.

272 Cuba: A Brief History of the End

I have already mentioned that I am staying privately on the island and trying to avoid the state-run hotels. The exception is Los Jazmines. Once I couldn't resist paying for a night there. It came to ninety euros, more than three times what it would cost to stay in a private guesthouse. I did it for two reasons. First, it has an unrepeatable charm as a kind of informal gateway with a wonderful view of the Valle de Viñales. The second reason is that an episode of the TV series about Major Zeman was filmed here in the second half of the 1970s. That's why I decided to explore this place a bit more and to be on the safe side, I was going to spend the night here.

The movie director Honza Gebert and I sat in the hotel bar in the early evening, drinking a strong dark lager Bucanero and chatting with the two bartenders. We were almost the only guests and the guys were bored. At first we were surprised that one of the bartenders was trying to set us up with his casa particular, which we saw as a clear conflict of interest. But that's not how it works in Cuba. They don't take other things that way either.

"How many women can you have in your country?" asks a bartender in a white shirt with black hair slicked back with brilliantine.

At first we don't understand what he means.

"How many girls do you have in the Czech Republic? How many do you have now?" he turns to Honza. He blushes and slowly says something about his Swedish girlfriend.

"Only one?" the guy wonders.

"Well... one. Isn't that enough?"

"That's not enough here in Cuba, man. Here in Cuba we have one wife and at least two other mistresses. At least!" he says.

"Hm," says Honza. "You really are alphas, aren't you? "

"I would say so. All the guys in Cuba are real mujeriegos, man." The guy uses a word that could be translated as womanizer. They're just into women. I get the vague impression that we've both sunk pretty low in their eyes as the conversation stalls. We sip a strong, sweet beer, order another and discuss the next day's agenda. We'll meet Dagoberto Valdés in Pinar and then drive to Havana to meet Martha Roque.

"Are you going to eat?" a man with slicked-back hair suddenly asks.

Considering the quality of the food in state institutions, I immediately said that we were not hungry. We'll eat at a private paladar in Viñales. The bartender doesn't protest, doesn't try to convince us. He doesn't care. It occurs to me to ask about Major Zeman. Maybe there's someone working in the hotel who remembers the filming, who was there. I urge Honza to ask. He begins slowly:

"Once upon a time, the Czechs filmed a series here..."

"... el capitán Séman?" the bartender immediately drops out.

"How do you know that? Have you seen it?"

"Dude, there's a lot of people coming here from you, and everyone, everyone is asking about it. I haven't seen it. I know they filmed it here."

"Is there anybody here who has experienced this? Anyone on the staff?"

"No, buddy. It was a long time ago. No one like that who experienced it back then works here anymore."

Supported by friends, an old man on crutches walks along the Prague embankment. A woman approaches him with a white lion cub, and the man gently strokes it. It's a strange scene. I have no idea where the white lion came from. I wasn't there, I just found the video on YouTube. The man is surrounded by a crowd of about 20 admirers. There are several cameramen running around, letting you know that the old man is not just anyone. His name is Vladimír Brabec, and he was a major actor in Czechoslovakia in the 1970s. On the embankment by Prague's Štefánik Bridge in 2016, he attended a meeting of fans and actors who portrayed characters in the television series The Thirty Cases of Major Zeman.

The most expensive project in the history of Czechoslovak television, the series was made in the mid-1970s, and since everything had to have some political justification, the creators presented it as a gift to celebrate the thirtieth anniversary of the National Security Corps, the police force that had been under the control of the Communist Party of Czechoslovakia almost from its inception. The plot of each of the thirty episodes is set in a post-war year and has a criminal or espionage plot, which is solved by Zeman, his colleagues and friends. The ideological message was overseen by the State Security, the political police, the most feared organization in the country. Unlike most Czech and Slovak productions of the time, the budget allowed the filmmakers to shoot abroad, in some cases in the free world. At a time when most Czechs and Slovaks could not travel to the West, this was not only unusual, but contributed to the success of the series.

As a kid, I looked forward to it. In the boredom of those days, it was also exciting because of the places where some of the episodes took place. It was a glimpse into the "big world" of espionage and "sophisticated life," of which we had only a vague idea at that time. My younger brother Dušan, after one episode of Zeman, wrote down in his little address book the address of the guesthouse König in Täubchenweg 7 in Kiel, West Germany, where a part of the spy story took place. This fictitious address in his address book coexisted with several phone numbers of his real classmates and was a kind of unacknowledged expression of longing for the larger world in which the characters of this Communist potato soup lived.

Because even if I leave aside the political lies, Zeman looks ridiculous from today's perspective. I don't think my daughters have ever been able to watch a single episode to the end. They find Zeman simply boring and don't even see a certain perverse value in it, which I find strangely satisfying. I take it as an expression of poetic justice. The fact that such a bad work could be so successful in our country proves what an artificial world we grew up in. Between the ages of ten and fourteen, however, I devoured Zeman. It was only later that I began to understand the meanness of portraying State Security agents as sympathetic family men and heroes willing to die for the "camp of peace and socialism," while turning independent activists, artists, and dissidents into murderers, hijackers, and drug dealers in complete contradiction to the facts.

Two episodes of the series were filmed in Cuba, including at the Hotel Los Jazmines, which was given the movie name Bella Vista. The spy plot is a James Bond story turned on its head. Similar works inverting Western spy stories were made elsewhere in the Communist world. The most ambitious was the 1973 East German series Das Unsichtbare Visier, starring German star Armin Mueller-Stahl as East German Stasi agent Werner Bredebusch, who operated in West Germany under the code name

Achim Detjen. Another example of this genre that aired in the Eastern Bloc was the Soviet series Tass upolnomochen zajavit (Tass is authorized to declare), starring Vyacheslav Tikhonov.

The episode "Hostage in Bella Vista" takes place in the early 1970s in an unspecified South American country similar to Chile. Zeman is investigating a plot by the American CIA and German Nazis against Czechoslovakia. His colleague is sent to uncover the American sabotage. The trail leads him to the mountains of South America, where he is arrested at the Bella Vista Hotel by a Nazi in the service of the United States. A Cuban intelligence officer helps him escape. Like the myth of Che Guevara on the world left, some of the propaganda formulas promoted by the Thirty Cases survive in the minds of a significant number of Czech citizens.

This is also why the threat of Great Russian expansionism, represented by Putin, is underestimated by more people in the Czech Republic and Slovakia than one would expect after all that Moscow has inflicted on Central and Eastern Europe in the recent past. The series is partly to blame for the fact that the anti-Communist resistance group of the Mašín brothers, who carried out several years of anti-regime sabotage in Czechoslovakia and then shot their way into West Berlin in the autumn of 1953 under incredibly tense circumstances, are not generally revered for their heroism in standing up to tyranny with a gun. In one episode, the show's creators turned them into a bunch of bitter psychopaths and murderers.

At the Mercy of Greasy Hicks

About fifteen years ago, I had the idea of honoring the Mašíns with some kind of public tribute. Originally, I thought a prominent Czech politician would meet them in America, which would provoke a discussion about the myths of the Czech past. It would be a groundbreaking gesture. I consulted the historian Pavel Žáček, who was in contact with the Mašíns. Their relationship with their former homeland was notoriously distant. They were suspicious of Prague politicians. However, through Pavel I received a message from America that the Josef Mašín respected the then Prime Minister Mirek Topolánek and was happy to meet him. At the

NATO Days in Ostrava, which Topolánek once helped to organize, he gave a speech in which he was, I think, the first top politician to call the Mašíns heroes. Nevertheless, I was pleasantly surprised that Topolánek immediately agreed and adopted my idea as his own. At the time, I was working for the Czech government on an information campaign about a U.S. missile defense program. We were about to go on a trip to the White House, and Topolánek said:

"We're going to give Josef Mašín a state award. It will be for the whole group.

Ctirad Mašín was ill and his health was deteriorating, so it was clear that only Josef would come to Washington.

"But you don't have the right to give state awards," I objected. "The president does that, and Klaus will never give them any."

"Leave it to me," Topolánek smiled mysteriously.

He then had a special prime minister's citation made for the occasion, which he actually presented to Josef Mašín on our trip to Washington. Few Czech politicians would dare make such a gesture - rewarding the Mašíns is not something that scores political points. Topolánek met with Josef Mašín at the residence of the Czech ambassador, Petr Kolář, and presented him with the medal at a luncheon.

The night before, we went out for a beer with Pavel Žáček. Josef Mašín wanted to join us. He arrived at the restaurant in Washington's Union Station straight from the airport, where he had flown from his home in California. He was nearly seventy-six, moved briskly and seemed to be in great shape. He sat down at our table and shook our hands. The waitress came over. Pavel and I ordered beers, and Josef Mašín, whose body language and handshake made it clear that he was a lifelong soldier even though he had been in business for a long time, ordered a cup of hot chocolate with whipped cream. Hot chocolate with cream! A man whom enough Czechs still considered a murderer just wanted to sweeten his moment in an American station bar. He poked a spoon into the whipped cream scoop on top of the glass, spoke to us in perfect Czech, smiled sweetly, but held back. I figured he wouldn't let anyone in right away. He was the opposite of the outgoing Americans who, unlike most reserved Europeans, wear their hearts on their sleeves.

At the beginning of the 1950s, Josef and Ctirad Mašín's resistance group, which also included Milan Paumer, Zbyněk Janata and Václav Švéda, wreaked havoc on the Bolsheviks with sabotage and armed actions that resulted in the deaths of regime officials. On St. Wenceslas Day in 1951, during a raid on a police station in Čelákovice, Ctirad Mašín killed a handcuffed and drugged policeman, Jaroslav Honzátko, with a dagger, fearing that if he left him alive, their group would be identified and caught. This act was used by the Communists to portray the resistance group as terrorists. The killing of Honzátko, who was already disarmed, is highly problematic from an ethical point of view. However, if one considers it a simple murder, one has failed to understand the depth of the criminality of the Communist regime, its true nature, which Honzátko served at that time with a gun, in all its implications and dimensions. I did not live through that time and I do not want to judge Ctirad's action. It is a matter that he must have settled with his Creator when he left this world.

In the 1990s, the Mašíns made a number of somewhat hasty and simplistic condemnations of certain politicians and the Czech post-revolutionary development. They were unfair to Havel. The antipathy between them and Havel was personal and dated back to the time after the February 1948 Communist coup, when they were all classmates at the high school in Poděbrady. Some people who would otherwise have been sympathetic to them resented these statements. My attitude towards the Mašíns is due to their incredible courage. As their biographer Jan Novák writes, the regime declared war on them personally, their family and the memory of their heroic father, an anti-Nazi resistance fighter, and they took the Bolsheviks seriously and fought back as best they could. The Mašíns are not analysts of post-1989 developments, but soldiers who, like their father, were willing to give their lives for freedom. For what they did, they can say whatever they want. Their resistance group stands in the honorable line of soldiers alongside the Cuban Brigade 2506 and the guerrilla fighters in the Sierra del Escambray.

In the second half of the 1970s, when Zeman was filmed at Los Jazmines, the hotel looked a little different. It was painted a creamy white, now it's pink. There was no wall separating the pool from the front of the

278   Cuba: A Brief History of the End

building and the front parking lot. Nor was there an adjacent wall with a "New York" mosaic. The film crew, coming from Prague's world of scaffolding and crumbling facades, must have enjoyed filming amid the tropical colors and wild scenery. Their journey took them in the opposite direction from that of Guevara some ten years earlier.

In Czechoslovakia, Che concluded that our country was a caricature of socialism. In Matocha's book, Komárek recalls how naively romantic Che's idea of socialism was. He wanted to create in Cuba an intellectual community of the ancient type, where the country's elite would engage in philosophical discussions and devote themselves to the arts. This was to be paid for by Khrushchev, whom Che despised and regarded as a greasy hick. His statement about the need to catch up and overtake the United States was considered ridiculous by Che. He said that America was a hundred years ahead of the USSR, and Moscow would never be able to catch up. When Guevara described the ideal Cuban society as a Hellenic polis of spiritual and physical development, Komárek disagreed, saying that the people needed some economic stimulus. This only infuriated Guevara.

"'How much per capita GDP do you think Socrates, Plato and their Greece had, and look what kind of society it was!' I replied that he was leaving out the slaves who lived there. Guevara, with his sense of humor, replied, 'We can have them too - we're still on good terms with Mao Zedong, so I'll persuade him to send us fifteen million Chinese to work for us, and we'll just do culture, guard the island, and discuss,'" writes Komárek.

What would Che think of Major Zeman if he had the chance to see the series? Would this classically educated intellectual have considered it trash? A caricature of socialist art? Again, he probably would not have realized that the type of society he helped create in Cuba, and then tried to impose at gunpoint in Africa and South America, would logically tend toward the indoctrination of Zeman's type, just as it tended toward the stuffiness he experienced in Czechoslovakia in the 1960s. Che imagined socialism as a government of tough and uncompromising but thoughtful and elegant rebels, and failed to understand that power always and everywhere ends up in the hands of what he would call 'greasy hicks.'

What is striking about the radioactive Zeman lie is its long half-life. In 1980, the Czechoslovak Television Weekly printed a prophetic statement about the series by Colonel Milan Broumovský, editor-in-chief of the Central Editorial Office for Army, Security and Conscription of Czechoslovak Television, a kind of cog between State Security and production. Broumovský wrote:

"In retrospect, when we can evaluate the series in its entirety after all the creative discussions, I think the most important thing was its political significance. The fact that from the first to the last episode it strictly followed the basic ideological line we had set for it, i.e. to reflect the class struggle in this country, to generalize the experiences we gained in this struggle, so that years later it will still serve the ideological-political education of those for whom the times in which the individual stories took place have long since become history. The series has undoubtedly played an important role in the present, and I am convinced that it will continue to do so in the years to come."

The colonel said it in his own language, and he said it very precisely. Perhaps even he did not know that more than forty years after its completion, their work would influence the minds of people who did not experience the historical events, as well as those who lived during them but know nothing about them. Or rather, they know about them from works like Thirty Cases. The series served as an active measure of internal indoctrination. This is what the Soviet intelligence called the means of the disinformation war it waged for decades against the free world: aktivnye meropriyatiya. An important feature of active measures was their believability. The actors and writers of Thirty Cases emphasized that Zeman's stories were taken from life. They wrapped their big lie in a package of small situations that were true or seemed plausible. The most effective demagoguery is the kind that has some truth to it. The stream of Thirty Cases has flown into a torrent of expedient myths with which our modern history is saturated. Here, in Los Jazmines, the myths and lies of modern Cuban history have intersected with our own.

"We were real brothers," one such victim of false memory told me in Moncada's barracks in Santiago.

In the bar near the upper parking lot, we get up from our chairs and walk to the railing, to which the tourist binoculars are attached. For a few pesos you can examine the picturesque Viñales Valley in more detail through the peephole. But the binoculars don't work. Jimena talks to the two clowns for a while. They must be hot in their heavy gold and silver uniforms. Beads of sweat are running down their cheeks, melting their make-up. Strangely enough, they don't ask us for handouts. When we arrived here, I wanted to explain to Jimena why the Los Jazmines Hotel is interesting to Czechs, but in the end I don't. I will spare her a complicated story whose full meaning she might not understand. A world without hostages in Bella Vista makes one happier.

I wander around the capital, where we arrived from Viñales. Jimena has since left and left me a bag of legume chips as a farewell. She got through airport security and onto the plane without any trouble. The streets of the metropolis are busy, the siesta is over and people are heading out into the cooler air. Through the open windows I can see into the living rooms. There's a flatscreen TV on in front of more than one shabby couch. Today, the wonders of communication technology can be found amid the worst ruins. You may not have anything to eat, but in the back pocket of your shorts you have a smartphone in any ghetto anywhere in the world.
Poverty is rampant here in Cuba, but it's not the worst thing you'll encounter. There is poverty all over the world. There are countries that are poorer than Cuba. What makes contemporary Cuban society particularly repulsive is the combination of poverty with a dictatorship that stifles any creativity. People cannot discover and develop their talents, they cannot get a normal education, they cannot create dreams and bring them to life. Most are left to parasitize on a bankrupt system. This makes it difficult to have a normal relationship with anyone here. And it's the impossibility of human contact that gets to you after a while. Cubans see you as a way to help themselves. I don't blame them, but it's not normal.

"This car needs to be serviced after 60,000 kilometers."
A fat, greasy face. Dark hair. Uniform. The man across from me sits in a big chair, flips through the papers for a moment, then looks at me

again, bored. I'm sitting in a rental car at Martí Airport, returning the battered Korean. Filiberto and I drove around Havana for a couple of hours before we found a working gas station in Vedado on the waterfront. So I could return the white horse with the sick fender with a full stomach. So I wouldn't lose my extortionate deposit of seventy-five euros. I'm silent, but I'm beginning to see where this is going.

"And you drove..."

He looks at the paper theatrically. Bad actor.

"You have gone over sixty-one thousand on the car."

"Yes?"

"And you weren't in the shop."

"How should I know? You never told me."

He picks up the paper and pulls out the trump card. The ace of spades.

"It's in your contract. It's right here. After 60,000 kilometers, the car has to be serviced.

You should have known that."

He points to the back of the contract, where it is written in the smallest possible font.

"You should have told me."

The fat, greasy face falls silent. It could be dangerous to offer him a bribe now. It could be a trap. He may be playing with State Security. Maybe he's recording me. I'm silent. We're a bit like in a Soviet psychological movie. But then the silence doesn't last.

"What are we going to do about it?"

"What are we going to do about it?" I repeat.

Suddenly his eyes are not bored. For a split second, a wave of anger flashes through them.

"You pay the fine. One hundred dollars."

I wonder what to do. Hell, a hundred dollars. I'm more upset that I've fallen into their trap. They figured out how to squeeze more money into the budget of the generals and their tourist gold mine. Momentarily, I'm filled with rage, and although I'm not aggressive at all, I'd like to punch that fat, greasy face. And that would be a mistake. If there's one thing I don't need, it's a scene. I can't draw unnecessary attention to myself, I tell myself. I can't. I have to focus on the immediate goal, which is to make a smooth transition to the plane.

"All right, I'll pay the hundred dollar fine, but you'll give me a receipt."

The fat, greasy face takes a form in his hand and slowly begins to fill it out. The whole process takes an interminable amount of time. With great precision, Cuba will remind you of what it was like to live in a society where there was no recourse against the whims of fat, greasy faces. I usually feel miserable on the road when the date of my return to Prague approaches. If only I could stay a few more days...

But not this time. Suddenly, for the first time, I'm looking forward to going home.

Editorial Note and Acknowledgements

In addition to personal experiences from numerous trips to Cuba between the summer of 2012 and December 2022, interviews with many Cubans conducted in Cuba, on two trips to Jamaica, Prague, and the United States, this book draws on the contemporary press and several other books, most notably Pavel Matocha's excellent publication *Castro's Prisoners* (Jota 2001), Juan Reinaldo Sánchez's autobiography *The Double Life of Fidel Castro: My 17 Years as Personal Bodyguard to El Líder Máximo* (St. Martin's Griffin 2016) and books by Reinaldo Arenas, especially his memoir *Before Night Falls* (Penguin Books 1994). For factual and historical data related to the attack on Moncada's barracks, I used Robert Merle's book *Moncada: premier combat de Fidel Castro* (1965) as a source.

Many other books, including Castro's autobiography, Guevara's *Motorcycle Diaries*, Martí's poetry, a monograph on the Bacardí family (Tom Gjelten: *Bacardí y la larga lucha por Cuba*, Viking Penguin 2008), as well as documentaries and feature films (such as *Before Night Falls*, dir. Julian Schnabel, 2000), have provided me with a basic orientation to modern Cuban history and culture. An invaluable source of additional information for anyone concerned with human rights in Cuba is the Memory of the Nation website, specifically the project "Memory of the Cuban Nation - A Tool for Transforming Cuban Society Towards Real Freedom" by Post Bellum, a Czech NGO.

In the first and especially in the second chapter, I use adapted and revised parts of the second chapter (Havana Blues: You Can't Falsify a Face) from my previous book, *Maybe the Dictator Will Come* (Bourdon 2017).

The book would not have been possible without the help and cooperation of several people, to whom I am grateful for their time, knowledge and experiences, which they generously shared with me, for their valuable comments on the first version of the manuscript, and for their organizational help in preparing and coordinating the trips themselves. They include the following friends, colleagues and collaborators (like the names of some of the people in the book, some of these names are pseudonyms, which I include here for good reasons):

284 Cuba: A Brief History of the End

Madeleine Albright (in memoriam), Lucia Argüellová, Matěj Bartošek, Jan Bubeník, Francisco J. Casas, Jimena Cervantes, Jiří Dědeček, Andrea Fajkusová, Sofía García, Clara González, Jan Gebert, Petr Gandalovič, Pavla Holcová, Ondřej Juřík, Karolína Kvačková, Esteban Madrigal, Šimon Pánek, Petr Pithart, Jiří Pehe, Petr Pietraš, Petra Průšová, Tomáš Pojar, Martin Palouš, Karel Schwarzenberg, Marek Svoboda, Stanislav Škoda, Šárka Vašíčková and Pavlína Wolfová.

Special thanks to my publisher Ivan Pilip, who inspired the book, helped with advice and shared his experience and knowledge with me. For their brave and generous support, as well as for their comments on the first version of the manuscript, I thank my wife Beata Berníková and my daughters Isabela and Sarah Klvaňová, who worried about me during my travels but never tried to discourage me.

I dedicate this book to the memory of Petr Přibík (1937-2014), who served as head of the Czech diplomatic mission in Havana from 1996-1997. Because of his support for dissent, he did not receive approval from the Cubans to act as ambassador and had to leave the country. I met Petr in the editorial office of Radio Free Europe in Munich in 1990. We became friends, on Cuban missions also because of him.

Milton Keynes UK
Ingram Content Group UK Ltd.
UKHW021208160524
442712UK00003B/8/J